# AN ISLAND PREOCCUPIED

Arthur De Caux

ELSP

Published in 2008 by
ELSP
16A St John's Road
St Helier
Jersey JE2 3LD

Origination by Seaflower Books, Jersey

Printed in Britian by
Cromwell Press
Trowbridge, Wiltshire



ISBN 978-1-906641-01-6

*Front cover: Photograph courtesy of the Société Jersiaise Photographic Archive*

# Introduction

The Occupation of the Channel Islands figured largely in the vivid and emotional memories passed on to me by my parents and others during my early youth, for I had been born in Jersey in 1943, almost three years into life under the Germans and over two before Liberation. Minds were fresh and the desire to tell and retell events to the new generation went on into the Fifties. Much of Jersey life did not change immediately after the War and characters from my parents' stories were all around me so that it was not hard to form a full picture of the time they spoke of, a time which had marked them so deeply..

As I grew older, the notions behind the stories fascinated me and I became particularly interested in the period of 'pre Occupation', those few weeks in the summer of 1940 as the Germans moved inexorably towards the Normandy Peninsular and possibly the British Channel Islands lying just nearby. The drama and heart searching that went on against the backdrop of history unfolding was constantly referred to by my parents. They were typical of other island families in that they had to face the dilemma of staying or going. Either way they would face an uncertain future – staying to await the enemy's arrival and unforeseen consequences, or leaving everything, probably bound for England, where very few islanders had any contacts or had ever contemplated visiting before. Jersey may have been loyally British but the mentality remained specially 'Jersey'.

The drama, fear, questions and panic of that June form the basis of this novel. Speculation and rumour abounded. What makes people act in one way or another? Decisions were made, some in haste, on a whim or by default, some because of age, gender, family situation. And the import of those decisions was to be played out over the following five years. I've chosen to present these disparate viewpoints as a novelised account, where the characters can be seen to follow their own reasoning, instincts or motivation. The aim is to paint a true picture overall but not true at an individual level, and to tell a good story. The characters are the product of my imagination and are not a representation of any persons, living or dead, but the ways in which they react and behave in the novel are based on perceptions by members of my family at the time. Details may often be true but remixed. A certain contemplation at a more abstract level on some of the issues is my own.

The tale which, more than any other, prompted me to write this account, happened to my father. In the confusion and misunderstandings of the dramatic few days when the evacuation was in full swing he, and other young men from his part of the island, were rounded up and taken down to the harbour at a moment's notice to board a boat for England. He waited for his brothers-in-law from other parishes to arrive. When they did not come he checked further and discovered that a mistake had apparently been made at a higher level where it was thought that all men of military age 'had to go'. Several of his fellows did not get off the boat in time and presumably spent the war in England. I am very conscious that had my father been one of them, leaving my mother behind, the chances of my being born were not too promising.

In contrast to the characters, the historical background to the novel is based on fact. I have researched and recounted the advance of the German armies and many of the actual events in Jersey over the month of June. The States of Jersey announcements, the letters in the Jersey Evening Post, the bombings, the painting of the white crosses of surrender for example are all facts gleaned from historical accounts and newspapers at the time, but their impact on the characters is again based on what I heard from those who lived through it.

Finally the special character of Jersey and its people, their shared values, their idiosyncrasies, their divisions, together with the beauty of its fields and coastline - I hope I have conveyed some of this in the book and my love for it. Perhaps it is only with the distance of decades that one can give a true perspective of those years to people who come to it for the first time and have little idea of the turmoil of the past.

*Arthur De Caux*
*March 2008*

# Position of the British Channel Islands, 1940

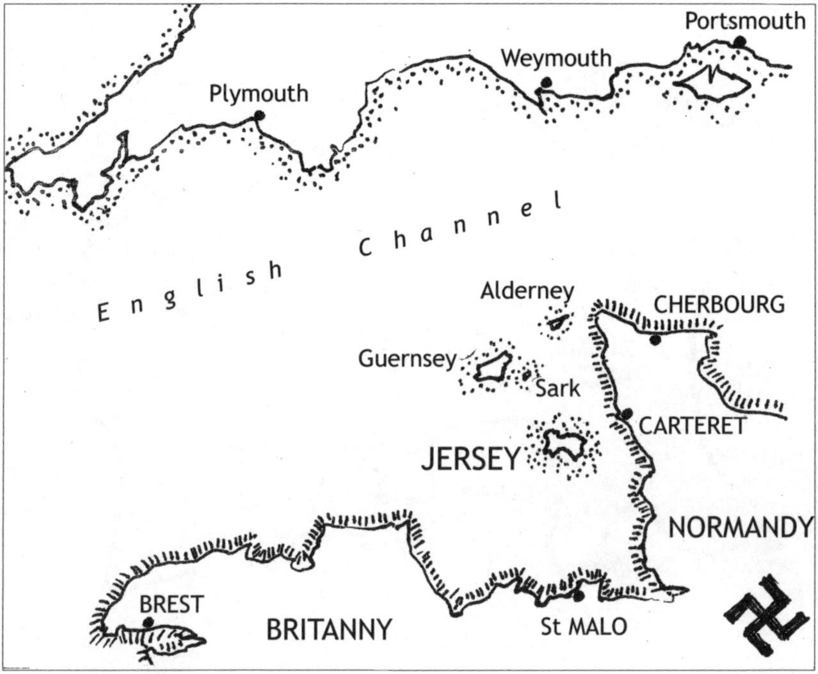

# Island of Jersey

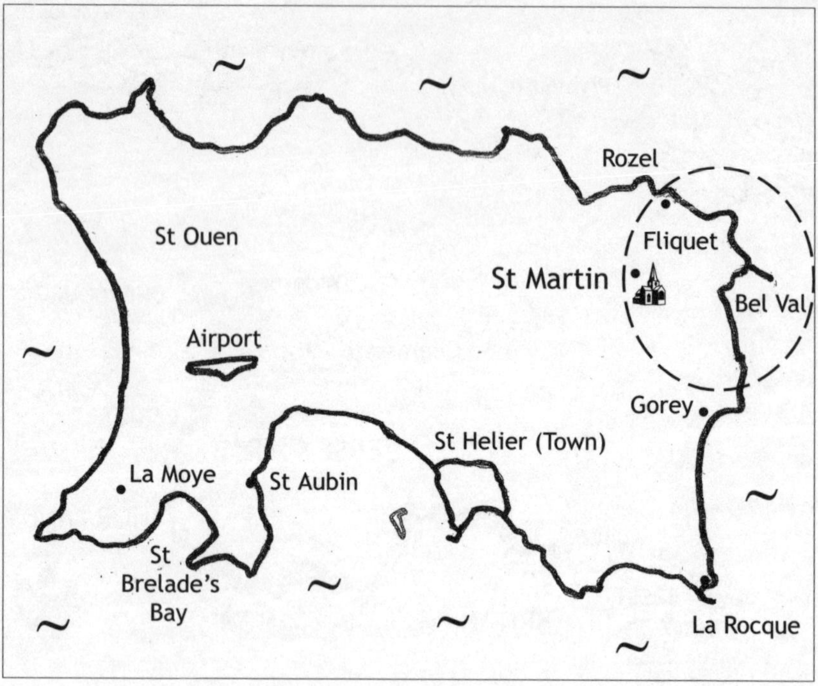

# ONE

*Thursday 13 June, 1940*

The rough-hewn Jersey men, many unusually accompanied by their wives, stood speaking and drinking as if drinking and speaking were about to end. By contrast, a few silent ones gazed into their rums, beers and pernods with the look immortalized by Degas in his painting of L'Absinthe. They were waiting for the war to reach them.

In spite of the solemn mood, Jacko, the rotund publican of the Royal, pulled a pint with the enthusiasm of knowing that people were drinking elbow to elbow as they had now for several days. Around him the gloomy paint and faded wood offered a fit setting for the tentative, fearful debates of this first wartime summer. Normalcy seemed to take on a greater intensity. More dogs than usual, most the hairy results of indiscriminate breeding, lay heaped on feet or wrapped around table legs. More glasses were spilt. Voices grew louder and harsher and a thickening film of cigarette smoke seeped into pockets. At twenty past nine, the erratic cuckoo emerged from the battered Swiss clock above the bar but failed to make itself heard.

After several months of declared war which had largely consisted of naval activity, the previous month had seen the invasion of Holland, Belgium and France and fear had arrived in the Channel Islands with a momentum which matched the blitzkrieg. In this atmosphere of barely suppressed nervousness, the locals of St Martin in the north east corner of Jersey, like others all over the island, drank too much and smoked too many, the twin benefits of the tax free.

Jack Birel stood and observed his fellow islanders. Trained in England, he was a teacher at the nearby elementary school. Broad back against the bar, heel wedged over the footrest, he could hear snippets of conversation which both amused and amazed him. When not manning the worm-infested desk in his classroom or controlling other pests in his half-kempt garden, he dabbled at writing, mainly short stories set in Jersey, but was too nervous to allow anyone to read his work. His slightly droopy eyes moved through the blue haze of the room and rested momentarily on a leg, neck or wisp of hair. His mind, though, was restless.

'If only I could capture all this tension,' he thought. 'The outlandish worries and half-baked ideas. I must write something decent soon, I'm thirty bloody three.'

So, in the reflective contemplation of a pint of Randalls, he determined to record a journal of whatever the future might bring to this little, close-knit community. Eyewitnesses to history, he thought, just need to be there and to decide to record it.

The energy from his decision stirred him into listening more attentively, not too easy in the hubbub. He could just make out the loudest voice saying in slow Jersey tones:

"They could kill us all, eh, it would be dead easy for them and like that we'd give them no more trouble. I mean men of military age."

"Why not kill everybody?" someone retorted. "Like that they'd have the whole place to themselves."

It was not easy to just shake off the implications of these threats. Jack was of military age, tall, educated, not too far from fit. The war came a step nearer in his mind. In the past few weeks, although his thoughts had often turned to the fighting and suffering, particularly in Holland, he had only recently begun to believe that Jersey could be caught up in it.

But now people were starting to question more and more whether they should leave the island, an anxiety which pushed them to public places to hear and share the worries of others.

As if echoing his own thoughts, Jack heard young Percy exclaim with a slight puff of the chest:

"Well, I reckon I'm going, me."

The lad had left school at Easter to start what was called 'a good job' in a bank in town. Alan Le Grand encouraged him with a hearty bang on the shoulder.

"I'd go like a shot, me too, if I was your age."

Alan was an energetic farmer in his late thirties who drank in moderation and was credited with good sense. He had the parchment coloured features of the islander, Norman and Breton ancestry buffeted by sea breezes and tanned by the sun beating down into tomato fields. His wife, Yvonne, an excitable little woman from Perros Guirec, interrupted in what Alan called 'ruptured English.'

"But, and your mother, Percy, you can't be leaving your parents that way. It will her heart break. She has only you."

Alan made a loud 'pah' noise of disagreement. "Everybody's got to leave home at some time. If the Germans do him in or cart him off, what will his mother think then? I bet she'd rather he was safe in England."

Alan's wife retorted that the Germans wouldn't come but already the essence of their discussion had spread to other groups, becoming more confused and uncertain as the cuckoo maintained its unique pace of three appearances an hour.

Jack shook his head in slow disbelief at the facility of his fellow human beings to form firm opinions on the slenderest of evidence or whim. But how else could you decide whether the Germans were likely to come, and, if they did, whether they would kill you, incarcerate you or leave you to carry on pretty well as before?

He placed his glass purposefully on the counter and nudged it towards the vivacious Mary, like a chess player edging his queen into a checking position. She was everything of the cliché of the barmaid, a coarse voice, hearty laugh and curves which rested with generosity on the bar. In spite of it being a Randall's pub, Jack always asked deliberately for the rival ale, Mary Ann, just to be able to say, "another Mary, Mary please."

Would either brewery go on brewing if the Germans came? Would pubs even be allowed to stay open? There was a sobering thought.

"A penny for them," said Mary.

"I was just wondering if the pubs will stay open if the Germans come."

"Does that mean you think they are coming, Jack?"

"I reckon so," he said with a shrug of helplessness. "It's beginning to look as if France has had it. The Germans have already crossed the Marne."

"You know my geography's useless, Jack. Where's the Marne?"

"The Marne is close to Paris. It's where soldiers were rushed up in buses and taxis in the Great War as a last ditch defence of the capital. Once the Germans get past there, they'll be across Normandy before you can say Jack Huet, then getting into boats at Carteret."

As he spoke, the Bigou brothers, who made little pretence of farming the tumbledown property near la Préférence while they spent their inheritance, looked up from their glasses. The older aggressive Luc, his drinking unimpaired by thoughts of war, sneered through slug-like lips. "Why should they want to come to a small island like this? Can you tell me that, Mister Schoolmaster?"

Chairs swivelled to face Jack and conversations stopped.

"Go on then," urged the brawny farmer, "tell us."

Jack, uncomfortable, took another drink, wiped the froth brusquely with his arm and turned away saying: "Don't be so bloody silly."

But a young and polite voice spoke through the strong light above the bar billiard table.

"I'm a bit worried too sir, I'd like to know what you think."

Jack recognised the voice of a former pupil. He was at once annoyed and excited. In most teachers there is a speechmaker waiting for an audience which doesn't sniffle, fart or suck sweets. He peered nervously into the shadowy areas of the room unlit by the strong light. Mary pressed his arm encouragingly.

"Go on Jack, what do you think?"

He thought as fast as he could while performing a number of slow movements, a swig of beer, a finger through the hair, a rub of the nose, a tweak of the chin then, barely conscious of having started, he said: "For a start I'm not an expert and, in any case I can't answer the question you most want answered. If they are going to come is it best to stay and see what happens or to get away to England before they arrive? You can only answer that one for yourselves."

He leaned over towards the green baize table and shaded his eyes again. "Luc behind me and Fred over there with the golden cue at the bar billiard table have asked me whether the Germans will be coming here or not. All I can say is, if France falls, and we've all heard on the wireless that Paris could go any minute, then, in my opinion they will be here in no time." The silence seemed to congeal. His words had not surprised anyone but they had now been voiced aloud and authoritatively. At that moment everyone felt them to be true. It was that kind of statement at that kind of moment. Jack looked up again.

"Most of the British army, as you know, had to get out of France at Dunkirk the other week in a helluva state. Belgium and Holland have had it. So, once Paris goes, the Germans are bound to head in all directions across France and I can think of several reasons why they would want to come here."

The teacher had taken over. He moved from the bar and pointed vaguely towards France.

"We won't simply be a dot on the map anymore. They will be able to see us from the Cotentin and it just doesn't happen that an army stops and leaves a tiny bit offshore untouched. No commander in his right mind is going to leave islands unoccupied lying just off his coast for the free use of its harbours and airport by the enemy. On top of that we are British, so imagine the propaganda boost to the Germans to goosestep about on British soil."

This is beginning to sound too much like a lesson," he thought, turning to the bar.

"Another Mary, Mary, please."

The seated drinkers, who had eased their bodies slightly forward as they listened, sank back in unison. There followed a rush for refills, just for something to do and the conversation started again even more volubly than before.

"T t ternelle m mille bb bougre" swore Adolphe in Jersey-French. "If J Jack says they're coming they're c coming."

Jack felt uneasy with all the eyes on him again. He moved over to the bar billiard table and clapped a hand on the shoulder of his former pupil.

"Come on Fred, why don't you thrash me at this? You are a lot handier with a cue than you were with a pen."

Fred agreed with a sheepish grin which helped to hide the anxiety he felt as he asked if his teacher was intending to leave the island.

"I don't know, Fred, to tell you the truth. Like everybody else, I've only just begun to think about it. You must think about it too, young man. It may not be much fun for somebody of your age to stay here. Come on. Set up those pegs and let's see if I can still play."

The boy potted steadily and carefully, building up twenties and thirties in the corners of the table. Jack tried too cleverly for fifties and hundreds and twice knocked the side peg over, then, inevitably, the black one; a Nazi peg, he thought which simulated death too closely, wiping out your whole score just as you were in reach of something.

"You're not on form, Mr Birel."

"No, Fred, I'm thinking too much."

Jack took games seriously and was often accused of having an excessive determination to win, so he was surprised at his reckless play. Surely that couldn't be put down to the war? Yet the atmosphere was undoubtedly odd, odd enough to have prodded him into giving the whole pub his assessment of the invasion prospects. They'd come in here for mutual comfort and he'd virtually confirmed their worst fears.

Fred was tapping his shoulder: "Are you OK, Mr Birel? It's your go."

"Sorry, Fred. Listen. Would you have thought the Germans might be coming here if I hadn't said anything just now?"

"Not really, Mr Birel," replied Fred a little confused.

"Then why have you decided now that they are coming?"

"Well you made it seem pretty certain," said the young man.

Jack was stung with panic. He banged the wooded surround of the table with his cue.

"Listen everybody." He called to two people about to leave the pub to stop, admonished the Bigous as silly twerps for getting him into this and continued: "This is too serious a matter for you to just think that what I have said is right. I don't know any more than anybody else."

With a little jump he sat on the bar and spoke, more quietly but moving his hands a lot.

"If I've helped you start thinking things out a bit more clearly, that's fine but it is no more than that." He could feel he was about to repeat himself and made a gesture of turning his collar around. "If I'm not careful, I'm going to start making a sermon."

"That'll be the bloody day!" roared Baptiste, the postman.

Above the laughter Jack shouted a final thought.

"Whatever you do, don't start or pass on rumours. Nothing could be worse at a time like this. Let's all have another drink and sing a bloody song."

For the last half hour the pub bulged with chorus after chorus: Tipperary, Auprès de ma Blonde, echoes of war. Mary was called over to the piano where the men jostled for a position in line with her seated bosom. Voices crackled like a badly tuned wireless across the churchyard, a welcome release of pent up tension.

At eleven, they bundled out in party mood, cracking jokes, cuddling wives and girlfriends amid much squealing. Young men leapt on walls and danced precariously. Rude suggestions were yelled in the night at Adolph Hitler. Baptiste made everyone laugh with his assessment in Jersey French:

"Il est si bas tchu, quand i'pète i'fait l'ver l'ponsi- he's such a shortarse, when he farts he blows up the dust."

Jack walked home briskly, filled with an inner excitement and enthusiasm to start his diary straightaway on the crest of a new creative purpose.

His wife Alice, unusually tired, had stayed in and was well asleep. What to tell her of these stirring events, of his addressing, twice, all those people in the pub? Should he tell her about the diary? What would she say?

He boiled the kettle, emptied the teapot and ladled in far too much tea as he gazed absent-mindedly into the twilit garden. Then with one hand he tried to take a cup from the cupboard but it fell to the floor and smashed into black pieces. Words like 'omen' and 'sinister' leapt quickly to his mind. Perhaps the wireless would have better news.

Jack learned that Churchill had met with the French leaders and spoken to them in forceful terms about continuing the fight. He was a better bet than Chamberlain, the poor sod, thought Jack. 'Never stood a chance against Hitler, too much of a gentleman. A bit like the headmaster in a way! When you are dealing with a nasty little bugger like that, you've got to be a bit of a bastard yourself. Teachers are more aware than most of the folly of allowing someone to get away with wrongdoing in the hope that they are just going to stop it. 'Blood, toil, sweat and tears', good stirring stuff but we haven't finished giving it yet. And the French Maginot Line! What a farce! A piece of barbed wire would have been as good. A blessing in a way that poor old Maginot hadn't lived to see this. Haven't been so keen on oysters since I read he died eating them at a New Year's party.

Anyway the French could crumble at any moment. What then? What's the point of leaving Jersey? To go where? And would we even get there?'

He stopped himself thinking and switched off the wireless. Would there still be football matches in England? He was thinking again already. He finished his cup of tea. If he didn't start his diary now, he never would.

He found an unused notebook and a pen and began:

*First Fears: For the moment I can't say Journal of what. It is meant to be a Journal of the German invasion and perhaps, occupation of Jersey. In spite of what I have just said in the pub, they may not come. The British may defend the islands successfully. Once France is taken, there may be a negotiated peace or whatever they call it. The best outcome is that not long after I start this journal, there will be nothing to write about and life will have got back to normal. Circumstances may be such that I (we) will be evacuated from the island, willingly or unwillingly. In that case my journal, if I continued it, would become something completely different.*

*How does one write a Journal? The few precedents I am aware of go back a bit; Samuel Pepys' Diary and Daniel Defoe's Journal of a Plague Year. More recently there are some harrowing diaries of life in the trenches in the Great War. I must see what I can find in the library. If the Germans do come, will the library remain open? Already it is clear that there are hundreds of questions to be asked. Will we be able to do this or that if the Germans come? Those questions and answers will be at the heart of my journal I suppose. I must also keep a note of what people say and think as things develop. Already I have a small collection of comments I jotted down in the pub on my cigarette packet:*

*"We'll all be slaughtered like pigs."*

*"The sea will save us."*

*"I'm not going to England, me. I've never been there and I'm not going now."*

*"If the Germans look like coming, I'm off."*

*"I bet we'll all get called up."*

*Equally I must record as faithfully as I can what these as yet unknown events will mean for the island as a whole, for the people of the little community here at St. Martin's, for members of my family and for me. I must try and discipline myself to write something every day, otherwise I know what will happen.*

*Perhaps I should start with a few thoughts about who I am in the context of a possible German invasion. I am a male and thirty three. I don't think I am particularly brave but I hope that, as a teacher, I would be able to show some moral leadership when it is required.*

*I have called today's entry 'First Fears' because, for most of us, the realisation of what might happen has only just come home. The key question everyone faces is:*

*Should they abandon their island, their homes and most of their possessions to go to England, or even further afield, or should they stay and see what happens if and when the Germans arrive? My own instinct as regards evacuation is that l just can't imagine leaving my island or my job as a teacher. If Alice wants us to go that would be a completely different matter. I haven't discussed it much with her yet but I doubt that she would want to leave her parents and go off to an unknown future in England, to which she has never been, even on holiday.*

*I can understand why Pepys kept writing 'and so to bed' because if you write a diary or journal at the end of a day's events, so to bed it is!*

Alice woke up in spite of Jack creeping upstairs on slippered toes. Her sleep had come with difficulty, affected by the ceaseless talk of war in the papers and on the wireless and the worry of what might happen to Jack. She was slim, attractive with waves of long blond hair and an ever-cheerful personality. They had been married seven years. As he came into the bedroom the sudden and awful thought came to Jack that a German might touch her and that he would want to kill him. His body stiffened at this realisation.

"What's the matter? Are you tight?" Alice asked.

"Not in the slightest. Just momentarily struck by the thought of what I would do if a German laid a hand on you."

Alice propped herself up on the pillow. "What would you do?"

"I'd kill him," said Jack.

Alice laughed.

"It's not funny, darling, I have just realised that I would actually want to kill somebody."

"What brought all this on, for goodness sake?"

"People talking in the pub. It's been a strange evening. I hope I haven't made matters worse."

"What on earth did you do?" asked Alice with a worried frown."

Jack related his intervention. "They were staring at me as if I was Moses coming down with the tablets of stone. Then we sang our guts out and I've decided to write a journal."

He stopped, conscious that he sounded like an excited child, everything rushing out at once. He got into bed. All over the island husbands, wives and lovers were worrying, discussing and arguing – the early stages of what would lead to the most critical decision of their lives.

# TWO

*Friday 14 June, 1940*

Jack's brother-in-law, Henry Falle, was out in his field by the church soon after sunrise. A man of the soil, alone with nature, is well placed to mull. Row after row stretches out ahead waiting to be picked, tied or hoed. He sees things growing, things dying and birds and worms and mice. A silence takes him to the beyond, the meat and drink of philosopher and poet.

But Henry was not a man to mull with profit. Too often, he simply fed his penchant for depression. He could barely cope with the cinema newsreel images of the German bombing and invasion of Holland which he kept seeing in his mind.

Jack emerged from his back door onto the narrow cobbled path running by the wall of the field.

"These tomatoes are doing well. Why don't you leave them get on with it and take my place at school while I go down to the beach?"

"We could do with some rain," muttered Henry.

"What a typical farmer," laughed Jack, "Everybody else is saying what a wonderful summer it is and you are doing rain dances behind your shed."

Henry nearly smiled but grew quickly serious again, his large unshaven face seeming to droop.

He asked Jack about the breaking news on the wireless that Paris had been declared an open city and that the Germans had just marched in.

"There's not much good news about," he added. "Some lorries of spuds were turned back at the pier yesterday and the price has gone down from four pence to thruppence ha'penny a pound."

Only Henry could switch from the fall of Paris to the fall in the price of potatoes in the same sentence.

Jack tried to change the subject. "Did you hear that Baptiste got the Derby winner yesterday? When he saw there was a horse called Pont L'Evêque, he backed it like a shot. He was telling everybody in the pub last night that a piece of cheese had won the Derby."

This time Henry did manage a chuckle then added: "I've been told you made a speech about the Germans coming and God knows what."

"Somebody's already spoken to you about that, have they?" said Jack, alarmed. "I hope there are not going to be all sorts of stories about what I said."

"People are funny like that. You'd think when not much happens they would get it right, but bah."

Jack smiled wryly because his brother-in-law was describing himself perfectly.

Henry went on to ask if Jack was going to say anything to the kids at school.

"All one can do," said Jack, "is try to reassure them and counteract the nonsense they might hear elsewhere. If the Head says anything he could easily make a 'foutaise' of it. He's a lovely man and a damn good teacher but he's hopeless talking to the whole school in assembly."

"Don't remind me about school and headmasters," said Henry. "You don't know how lucky you were to have brains, you."

Jack smiled and walked into the main road. He had neither the time nor the inclination to let Henry get started on his schooldays.

Within twenty yards a group of children had gathered around and nearly deafened him. "Hello sir, look sir, why have we got to go to school today sir?" They were still chirpy and friendly but he feared for what might happen to them. They skipped, jostled to carry his bag, show him a beetle, a matchbox, a drawing. Might they do something thoughtless and suffer dreadful consequences? 'Boys will be boys' and 'you're only young once' were concepts suspended in wartime. Life is strange. If a photographer snapped this scene and showed it to people in fifty years time, would they not say something like: 'how charming! a teacher without a care in the world strolling to school with his pupils on a lovely summer's day.'

At school he slinked, or was it slanked or slunk, into the empty untidy staffroom unable to rid his mind of what might happen to the children. Perhaps they should all be evacuated but what about their parents? Should they be allowed to accompany them? Would there be special extra boats? Would there be room for all who wanted to go?

"Sorry, I was just thinking," he said to a colleague who had walked in and looked at him curiously.

"Nothing serious, I hope," said Miss Cooley, the Senior Mistress.

"Only if you call war serious," replied Jack, uncharacteristically curt.

~

Meanwhile Henry hacked and hoed at his weeds, all the more miserably when he rounded the bottom of the field and the cross of the Great War memorial came starkly into view. The inscribed names were all familiar to him, though thankfully his older brother and uncle had survived. So had his teachers, men like Jack, who, after years of training had been diverted from the classroom to the mud and suffering of Flanders. It made you wonder what education was all for. A few years older than Jack, Henry had seen his schooling left in the charge of the clever girls as they reached school-leaving age while the then headmaster, the only man left in the school, kept discipline with large hands fuelled by bottles of gin.

The clatter of a bicycle followed by the appearance above the wall of a hearty red face under a postman's cap brought him back to the present.

"Ah, by goodness me, bougre," said Baptiste Bartel, "you talk about it's hot today, you, and all go, eh. Everybody's gone mad writing twice as much as usual. I'll have to get a bigger bag."

"Why's that then?" asked Henry.

"Ch'est la dgerre, the war. By cri, it's worse than Christmas. They're all writing to relations in England and getting answers back. There's no sense left anywhere. You know the Colonel's widow down at the Hall is starting to pack her bags?"

"Go on!" said Henry.

"Yes," continued the postman, lifting his cap to wipe a welcome sleeve across his forehead.

"She's off. 'Those Germans are not nice, Baptiste,' she told me."

"Well you can understand her," said Henry sympathetically. "An old woman on her own like that. She doesn't want to be bullied about."

To Henry's surprise, Baptiste disagreed. "I don't see why we should panic, me. You should have heard the 'niolîn', the tripe talked in the pub last night after Jack had spoken. I reckon the Germans are just ordinary blokes, some of them are bloody postmen and farmers like us. They can't help being called up. They won't stay long, they've got wives and kids back home."

Henry pointed to the War Memorial. "A lot of them had wives and kids back home too."

"Yes," conceded Baptiste, "but just think about it. What would the Jerries want to hang around here for? When Hitler's got what he wants, the whole thing will finish and that will be that. It's daft for an old woman to uproot herself at her age."

Henry listened, leaning on his hoe, his eye fixed on a swallow darting in and out of the headstones in the cemetery. More opinions ! Who was right, his brother-in-law, the old lady, Baptiste? Nothing bothered the postman in any case. He took life philosophically and shaped it into something humorous. He and Henry had shared their impoverished schooldays. Baptiste had been a 'tearaway' then, a handy chap for smearing cow dung in unexpected places like wheelbarrow handles.

"Are you going to do your cowshit tricks on the enemy ?" Henry asked him.

"My goodness me, that's a bloody good idea, buggered yes. Where are your cows? I must get my hand back in." He smacked his leg several times laughing uproariously and pointed to the pub. "It should be open, I'm going to check the barrels are not leaking. D'you fancy a break, you?"

Physical work, mental turmoil and the heat had quite exhausted Henry. He jumped down from the wall and banged his boots loudly in the road to shake off the ground.

"You sound like the Nazis by cri, goose stepping about like silly buggers," remarked Baptiste.

In the pub the semi-permanent occupants, the parish workmen and the gravedigger, were well in position. Baptiste shouted to the latter: "You ought to change your name,you, Adolphe or people are going to start sticking their arms out at you."

"D d don't be d daft, you tchu Baptiste, I'm not changing nothing for nobody."

No one had seen Adolphe without his wellingtons, the colour long-hidden under the caked ground from many a grave. Rumour had it that he had not taken them off for months. Their present hue matched his two remaining front teeth which did little to help the passage of his stammered utterances. His spiritual condition generally vacillated from not too drunk to very far from sober. Pint after pint went down punctuated, when he had the money, by flasks of rum. He used to shout to passers-by, that he was playing the bugle as he swayed bottle to mouth, on a pile of earth he had managed to dig out. The vicar was resigned to the possibility that one day a coffin would not fit into a grave which had been inebriately dug. With the pub so near to the cemetery, it was only a matter of time before Adolphe drank himself into one of his holes in the ground.

Baptiste bought a further round on the strength of his Derby winnings, not without suggestive remarks about the mobility of Mary's sweater. She told him firmly to stop his nonsense and repeated the news that the Germans were definitely in Paris, adding: "To think that we were there on honeymoon only the year before last!"

Talk of honeymoons could only provoke Baptiste and he did not disappoint. Nothing could make him concentrate for long on the war. Henry on the other hand, showed immediate concern and pressed Mary with questions. She replied that hundreds of refugees on the roads out of the capital, walking with their possessions loaded on carts and bicycles, were being machine gunned from the air. "The German planes were just flying over and shooting."

This chilling news brought the reality of war much closer. Few in the pub could have placed Poland or Czechoslovakia on a map of Europe, but Paris!

"Jack said last night that if Paris fell, the Germans would soon be here", said Mary. "They could shoot us all."

A moody silence fell over the assembly.

~

Alice was due to have dinner at her sister's with Jack and, in brilliant white blouse and red skirt, she started across the field which ran from the back of her little house to Henry and Jeanne's farm. Henry had returned to hoe with much diminished enthusiasm. The bell rang out from the catholic church behind the trees and, although Alice no longer practised the religion of her mother, the ringing reminded her of Millet's painting of the Angelus which had hung over the old iron bedstead of her childhood. After a brief reflective moment, she called to Henry. He welcomed a further chance to leave his work.

"Look at the sky and those birds, Henry; not even the Nazis can paint the sky black, trample every flower or butcher every bird."

"You ought to write poetry, you," said Henry.

"Hah! It's bad enough having one frustrated writer in the family."

They walked for a bit in silence towards the farm when suddenly Alice squealed and rubbed her leg hard. "Damn stinging nettle, I haven't been stung for years. There I was just admiring how wonderful nature was and one of its nastier species stings me without warning. I hope it's not an omen."

Fortunately Henry didn't worry too much about the inexplicable.

"You've just been stung that's all. I get stung, me, at least once a week. When I was four I sat in a clump of nettles with no clothes on."

In spite of her discomfort, Alice laughed. "I hope it didn't do any permanent damage."

"Ah bah," mumbled Henry, "here's a dock leaf; rub that on."

At the farmhouse they ran into the uncoordinated assault of children, dogs and goat. Jojo, three and Louise, nearly two, clutched at legs and squealed with pleasure. They were carried into the kitchen where Jeanne was cooking with quick flustered movements. She had been for a walk with the children, dinner wasn't ready and Henry didn't usually come back that early.

He replied tersely that he was fed up working in the field, that he could jolly well come in when he jolly well felt like it and that he kept thinking about the Germans.

"That's why I went out too," said Jeanne, "to try to get my thoughts together."

She turned to her sister. "Have you spoken to Maman and Papa about anything? What are they going to do?"

Alice wasn't at all sure.

"Ah bah! Let's not talk about that," Henry snapped miserably.

Jack's arrival for dinner helped to lighten the atmosphere. He lifted Jojo on his shoulders and galloped around the room before collapsing into an armchair.

After a sip of the proffered Dubonnet he beamed and said: "Well, we had some fun at school this morning. I told you, didn't I Henry, that the Head might make a mess of things if he talked to the kids about the war? Well, he hit the jackpot."

Alice was eager to know what Mr Stevens had done.

Jack continued: "When I got to school, I was a bit upset because I had started thinking about what the Germans might do to the kids if they behaved badly. Stevens asked me into his study and began to shuffle about like he does. Eventually he said: 'I hear you told people in the public house....' - you can imagine how he said 'public house', you know he doesn't approve... where was I? ah yes... 'I hear you told people that the Germans will be coming here,'. I explained what I had said and why. He didn't agree. He reckoned they would stop at Carteret. I tried to point out that they did have planes but he said that we could shut the airport. Jack put on his posh English voice: 'Awfully sorry, Herr Hitler old boy, but we are closed. You can't land here.' Anyway, I asked him why, in that case, the French had not asked the Germans not to go round the side of the Maginot Line He stuttered a bit and went on about loose talk and starting rumours, which upset me and I told him that I had specifically warned people against passing on rumours and that he had better get his facts right. Can you imagine anything like this happening normally? He's a good man, I just don't know what got into him."

The meal was ready now, though Jeanne was still flapping. The plates and pots were brought to the table and, after a mouthful or two, Jack spoke again.

"The assembly started normally enough, heads drooping, eyelids closing, when Stevens announced from his lectern arrangement that he had something to tell them about the war.

'Some people,' he began, 'have been saying that the Germans are going to come here, perhaps tomorrow.' That woke the kids up, I can tell you. They looked horrified, I could hear them whispering 'tomorrow?'

Stevens had a helluva job shutting them up. 'Be quiet. Be quiet,' he kept saying. 'I am telling you that they are not coming, I repeat, not coming.' Then little John Leconte asked quite innocently, 'How do you know, sir?'

'I know,' then he paused before adding, 'because I am the headmaster of this school.'"

The family laughed as Jack took another mouthful.

"But hang on, that's nothing yet," he continued, showering some potato on the tablecloth and turning to the children saying:

"You see what happens when you talk with your mouth full. Philip Machin then put up his hand and instead of ignoring him as he usually does, Stevens said: 'Yes Philip', and Philip said... listen to this... 'My father told me that Mr Birel told them in the Royal last night that the Germans are coming.'"

"Oh no," moaned Alice.

"Old Stevens was rattled now. Remember we'd had that little contretemps before assembly. He looked in my direction. I was trying not to laugh. He then said: 'People who go into public houses hear all sorts of things. They are the last places where anything sensible is said' and Philip called out: 'But my dad goes to the Royal every night, sir' and sweet little Joan added: 'So does mine.' Stevens did his best: 'I didn't say they shouldn't go there, only that they would hear some funny things said.' 'But it was Mr Birel who said it,' insisted the kids. Then Andrew, you know, the English chap, leaned across and whispered to me: 'There's no answer to that.' I just exploded into my handkerchief," added Jack as he tucked into his food.

After dinner, Jack had barely turned into the school entrance when he was met by Mrs Stevens, apron flapping and hands wringing as she dashed from the school house.

"Oh, Mr Birel, my husband's sorry but he's had to go to town with Miss Cooley to a meeting of the Public Instruction Committee about the war. He says would you mind keeping an eye on things this afternoon. I don't know what they want to see him about, they phoned twice, he wasn't there the first time, I had to go and find him with the caretaker looking at something in the playground then they phoned again just as he was going to eat, I had to put everything back in the oven. And, I nearly forgot, there are some people waiting to see you. I asked them to wait by the study. I said they could come back when my husband was there but they said no they would see you, I don't know what they want."

"That's all right, Mrs Stevens," said Jack, as she paused momentarily for breath.

There was a little group of visitors near the study. Jack recognised Bert Grayley, a farmer from Rozel, then his heart sank at the sight of Mrs Le Brun, hidden for a moment behind the others.

"Are you all together?" asked Jack.

They gave a nod and filed into the study. Jack sat behind the desk amusing himself at looking important. The parents looked at each other. Had Bert Grayley been Mrs Le Brun's husband, she would have spoken first. She always spoke before her husband and after him and, more often than not, whilst he was speaking as well. But, as this was sort of official, she believed a man ought to speak first and she turned to Bert as her chosen man. With a resigned gesture of the hands, he said: " Look, Jack, we don't mind talking to you but it's Mr Stevens I'd like to complain to, I don't know about the others"

Further nods of agreement. Jack placed his hands together under his chin. Bert continued:

"My son's come home for dinner with all sorts of stories about the Germans and God knows what. I know he tends to screw up half of what you tell him but it still seems to me he's been told a load of codswallop."

Mrs Le Brun now felt the man had had his say and her whining voice began as if pumped by the heaving of her aggressive breasts.

"Anthony told me that the headmaster said the Germans were coming here tomorrow. Why haven't we been told before? The Bailiff must have known."

Where do you begin, thought Jack, when a child tells his parents the opposite of what the headmaster had said but what the headmaster had said was probably nonsense anyway? The Jersey-French expression to describe a mess of this sort, 'une tchéthue à tchians', a dog plough, came to mind.

Jack made a spirited and supportive attempt to unravel the head's position, commented on the irony of causing panic by trying to avoid panic and offered to speak again to the children himself that afternoon.

And so, for the second time in two days, Jack addressed an audience about the likelihood of Nazi Germany invading the small Channel Island of Jersey. He bolstered the head's position by stressing that what he had really meant to say was that there was no immediate fear of the Germans coming, certainly not the next day, so there was time for everyone to consider carefully what to do. Basically no one knew what was going to happen but if it looked as if the Germans might come at some future date, the Bailiff and the States would inform everyone what to do.

He stressed these points several times and repeated that there was no need to panic and to be very careful about passing on rumours.

Andrew came up to Jack afterwards. "Well done, old man, that should sort it all out. Old Stevens lost the plot a bit. Well, better go and do a few sums to take their minds off the war. By the way d'you think I could have a word after school - just a bit of advice; for me that is, not you. Could be ambiguous that."

Jack nodded and went off to his own class. The children seemed content enough, labelling pictures in French while he went over a few things in his mind. Later, pleased with the small reins of power entrusted to him, he let the children go home ten minutes early. He stood at the door and watched them run out of the gate. They always ran out and always would, however much you yelled at them.

"Have you a minute, Jack?" It was Andrew.

"I can't very well say 'no' since I've just given us all ten," smiled Jack.

"True, true, jolly good scheme, thanks. Know you can't really help and all that, nobody can, but just need to talk this out, get my ideas straight."

"Fire away."

"Well, you know, I'm English," began Andrew. "Came over here for a change of scenery and all that, knew the island a bit, dragged round the place when I was eleven by an aunt who liked climbing cliffs. Cut a long story short, thought I'd stay here about three years, then this business has to happen."

"The invasion of France, you mean."

"Yes, the whole bloody war business."

"The war started last September, of course," interrupted Jack.

"Yes, the day after I got here, in fact. Woke up, strange room, strange bed, to hear that the Nazis had smashed into Poland. Miserable affair of course, but thought nothing further likely to happen, Poland so far away. Thought they'd fix things like at Munich. Until this month nothing much has happened and now the damn Germans have marched into France and, I agree with you, are pretty likely to come here soon."

Jack nodded in agreement and sat on the steps. Andrew was in full flow, leaning against the wall, his hands deep in his pockets.

"Puts me in a bit of a spot. Like it here very much but more to the point, I'm going quite strong with Kate."

Jack had not been sure about this, although a certain amount of eye flashing between the two colleagues had not passed entirely unnoticed.

"Tried not to advertise it too much", continued Andrew, "teaching in the same school and all that, strictly Mr Durridge and Miss Le Couteur stuff."

He smiled seeing Jack's face. "Sorry, I'll never pronounce it properly."

"That's one good reason for staying to change it," said Jack, "plus the fact that you are an asset to any sane teaching establishment."

"Thank you. Jolly nice of you to say so. But you see, might not be too clever for me to stay here, an Englishman of military age. Nazis might do anything, mightn't they? Another thing. Whole family in Reading and, you know, if it comes to a proper war, feel I would want to join up or something. If there was a sort of battlefield like in the last war that everybody went to, it would be much easier to decide. Just turn up and get on with it."

Jack understood Andrew's dilemma but there were just too many unknown factors and emotions pulling in too many directions for anyone to be able to help him. For once the status quo seemed marginally more hazardous than taking some kind of action.

"Why not come over for a bite this evening? We can carry on chatting things over"

"What about Alice? Can't put her out like that."

"I'm sure she will be only too pleased to escape from her sister's. Things are a bit gloomy there at the moment. Jeanne hasn't been too strong since the second kid was born and my brother-in-law is on a bit of a downer. We can pop in and ask her."

Tea arranged, Andrew happily fell in with the suggestion that they go to the beach. The two men collected costumes, bikes and towels and were soon pedalling towards the coast. It was virtually downhill all the way to Bel Val. Ten minutes later, after a little cold shock on entering, they were enveloped in the refreshing azure sea. After swimming out to the rocks and back, they lay down on the sandy bit of the beach. A few mothers with children, pushchairs, buckets, spades, deckchairs and sandwiches were scattered about near the slip. Holidaymakers from the mainland were conspicuously absent.

Jack began. "Look across there at the coast of France. That's Carteret. Most Jersey families go over at least once a year on the boat from Gorey. My parents used to take my brother, Jim and me as a birthday treat. My father loved it."

"Do they still go?

"No," said Jack sadly. "They both died within a couple of years of each other not long after I was at college. My mother was taken ill in my last year. I felt it best to come back to the island rather than start teaching in England. Luckily there was a vacancy here. Jim, my brother, was only eighteen. He was a bright lad though not in the academic, passing exams sense. You'd have to practically chain him to a book to get him to read it. Nevertheless I hoped that he would do some sort of higher education or at least leave the island for a bit."

"From the way you are speaking it sounds as if he didn't go to college."

"Sadly, I never managed to persuade him," said Jack with a small shrug. "After leaving school, he worked with my father on the farm. He was a natural herdsman. What he doesn't know about cattle isn't worth knowing. But my father only rented the farm and after he became ill, the little money he had disappeared very fast. When dad died, Jim was at a bit of a loose end. He didn't want to work on a farm for anybody else, so he got a job on a building site at Red Houses, between the Airport and St Brelade's Bay. I think he worked on the Bailiff's new house too. He also worked for Jersey Airways at the Airport."

"I'm sorry to hear about your parents," said Andrew with some feeling. "It must have been very difficult for both you and your brother."

"Anyway, enough of that." interrupted Jack, "It can be a funny old crossing to Carteret in rough weather but it's a damn good day out and not too expensive. I wonder when we'll be able to go again."

"Clearest, I've seen the French coast," said Andrew. "Sand very bright. Is that a train, that smoke there?"

"Yes, it is, but do you realise that somewhere behind those cliffs are thousands of Germans in tanks and things heading in this direction. It doesn't seem possible, does it?"

Andrew agreed. "All is still upon the summer's day. Not a hint of menace to be seen."

"No, and the bastards are in Paris," said Jack forcefully, "wonderful French Paris where we spent our honeymoon along with half the population of the island. Not at the same time, of course," he added with a laugh. "I spent a bit of time there as a student too. There is nothing German about it." He smashed a stone down on the rock, feeling his anger rise inside him.

"Everything about Paris breathes art and culture. Anyone, even Germans, in love with history or philosophy, painters, writers, musicians, have always flocked to Paris. It is wonderfully vibrant and alive and now jackbooted krauts will be marching about the boulevards with their steel and efficiency throttling its life."

Andrew was silent, just listening to Jack, very serious, in spite of his natural jocular manner.

"Tell me Andrew," Jack continued, "what can you say to an intelligent youngster about all this? How can you tell him or her that Paris belongs to France, not because it is within the boundaries called France, but because everything about it, down to the last miserable Gauloise butt in the gutter is part of the soul that is France? And what if the same intelligent youngster asked you why the French didn't fight every inch of the way to save their capital if it means so much? How do you answer that one, Andrew?"

"If the French had fought for Paris, it would have been destroyed, so, now, when it's all over, Paris intact will go back to the French one day," Andrew suggested, throwing a pebble despairingly into the sea.

Jack continued, almost breathlessly: "That's what I thought at first when I heard the news this morning. But then, what about all those people who have made Paris what it is? What would they say? All those who have manned barricades, the men of the Bastille, of the Commune, the taxi drivers who took soldiers to the Marne in 1918, the intellectuals whose minds have imprinted themselves into galleries, bookstalls and on the walls; all those poets, painters and film directors. What would all those people say about just handing it over?"

After a few moments' silence, Andrew said quietly: "I don't know."

Even though they lay back in the sun, they could still see France because of the steep angle of the beach.

"They could really be here any day now, running up this beach even," mused Andrew. "Can we talk things over a bit more so that with your wife later we'll be able to concentrate on happier matters?"

"She's had one good laugh anyway today. I told her about assembly this morning."

"Extraordinary affair," said Andrew, with a huge grin. "Told Stevens as politely as I could that he'd made a bit of a fruitcake of it. He didn't get angry, just embarrassed. Felt a bit sorry afterwards. Nice old boy really."

"I know," agreed Jack, "the whole thing was amazing. I thought it best not to comment because I might not have been as polite as you."

He turned and shielded his eyes from the last rays of sun as it sank out of sight behind the high bank of trees at the top of the beach. The last family got up to go back for tea. A little boy ran down to collect his ball which Jack had stopped from rolling into the sea.

Andrew asked Jack how he saw things happening when the Germans came. Jack took a little while to reply, partly because he was watching the young mother trying to cope with bag, pushchair, larger child and ball up the slipway.

"I wish I knew, Andrew. I suppose the most vulnerable people are men of military age."

"Us."

"Yes, us. The Germans are unlikely to worry too much about the elderly, women and kids. They might put all men between say sixteen and forty five into a camp of some sort like the one at Grouville where we have already interned all the Germans and Italians on the island. Or they could ship all the men over to France or Germany."

"Or just shoot us." said Andrew.

"Or just shoot us. Somebody raised that possibility in the pub last night. But, I don't think they will. For no logical reason, mind you."

"I doubt if even the Nazis would systematically start killing people in cold blood but they could easily do so by way of reprisal if the population doesn't comply with all their demands."

"You are probably right. We will soon know how they are going to behave in France."

"Think my being English will make me more vulnerable?" asked Andrew.

Jack thought it was unlikely to help.

Andrew pressed the point. "I don't want to go on about it but do you think they really are going to intern all the men, Jack? That could mean years off your life."

"No, I don't."

"Why not?"

"No logical reason as I said before. Possibly just wishful thinking. When I was talking about Paris, I might have said yes, but now I just think they won't. What you said about reprisals is probably right though. It would certainly be a lot easier to just shoot, or, let's hope, imprison a few people who transgress, than to have to look after thousands of men getting more and more restless in camps."

"Somebody does something stupid, though, and it's men of our age for the high jump, right?"

"Almost certainly," agreed Jack. "At the moment, I think I'm prepared to risk it. It's pretty scary though, if you dwell on it too much."

"So where do we go from here?" asked Andrew with a shrug of helplessness.

"Well, Andrew, it could come down to asking yourself how much Kate means to you, because everything else seems to point to your leaving. You are English, male, young, family on the mainland and you feel you might want to join up. Lined up against that is a lovely woman. Shakespeare has probably written a play about it. You can, of course, always take her with you."

"Will she come, though?"

"Ask her. I don't know her terribly well. She's a good bit younger than me for a start and comes from St Ouen's - wild lot out there."

Andrew laughed. "Can't be that bad, it's only eight miles for goodness sake."

"But those miles make all the difference, you mark my words. I've played football against them. When you run out on their pitch, fern and moss kept together with cow dung, you take your life in your hands. The main cry of their supporters, in Jersey-French of course, is: 'Reste pas la à gober la leune, co-d'pise-li dans l'ventre - don't stand there gawping at the moon, kick him in the guts.' Any team who played against them needed a goalkeeper as big as Jacko from the Royal or he'd end up in the net, with or without the ball, at every corner kick."

"OK, OK," said Andrew. "Got the score, no pun intended."

"Sorry, I got carried away," said Jack. "She's a smashing girl."

"Just have to ask her," declared Andrew.

Alice was back from Jeanne's and moving busily around the kitchen when they came in. It was the first time that Andrew had stayed longer than a few minutes in the house.

"Dubonnet, all right?" asked Jack. "We drink bottles of the stuff."

"You make us sound like alcoholics," chided his wife.

"But we are! I have every intention of carrying on where Adolphe leaves off. You know Adolphe, don't you Andrew? The gravedigger, not the German version."

Andrew nodded with a smile.

Alice sat opposite the two men at the table. They had plenty to tell her of the afternoon at school and on the beach. Naturally Andrew's involvement with Kate was of particular interest.

"I warned him about les St Ouennaises, but I don't think he believes me," said Jack.

Alice giggled. "We call it the wild west. They eat raw limpets out there."

Andrew held up his hands. "I'm convinced."

Two treats were announced for tea. Paul Vigot, from Greencliff, had brought some mackerel straight out of the sea. They could smell it frying nicely. Funny word 'waft' thought Jack. A more unusual gastronomic feature were medlars from Alice's uncle's garden. Andrew had never heard of them. They could be mistaken for small apples and, after initial doubts about swallowing something which had to more or less rot first to taste their best, he quite enjoyed them.

Alice was far too excited by Andrew and Kate's future plans in such uncertain times to allow the subject to rest. "Are you going to stay over here do you think?"

"Don't know, been discussing it with Jack, much confused at the moment, with the Germans so jolly near."

"What about family in England?"

"Teaching dynasty, I'm afraid. No surprise to them if I start courting another teacher. Both parents teachers, father retired now, mother part-time, mother's father was a headteacher in a small village near Guildford at the turn of the century."

"Do you think Kate would be happy to up sticks and go to England with you?"

"That's the question isn't it? Don't know again, don't know much do I? Haven't asked her, didn't want to pressurise her but now, with Paris gone, things starting to move pretty quickly, have to ask her. Another sleepless night I suppose."

"What about your parents, wouldn't they want you to come home?" pressed Alice.

"Course they would," said Andrew very quickly. "That's why it's all jolly difficult. Anyway, some meal, that, fresh mackerel a bit scarce in Reading and, as for medlars, something to talk about." He shook his blond hair in mock disbelief.

"Tu n'as pas acuou veu la grosse bête qui t'mangera" said Jack.

"Made that nonsense up, I'll be bound."

"You can't make that sort of stuff up. It's what you say when someone claims they've never seen the likes, or they've never heard of such a thing. 'You haven't yet seen the big beast that's going to eat you.'"

"La grosse what?"

"Bête."

"Hope 'la grosse bête' is not the Germans. Let me take you to the pub for a nightcap."

"I'm not sure I dare after last night," said Jack.

"Worried about giving the headmaster cause for another assembly?" laughed Andrew.

Alice's casting vote decided Jack, more reluctant in the word than in the intention. She clung to her husband's arm as they crossed the churchyard.

"I never walk through here on my own at night, even in summer. It's so spooky."

Then she started laughing. "Last year, our neighbour, he's quite serious, a bit stuffy you know, it was some time in winter, wasn't it Jack? Anyway, it was raining, really pouring down and he was coming back from somewhere or other, not the pub, because he doesn't drink, through the churchyard and he fell into an open grave which Adolphe had left uncovered. Luckily, there were a few people about and somebody heard him shout. They actually came to our place to fetch a ladder to get him out."

Jack carried on the story. "The funny thing was, when we got there with torches and so on, he was normally so prim and proper, a solicitor's clerk, not that that means anything necessarily, anyway he was covered in mud and I mean really covered, and soaked and holding his leg and swearing like I've never heard swearing before or since. The dead were sitting up that night, I can assure you. I think it was this grave here," said Jack, pointing to a few dead flowers.

An observer of this scene would have been surprised, perhaps shocked that people gazing at a grave could be laughing so much. "He didn't speak to any of us or thank us or anything," continued Jack. "He just kept putting all the swear words at his command in tremendous combinations. He hobbled off like Charles Laughton in the Hunchback of Notre Dame. Have you seen it?"

Andrew nodded.

"Belheche - that's his name - headed for the pub. We sensed something was going to happen and followed him in. He was already shaking Adolphe by the collar and calling him unbelievable things. The pub was in a helluva stir. Imagine it, the drinkers had been standing around happily downing pints when the door burst open like in a Western and a normally respectable man, who was known not to drink, had come limping in, covered in mud, gone straight up to Adolphe and grabbed him by the throat, calling him obscenities."

Andrew could only cry 'stop, stop' as he clutched his aching sides.

"Looking back on it, I can understand now what old Stevens meant when he said that you didn't hear anything sensible said in a public house."

They pushed open the door of the Royal. The atmosphere in the smoke-filled room was much the same as the previous evening - lots of people and much jostling and argument. The words 'Germans', 'Paris' and 'evacuation' seemed to dominate every sentence, along with expressions like 'getting bloody close' and 'won't be too hot here.' The gravedigger was half propped against the bar, his nose buried in a tall glass. Jack asked him, mischievously, if anyone had fallen into one of his graves lately. Adolphe spluttered in his drink.

"B b bloody hell! C cor what a night that was, you. I thought the b b bugger'd gone mad. D did he shake me! And the n n names he called me, you. For m months when he saw me, he would sh sh shout and wave his fists."

Mary was listening with her best beaming grin.

"It's good to have a laugh with all this worry about. I heard more words that night than I ever knew existed. And from such a strict man."

"Right, Mary, a Mary," said Jack. "What are you having, Andrew?"

"What's that stuff Adolphe's drinking ?"

"It's a b b brown b boiler."

"OK, one of those please"

"I'll stick to Dubonnet," said Alice.

"Du dubonnet, it nearly killed me that stuff," said Adolphe.

He, of course, did not mean it in the sense that most alcoholic drink was nearly killing him all the time. He continued with his story, lapsing occasionally into Jersey-French made all the more amusing by his stammer. He had gone to Carteret on a day trip with some fellow drinkers and they had got no further than the Café du Port, where they spent the day eating and drinking. They were at about peak intake when a local, of similar bent, had started them off on Dubonnet. The result had been a desperate zigzagging charge towards the boat which was just pulling away from the jetty and Adolphe had ended up in the harbour.

"What a b bloody hoo ha, you," he continued, "they k kept me in prison overnight."

Andrew just managed to say that he had never laughed as much in one day. Jersey anecdotes just seemed to trigger themselves off one after the other.

Mary repeated: "We need a good laugh these days."

In spite of that, the pub hummed anxiously around them. People seem to talk louder when they don't know what they are talking about. Arguments broke out easily. Jack avoided talk of the war by introducing Andrew to bar billiards.

Later, after steering Andrew homewards, Alice said: "Well, well Andrew and Kate. What are they going to do? He's so sweet and cuddly."

"I sympathise with him," said Jack. "Everything he's got, except her of course, is in England."

"She'll go with him, if he goes, won't she? It won't be much fun for her if he's called up, though."

"He's very English," added Jack.

"What do you mean by that?"

"The way he speaks mainly, his accent, his crisp phrases, his sardonic sense of humour and the way he carries himself."

"Well I think he's sweet," repeated Alice, "much better mannered and more civilised than most men around here. Did you notice how he stood out in the pub?"

"That's not very fair love. I mean, next to Adolphe, anybody would stand out as pretty civilised."

Alice giggled at the thought and offered to make a cup of tea while Jack settled down to his diary. Then she said suddenly:

"What about us?"

"What, going you mean?"

"What else can I mean?"

"We were just comparing Andrew and Adolphe."

"Well!"

"Well what?"

"What do you think about going?"

"I don't really want to go anywhere unless something dramatic forces us out."

"Like what?"

"I don't know, that's the trouble," said Jack becoming a little agitated.

"Well I don't want to leave my parents," said Alice, "but I'm worried about what might happen to you. What about your brother? Jennifer won't want to leave now any more than she did when he was working at the airport. We'll have to talk about it again. Don't be too long."

*Journal*

*Fall of Paris*

*The tragic news today is of the fall of Paris. It was declared an open city and the Germans have just marched in. I feel a certain relief that the city and its beauty has been saved but a great sense of misery that jackbooted soldiers are marching and laughing in places I know so well, the Champs Elysees, the Tuileries, Montmartre, Notre Dame, the Boul Mich, up the Eiffel Tower even. How many people have left, I wonder?*

*..I don't regret speaking in the pub last night although I am concerned at how easily rumour and misinterpretation can take a hold. The arrival at school of several parents whose children had given them completely garbled information of what the headmaster had said was quite extraordinary. There is a lesson to be learned from that about how we communicate. Some things will be just too serious to entrust to the children.*

*..Already dilemmas are beginning to show. Andrew, an English colleague at school, is having to weigh up where he stands. He has made me think about what might happen to men of military age on the island once the Germans are here and whether some people might be better off leaving. I haven't mentioned it to Alice yet but we might have to face the fact that I could be interned somewhere.*

*It looks as if the Colonel's widow from the Hall has decided to go. What an upheaval it will be for her! Andrew also asked me about my parents. It made me miss them more than I have for a little while. How would they have coped with what we may be going to face? (What sort of sentence is that? A past conditional future subjunctive! ) How well will the Germans speak English? Not many islanders speak German, that's for sure. Perhaps French will become a common language? And Jersey-French behind their backs! More questions.*

*..We are going to need some earthiness and humour to help get us through the days ahead. Baptiste, our postman and fount of all known information and Adolphe, the gravedigger (what a cracking name), will provide plenty of that.*

*..At school today I kept worrying about the children. How will they cope with an occupation? It is such a dreadful, alien thing to have youthful*

*freedom curtailed in this way. I know war is horrible and already thousands of people have been killed but it is almost impossible to conceive it happening here on a small, peaceful (and beautiful) island. War, sadly takes little account of beauty, or only hangs on to it at a cost, as in Paris.*

Later in bed he whispered to Alice that if the Germans were going to ban lovemaking, they ought to get in as much as possible while they had the chance.

# THREE

*Saturday 15 June, 1940*

Like many inhabitants of the country parishes, Alice and Jack went into town on Saturdays. The buses were often crowded, even more so today, with anxious people shuffling at bus stops, talking in stunned and sad disbelief about the fall of Paris and what might happen next. After the frightening news of the invasion of Poland, which had shaken everyone several months previously, the curious period of the 'phoney war' had lulled them into thinking things might not be so bad after all. Then, with dreadful suddenness, had come the invasion of France, the disaster at Dunkirk and now, Paris.

The wireless and newspapers were full of the occupation of the city, with pictures of the triumphant German parade through the Arc de Triomphe and down the Champs Elysées. Surely France was finished, in spite of its government remaining on the move, first to Tours now to Bordeaux. Mary, sitting at the front of the bus, was telling the deaf Mrs Long how the Germans had killed hundreds of ordinary people, including women and children, as they fled along the roads leading towards the South and West of France.

The bus, already full at St Martin's, sped past outstretched hands to the terminus at Snow Hill. People in King Street and Queen Street scurried everywhere like clichéd ants to stock up with goods, to pass on information or comfort but only too eager to feed on the wildest rumours before a more vicious breed of ant dislocated their lives.

French Lane, as Hilgrove Street was popularly known, was packed with Breton workers standing in little groups, their faces shining through years of cider and rough red wine. They knew even less what to do than the locals, with their capital fallen and Brittany now obviously vulnerable.

They were arguing furiously as they always did, only this time, at least, they had something to argue about. Jack and Alice pushed their way past the garlic fumes into the market where Jack, standing around as bag holder, was able to admire one of the few buildings in the town of outstanding architectural interest - a fine feat of engineering by TW Helliwell in 1882 to fit into an octagonal site amid Georgian and Victorian houses and shops. The stalls, gathered in the cruciform central area competed with the colour, variety and presentation of their produce. The centre piece, against which Jack was leaning, was a fountain-cum-rockery with ironwork imported from Yorkshire. A local iron-founder, George Le Feuvre, however, had been responsible for the external gates and railings, depicting heads of sheep, deer, bulls and lovebirds with pendants of bunches of grapes, vine leaves and fleur-de-lys. Several times Jack chatted and passed the time of day with children from school and their parents. They were all buying food furiously in a manner reminiscent of Christmas. Was this the beginning of a big stock up Jack wondered? More and more, he found himself pondering on whether the scene, building, activity or people currently under his gaze, would continue unaltered when the Germans came. Would there be anything to sell in the market? Would the clocks stay at British time? Would the fountain splash on unabated?

Lost in his random musings, he was not quick enough to take evasive action as the headmaster bore down on him like the proverbial Assyrian.

"Ah Mr Birel," said the Head.

"Good morning, Mr Stevens, lovely day isn't it?"

"Yes, isn't it?"

How very English we sound, thought Jack, smiling at the idea of the Bretons saying to each other: 'Beau jour, n'est-il pas? Oui, n'est-il pas?'

There was a silent pause as both men began to fidget. Jack focused on the curious little fat cherubs which held up the central fountain.

"That, er business yesterday," the Head began, "I spoke to Miss Cooley last night. She came to see me. Thank you for what you said to the children in the afternoon, it obviously helped a lot."

Jack waved a nonchalant hand, embarrassedly.

"I just don't know how I came to confuse things so much. I thought I was acting for the best. Anyway I want to thank you but I'm still not sure about your assessment of the likely turn of events. Now, I've got a bit of news you might be interested in. At the meeting I went to yesterday we were told that British troops would start arriving today to defend the island. There's going to be a curfew too, and, something which affects us directly, the school holidays might start soon at very short notice."

Jack could barely conceal his excitement at hearing some real news.

He thanked Mr. Stevens and repeated what he had heard to Alice who had called him over to take charge of brown bags, filled with vegetables not available in Henry's patch.

"How will the soldiers coming affect us?" she asked.

"The worst scenario is if we have some kind of battle because it could be a massacre. How can an island this size be defended against the type of bombing the Germans have been doing?"

Before Alice had time to dwell on this awful prospect she felt a hand on her shoulder and turned to see the smiling face of Jack's brother, Jim, as dishevelled as ever, as if he had struggled through gale force winds.

"You haven't seen Jennifer have you? She's run off with all my money on the pretext of buying food. By the way, have you been down to the pier?"

"No, why?" asked Jack.

"It's all happening down there. We saw a crowd of British soldiers coming ashore and lots of military equipment being unloaded. The War Cabinet or somebody, some bigwig soldier, has decided to send an army battalion to Guernsey and one to Jersey. Those arriving today are the advanced guard."

"How many is a battalion?" asked Alice.

"Don't ask me. Do you know, you, Jack?"

"Haven't got a clue, but it must be quite a lot if they are serious about defending the islands. We must go and see," he added keenly, thinking of his journal.

"And that's not all," added Jim, "the queue for boat tickets at the Southern Railways Office in Bond Street stretches well into the Royal Square. Most of the people look English, mind you. They want to get home as quickly as possible."

"So an evacuation has started already," remarked Jack, partly to himself.

"Yes, by cri," said his brother, "things are moving all right. We came down with a young couple on the bus. They are from Brighton, they told us. They had just walked out of their rented place and left everything. When we got off the bus, they went straight to the back of the queue for boat tickets, just like that. Still, I suppose they've got somewhere to go to."

Jack agreed that Jersey people would not find things so straightforward if they rushed off and became refugees needing looking after in England.

The brothers arranged to meet up later and Jack almost hauled Alice in the direction of the pier.

They half-ran along Conway Street to the Weighbridge. The harbour at St.Helier is on the southern end of the town. Above it to the east is a high cliff topped by Fort Regent, still used, not long ago, as an army barracks when a regiment was permanently based on the island. Now it housed the Jersey Militia, which had been mobilised in September 1939 soon after the declaration of the war. Presumably, the arriving British soldiers would join them.

The harbour below was divided into three sections and the main basin. The Albert Quay formed the final edge of St Aubin's Bay which swept round a good third of the island's southern coastline. Not far from the harbour entrance on a rocky islet stood Elizabeth Castle, once boasting Sir Walter Raleigh as Governor of Jersey and Charles II in exile.

Jack and Alice walked past the abattoir which ran the whole width of the quay to the harbour itself. A small crowd had gathered on the quay to watch the soldiers load up lorries with military equipment. The noise of shouted orders seemed incongruous and a little frightening as it brought home what was really happening.

"Look at that young officer," said Alice. "There's certainly something about men in uniform."

"Only ours I hope," laughed Jack.

He began scribbling notes for his journal. As far as he was concerned, this was the first 'event' of the war. The arrival of these men only intensified the conflicting calls of duty. If they were coming to defend the island, then the young Jersey men of military age, in addition to those in the Militia, must have some obligation to stay and help them. Yet it could equally be argued that it was preferable to escape from the threat of occupation in order to be of greater long term use elsewhere.

"I don't understand why they are sending troops here," said Jack again with a puzzled shake of the head. "The military must be able to see that you can't defend an island this small against planes."

"Well I prefer to think that something can be done," said Alice stubbornly.

"I prefer that as well, but preference doesn't come into it. Surely if this place is a lost cause all the soldiers being sent here would be better deployed in the defence of England?"

"In that case," repeated Alice, "since they are here, it must mean that they think the islands can be defended."

Jack might not be the Chief of the Imperial General Staff advising the War Cabinet but he remained unconvinced.

When they reached the Shipping Office the queue was longer than for a new Fred Astaire film. Jack spotted several acquaintances including a former football team mate who worked for the Electricity Company.

"So, you've decided to go, Alec?" said Jack.

"Yes, I got up this morning and thought hell, this is it. I don't fancy starving."

"Well, good luck."

"Thanks, you're staying are you?"

"I think so, but there's time yet," said Jack, suddenly unsure of himself.

"Maybe, but I don't want to be caught on a cattle boat or something at the last minute. I'm an Englishman, I'm going home."

"Fair enough," said Jack as he warmly shook his hand.

Unlike the other public places where people were congregating, these men and women were no longer looking for answers and a sullen quiet hung over the queue. They seemed embarrassed, perhaps slightly guilty, at being seen to be leaving.

Jim and Jennifer were already in the Peirson, a pub of particular significance at this time. The Royal Square and the pub itself had been the main venue for the Battle of Jersey in 1781 when the English Major Peirson, a forerunner of these very men coming ashore that morning, had defeated the invading French and had died heroically doing so. The marks of the cannon balls were still visible on the walls of the pub. When at college in London, Jack had visited the Tate Gallery to see Copley's famous painting of the death of Peirson. It seemed impossible that the sound of shooting might once again fill this pretty square where old people and dogs liked to sit in the sun.

Jack bought a round and returned to the stool which Jim had cunningly hidden under the table. The place was full of anxious people talking about the arrival of the soldiers and the queues waiting to leave. Jim, who lived at La Moye in the south west of the island, had been through all the drama of decision making two months previously, when he had been working for Jersey Airways at the Airport. In April, faced with the rapidly worsening war situation, the airline had evacuated all its planes and staff to Scotland. Jim had been offered a free passage, home found, everything. Many of his colleagues had taken up the offer but Jennifer had resisted any idea of parting from her family and her island. Jim had found new work, lifting potatoes. Now the decision needed to be made again in different and more pressing circumstances.

He was just listening to Jack exploring the moral argument of staying to defend the island when a young man ran in from the square, paused only to regain his balance after tripping on the doormat and spoke breathlessly to the vivacious barmaid.

"Come on Veronica, we're off."

"Off where," she replied, startled.

"To England of course. Come on, the boat could leave at any time."

"But, but," stuttered the girl as the pub fell silent and waited.

"There's no time for butting, we've got to go," he insisted.

"Why, but where?" The poor girl didn't know where she was. "What about my parents?"

"Do you love me or not?" asked the young man.

"You know I do," said Veronica blushing furiously as she realised she had the rapt attention of the whole room.

"So, come on then."

Veronica looked at her boss, glanced shyly at the people near the bar, picked up her handbag and walked out hand in hand with the young man.

The pub throbbed into conversation in their wake. 'So that was how you evacuated, you just went. Questions everywhere! Was she doing the right thing? How long had she known him? Who was he? He seemed a nice enough chap. Had they got anywhere to go? Wouldn't mind evacuating with her myself! Jack scribbled as much as he could.

As new customers came in, whether or not they made any reference to Veronica, the landlord would say: "Well I'll be damned! A moment ago Veronica's English bloke just came in and took her off to the boat. Well I'll be damned!" He thumped the bar, tugged hard on his thick bushy beard and turned to anybody near at hand to substantiate this extraordinary story. He repeated it so often that Jim remarked he was worse than a gramophone needle stuck in a groove.

"Remember you told me about Fred, your brother, disappearing in 1915?" Jim continued, looking at Jennifer. "He was only seventeen. What a bloody to-do, nobody knew where he was."

"Yes," confirmed Jennifer. "The Centenier questioned our family for hours."

"He must have done something like those two just now because the next you heard of him was a letter from England saying he'd joined up."

"Well, I hope you're not thinking of doing the same as him," said Jennifer.

"Why not? He came back unscathed and said he'd had a great time."

"You liar, it was dreadful. If you go, I'll never talk to you again."

"Pauvre tchu," Jim roared with laughter, "if I'm gone I won't be there for you not to talk to!"

But the mood became serious again as they settled back into their thoughts. Jack took more notes of the comments being made around him:

"...I can't see how they could land if the army's here."

"...there'll be boats to take everyone off."

" ...just push the buggers back into the sea."

"...a few weeks..."

"...I'm not going nowhere - they can shoot me if they bloody well like."

These snatches of conversation were halted by the heavy bluster of two men entering the pub.

"Those soldiers who've just arrived are not going to defend the island. They've been recalled to England."

"What!" cried many in unison.

"We've just seen Harold. His brother works in the States' Offices, he's not supposed to know this, but he says that the War Cabinet's changed its mind and all military personel, even the young blokes at that army technical school are going to be evacuated in the next few days."

"But surely," said the landlord, distracted for a moment from the precipitous departure of the most attractive member of his staff, "they can't have brought these soldiers here for nothing?"

"You can think what you like, but Harold's brother says that the phone lines to the War Office are red hot and nobody knows what's going on. Some people want one thing, others want another."

It took some time for reasonable humour and calm to be restored.

The two couples raced each other to the chip shop. Everything seemed to taste better than usual because they wanted it to.

"I wonder where the nearest German is," asked Jack between mouthfuls of chips.

Jennifer suggested two hundred miles.

"Correct to the kilometre," said Jack.

"What's his name?" asked Alice.

"It must be Fritz."

"Why?" asked Jim

"All Germans are called Fritz, aren't they?" said Jennifer.

Jim roared with laughter again. He had the kind of laugh clowns would have paid to have in an audience. "It's not Fritz Hitler is it, or Fritz bloody Goebbels! In fact not one of the big bastards is called Fritz."

"Well the nearest one is, so there," said Jennifer but her mood quickly changed as she said. "It's not funny is it? What do you really think they are going to do to us?"

"I normally look on the bright side, me," said Jim, "but I can't see them letting the men, anyway, walk freely about. After all, we've put all the Italians and Germans into that camp at Grouville in case they got up to something, so the Germans will probably do the same with us. They've even interned Miko from the café at St Aubin's and he could only harm you if he sat on you."

Jack smiled and admitted that he kept changing his view about the likelihood of internment.

"Still, it might not be so bad, you never know," he added nervously.

"Not much fun for us, though," moaned Alice.

"All the more reason for gathering the old rose buds while we've got the chance my little love, as the poet Marvell urges us in 'To his Coy Mistress', although there is nothing coy about the two of you, most uncoy, or is it decoy?"

"Please!" winced Alice, "just remind us what Marvell wrote again."

"Something like:

'Now therefore while thy youthful hue
Sits on thy skin like morning dew
Dee dum dee dum transpires
From every pore with instant fires
Now let us sport us while we may.'"

"Well, I couldn't have put it better myself," said Jim.

~

While they spent the rest of the afternoon in town buying little luxuries including enough notebooks to see Jack through an extensive period of journal writing, Baptiste, the postman, his round completed, was cycling past the Hall on his way to the Royal. He noticed the Colonel's widow picking flowers in her garden. Aware of her unhappiness and decision to leave the island, he decided to stop, though not in such a spectacular manner. Later he was to blame the Germans. Had their arrival not been imminent and had this not affected the old lady, he would not have wanted to stop so quickly. His carrier bag knocked the little catch on his front wheel into the locking position and set into motion a series of manoeuvres so popular in Hollywood comedies. The philosopher Bergson would have noted Baptiste as a man desperately in contention with his environment, the stuff from which all comedy ultimately flows.

Sadly there were only three witnesses, a sparrow which narrowly avoided decapitation, the child playing across the road who had simply seen the bicycle hit the wall and the old lady herself, who turned to see a large human form hurtle into her pond. So, nobody really had the chance to find it funny. The words, oft repeated, that 'it all happened so quickly' were rarely more applicable.

The child's mother and the old lady had helped Baptiste from the water which had just been deep enough to prevent serious injury. In the house, the first sip of tea taken, the damage, mainly bruising to his legs, was assessed and covered with disinfectant, butter and salt, plasters and bandages. Baptiste, a repaired man, was able to limp to the pub to tell his tale and claim to be the first victim of the forthcoming invasion.

He'd had time to work on the story, but there was little need for embellishment. He had managed to do every single thing which made the incident and the telling of it, a comic gem: locked wheel, struck wall, sailed through the air, landed in pond nearly frightening to death the old lady he was meant to be comforting. From the moment he walked in he had the gripped attention of the whole pub. Once again Mary was able to say: "We need a good laugh these days."

~

Inside the front room of the Hall, the old lady sat down a moment after ministering to the stricken postman. Her gaze remained fixed on the contents of her blue and white porcelain vase. The disposition, colours and texture of the flowers came together in a clear and beautiful picture she wished to lock in her memory and take away with her. This simple wish had sparked a certain excitement in a mind she feared dulled by too many years of monotonous widowhood. She got to her feet as fast as her arthritis would allow and, with growing impatience, hunted through the packed trunk in the corner of the room until she found the book she wanted. Cursing her fingers, she turned the pages to the 'Vase of Flowers' with which, long ago, an old bohemian neighbour had awakened her enthusiasm for the Impressionists.

Taking the book outside, she began picking and searching for missing flowers, finding them in the garden, cutting them to length and at last gathering them all up and taking them indoors. Her patient hands and eyes worked them into the vase until there, on the mantlepiece stood Renoir's painting.

~

Up the road, the headmaster stumbled down the uneven steps into the shop near the end of the little lane which led to the church. A large cheese and pat of butter took pride of place on the counter. Boxes, tins, buckets and implements with handles were strewn about the floor in a kind of organised untidiness. Long-forgotten items were not quite lost in obscure crannies. Mr. Stevens felt comfortable in this shop and in buying his tobacco, was partly escaping from his wife who sensed and fretted at his every change of mood, especially when he was just trying to think, as he was now.

He left the shop, again tripping on the step and slipped into the church where he sat in the darkest corner pew like a child scared to go home after a naughty deed, or a criminal of the Middle Ages seeking sanctuary before escaping down the 'perquage.' The twelve (Anglican) parish churches had a protected 'perquage' path leading to the coast where, if a boat could be arranged, a treasonable felon could escape to self-imposed exile. Mr. Stevens doubted if the Germans would observe such niceties. His thoughts dwelled on escape, not from the island but from the regularity of his life.

He knew he had allowed himself to become old and boring. Although his job was likely to bring worries if the Germans came, there might also be an opportunity to battle and reassert his bruised self-respect. Thus he prayed to God.

He felt a new confidence, a renewed readiness to face a difficult world. He no longer seemed to care what others might think. Outside in the sun, the world, for a moment, had become a better place.

"Good afternoon Mr. Stevens," he heard. It was Mr. Belheche, solicitor's clerk, earnest churchgoer and man who fell into graves.

"How do you feel about the Germans coming?"

"What do you mean? How do I feel? How do you think I feel?"

"Well," whined Belheche, "at least the riff-raff and criminal element will be properly dealt with."

"Is that all you can think about?" said the Head curtly and walked briskly home.

"Ah, there you are!" greeted his wife. "Parents have been ringing. I told them I didn't know anything. They say that all the schools are going to close and the children are going to be evacuated. Do you know anything about it? Why didn't you tell me? Are you going to have to go with them?"

"Where have they got this nonsense from?" said Mr Stevens angrily as he went out into the garden and sat on a bench, puffing his pipe. Evacuate all the children, really! The day trips to St Malo were bad enough and the kids were supposed to enjoy those. Where would they all go at the other end in any case? What if they were bombed or attacked on the way? Surely there was nothing the Germans would do to them which could be worse than wrenching them from their homes and parents?

~

Back in town in the Forum cinema, the patrons were enthusiastic for once to stand for the National Anthem, a welcome demonstration of patriotic spirit. Certainly if the Germans came there would be no more calling on God to save the King. There probably wouldn't be any more films unless they showed some of their own.

Jack and Alice, Jim and Jennifer filed out of the Forum in that strange silent procession by which a cinema empties, nobody wanting to be first to express an opinion or even give the next waiting queue any indication of whether they were about to be moved, amused or horrified. The two couples agreed that, at least, the film had taken their minds off the war.

They determined to keep in close contact, especially when the likelihood of invasion became more obvious. The buses back were again full to their different sides of the island.

Jack settled down with his pen.

*Journal*
*To defend or not to defend*

*..Being a Saturday, crowds in town but buying furiously, with more than a hint of hoarding about it. A day of turmoil and confusion. At first the word got round that British troops were arriving to defend the island and we saw them landing at the harbour. This raised the frightening prospect of fighting. I'm not a military man but the way the' Anchluss', I think it's called (must check the spelling somewhere) has swept through the low countries and France, how can we possibly defend an island this small against bombing from the air and artillery fire from the Normandy Peninsular? Would we really want to stay here, as we pretty well decided yesterday, if an actual battle was going to rage around us?*

*Then the word went round again, apparently from someone in the know, and confirmed by the Evening Post tonight, that the War Cabinet had reversed its decision and that the soldiers who had just arrived would be returning to England and that all other military personnel would go with them -demilitarisation I think it's called. It would leave us undefended but, hopefully, less vulnerable to bombardment, like Paris, I suppose.*

*...The Evening Post says that the British Government is deciding what to do with regard to the defence of the islands.*

*Extract from the Post: 'This statement, we trust, will reassure our readers who will realise that this vital matter is safe in the hands of those most competent to know how it should be dealt with.'*

*I wish I had the same touching faith as them in the powers that be.*

*...Not surprisingly, given the rumours and counter rumours, people are beginning to leave in bigger numbers but the faces in the queue for boat tickets look terribly sad.*

*While we were having a drink, the barmaid from the Peirson was just whisked away by her boyfriend. When it is all over (how many times will I want to write that?), it would be fascinating to know what happened to them, and to Alec, the electrician I spoke to in the queue for registration and the young couple from Brighton Jim talked to on the bus. Would they have been better to have stayed?*

*...Went to the pictures. More people than usual, looking for a distraction. Gustier singing with the organ! Their enjoyment of the film, if they were like me, was tinged with a feeling of fear in the stomach.*

*... I am still moved by the leader in the Times today:*

*'Paris has opened her gates to the invader. One of the great lamps of civilisation has been darkened but it shall never be quenched.'*

*Amen, I say to that. It has brought back so many memories of the time I was lucky to study there. I hadn't quite abandoned religion yet, otherwise I might not have made the rounds of Sunday morning sung masses at Notre Dame, Sacré*

*Coeur, St Sulpice, St Germain des Prés, St Germain l'Auxerrois, La Madeleine... with their wonderful choirs, even to my unmusical ears, and that splendid architecture to admire from the pews. Those hours, too, spent in the Jeu de Paume with Renoir, Sisley, Cézanne, Monet, Manet, Gauguin, Van Gogh and my favourite, Pissarro. They too, had to face the German invader in 1870. Paris, it seems as if I am writing your obituary. Your churches, monuments, boulevards, café terrasses, quais of the Seine - all reduced to a single word- 'Occupied.'*

# FOUR

*Sunday 16 June, 1940*

Jack had slept badly in spite of following the advice of the poet Marvel. His body satisfied, his mind had tossed and turned him into positions of increased discomfort. It was another fine morning so he enjoyed the relief of getting up early to escape from his dreams. No Sunday paper yet. When it came, would it be the last one he would see for some time?

He made coffee and sat munching toast near the window, watching people making their way to one of the places of worship in the village. There'll be a good crowd today, he thought, trying to find some sort of spiritual comfort. He couldn't stand the 'only when the going's rough' sort of religion. What an affront to God that was, scurrying into church for the first time in months or even years to ask Him for protection from the Germans! Jack had had his fill of organised religion. He wondered how the clergy would reconcile the view that if the Germans came it was God's will and He moved in mysterious ways, but if they didn't come it was thanks to all the churchgoers kneeling down and praying to that same God to spare them from the evil hour.

The size of the congregations looked as if they would come up to Jack's expectations as Sunday-best clothes increased in frequency past his window. How tempting to go and hear what would be said but it just wasn't done to slip into three different sets of pews to see how three denominations were preparing to face the foe.

The pretty Catholic Church round the hairpin bend was small but with a good congregation maintained by the threat of damnation if attendance was not clocked up every Sunday and holy day of obligation. The priests were French. What would they be thinking of the fall of their capital? Jack's in-laws would be there, two rows from the front on the right.

But most of the family groups passing the house were Anglicans, the congregation made up naturally of English residents on the island and members of Jersey's 'society.' A lot of the children were at prep school or at Victoria College, overlooking the town. In spite of the social bias there was still a good core of 'ordinary' islanders, whose ancestors, somewhere in the recess of history, had guided their steps through the lych gate and up the protestant path.

Down the hill, near the Hall, the Methodist Chapel stood solid and unadorned, one of many on the island which bore evidence to the spread of non-conformity, following the preaching of John Wesley during his visit to Jersey in 1787.

One of his pupils brought Jack from his reverie by pushing through the letterbox the Sunday paper flown in from London after all. First things first, the cricket scores!

Later in the morning Papa and Maman called after Mass. It hardly constituted a visit as the old couple remained in the car but it did not prevent Alice and her mother from both talking at once across a wide range of subjects. A rendez-vous was fixed for tea in the parental home as Maman let the clutch out with her customary jerk. Now seventy, she had been one of the first drivers on the island, before the inception of driving tests. Her driving then as now, relied on a hooter, a strong will and good fortune. Papa sat, as he had done throughout, tensely grasping the strap, hanging for that very purpose inside the car door.

At that moment Baptiste limped into view and had to leap hurriedly from the path of the advancing car.

"Your mother's still a bloody menace," he told Alice, "as if I haven't been injured enough."

Alice giggled and asked: "What on earth have you done, Baptiste?"

He repeated the now well-told tale of his visit to the old lady's goldfish.

"I've just walked past there again. You talk about I was lucky, you. I flew over the wall between the gate pillar and a tree, only just wide enough for a bloke my size to pass through. I caught my leg on some stones, look how swollen it is."

"It looks like gout to me," smiled Jack.

"Gout!" shrieked Baptiste. "You don't know what you are talking about. My uncle, do you remember him, no, pauvre tchu, he was dead before you were born, no he wasn't, well not long after in any case."

"Are you going to tell us anything about him?" asked Alice mischievously.

"Yes I am, if you give me a minute. He had gout, him. The booze finished him off in the end. I tell you what, I've got a helluva lot left to drink before I've had half as much as him."

~

At La Moye, in St Brelade's over on the west coast of the island, Jim and Jennifer were in the tomato field early. To supplement their income from digging potatoes they had taken on fifteen thousand tomatoes. It was far from loveable work, especially in the heat, the extra money just compensating for the monotony of hammering in fifteen thousand bamboos, tying fifteen thousand stalks three times each as the plants grew, side shooting all fifteen thousand at least twice, hoeing them at least three times and finally, stopping all fifteen thousand after the fourth flower. So they had plenty of time to think, sometimes together. In neighbouring rows, they often punctuated long moments of silence by suddenly asking each other virtually the same questions for which they did not know the answers.

Jack tried to work in his little garden but the irregular snipping and clipping belied less than full concentration. Usually his clear mind was able to see problems, break them down and start finding solutions but this business of the Germans made it difficult to rationalise properly.

It was but a small mental step to reflect that his schooling had informed him of when and where battles had taken place and odd little details, but nothing about the things that really mattered ... Waterloo (1815, Napoleon, Wellington, railway station named after battle, boots after winner, brandy after the loser). Next Crimea ( Balaclava, Charge of the Light Brigade, French General summed up the whole thing so well: 'C'est magnifique mais ce n'est pas la guerre,' helmet named after battle, wool after worst General, woollen garment after next worst and so on...) On to the Boers, then the Great War...but nobody tells you about what ordinary people were thinking and doing in the weeks before a battle arrived on their doorstep. What was half of Europe thinking as they learned of the approach of Napoléon's Grande Armée; and the Celtic tribes before Caesar, and the Saxons living around Hastings?

"That's the third time I've called, Jack. Do you want a cup of tea or not?"

He swept out of his thoughts and into the house.

"What is your mother going to do if we can't get tea?" he asked his wife.

"She'll be jolly miserable. She must get through a dozen cups a day."

"Necessity is the mother of invention. We'll have to use grated acorns or something."

"You're being very pessimistic, Jack."

"No, just realistic. I'm sure we'll to have to adjust our minds very quickly to what our real needs are without panic or hoarding."

"Oh yes," mused Alice, "and what do we do if everybody else starts panicking and hoarding?"

"There is no need for anybody to hoard anything."

"That is not an answer and you know it. Are we supposed to just sit here self-righteously whilst others eat?"

Jack replied in some frustration that if he were a politician he would say he did not answer hypothetical questions.

"We've been thinking too much about what they might do to us. What could be a lot worse is what we might do to each other."

During the afternoon, with these disturbing thoughts temporarily put aside, Jack and Alice walked to her parents' farmhouse at Fliquet through Le Pont, a footpath behind Rozel Manor across a little secluded valley. The universe had conspired to bring about a classic summer's day, ripe for warm and romantic feelings. The greenness and freshness of early evening, the stream, the fragrance of wild flowers helped to entwine the couple like the youngish lovers they were.

At the bottom of the path they sat on the low granite bridge and watched the water glide towards the sea at La Mare.

"Let's come back here when it's all over and sit here again," said Jack.

"When you say come back, do you want us to go away?"

"No, I meant, come back specifically here to this spot."

Alice could only hug him wordlessly suddenly afraid that something awful might happen to prevent it.

Then she said: "I don't want to leave the island, Jack."

"Nor do I, you know that."

"So, have we decided to stay?"

"Unless something completely unforeseen happens."

"Like what?"

"I don't know. The States might decide that the whole island should be evacuated."

"But, unless that happens?"

"Then we stay here," said Jack. Alice hugged him again and they began the steep climb out of Le Pont.

When they reached the farmyard, Alice's parents were carrying deckchairs in from the shade of the gigantic hydrangea bushes. Maman kissed her daughter. "Hasn't it been lovely! We've been sitting there reading since we got back from Jeanne's. Your father has dozed off a few times, the blue hydrangeas are so lovely again, it would be a pity if they got spoiled."

"Why should they get spoiled?"

"The Germans might drop a bomb on them, or something."

"Don't be silly, Maman, it would be a lot worse if they dropped a bomb on you."

"Well, they might do that too."

Jack tried to lighten the atmosphere a little by pointing to the curiously-coloured lily of mildly obscene appearance against the wall near the drive entrance.

"All we need to do is get the Germans to smell it and they'll all want to go home."

The old couple laughed. They had watched so many people walking past, attracted by the purple oddity to come and smell it then leap back clutching a handkerchief to their noses at the repulsive odour.

In the house, after the straightening of cushions and moving of armchairs, they sat in the front room with a cup of tea. First they re-established pleasure over the fine weather and state of the garden and amazement at how Jeanne's children had grown, before broaching the subject which worried them most.

Eventually Maman said: "We've decided that we are too old to go anywhere and we are going to stay here, and whatever will happen will happen."

It was obvious that not a lot of reading or sleeping had gone on in the garden. Alice took her mother's hand and said softly: "We guessed you wouldn't want to go but have you really thought of what might happen if you stay?"

Papa was clutching the arms of the chair. Jack had rarely seen him other than cheerful and jovial in spite of the cruel blows fate had handed out to them. The Great War had crippled and indirectly killed one son, a tragic accident had taken another. Now, as he spoke, he made no attempt to hold back tears.

"They can kill us if they like. We've had our lives. If they are the sort of people who kill off the old and they are going to take over the world, then we are better dead. What is hard to say, and I mean this with all my heart, is that if you and Jack want to go to England and if Henry wants to take Jeanne and the children, then you go with our blessing even though we will probably never see you again."

Only the ticking of the clock could be heard in the darkening room.

Alice was the first to rally. "What makes you think we should want to go to England?"

"Well," said Maman, "Henry seems determined to go. You should have heard him at dinnertime. It's such a shame, he's a good man and a hard worker but when he starts getting depressed like that..."

"I know," agreed Jack, "he's going to think of nothing else."

"He imagines all sorts of horrors the Germans are going to do."

"Well, I'm sure we are not going anywhere," said Alice, looking to Jack for support, which he willingly gave.

"Right then," said Papa, "let's talk about something else before we get into a stew."

For the next couple of hours, the sounds of three, four, pass, nap and misère took over. Maman was always happy and eager to play cards, even though she was an abominable loser. The young couple caught the last bus back from the top of the hill at Greencliff and Jack settled in his journal-writing chair with a cup of cocoa.

*Journal extract*

*What is Jersey?*

*... Sunday seems a day made for thinking. I mused for a while on what we know of wars and of how people faced battles or armies approaching their doorstep. Is evacuation simply running away? Should all Jersey young people stay and protect their island? But if, as seems to be the case, the island will be abandoned by the British Government, then will not young Jerseymen be needed to stand alongside English soldiers in the battle which might lie ahead for England? I discussed duty and, by implication, patriotism, with Andrew, my English colleague the other day. I know he is grappling with this question.*

*... It was good to provide a bit of cheer to Alice's parents. I think they had convinced themselves that we were all off to England. I have never seen Papa look so sad. He doesn't deserve any more knocks. But life and war don't distribute knocks on the basis of fairness.*

*... Now that I have managed a few days of this journal I am beginning to think it might actually be read by somebody, somebody English even, so I will make an attempt to put our island into context.*

*... We are not French because apart from a few years here and there we haven't belonged to France, or Anglo-Normandy, since 1204. We are not subject to French law, institutions or any form of direct influence, yet we are francophiles because a lot of us have or had French parents or grandparents. We usually go to France for day trips and, for those who can afford them, holidays. We get by pretty well in French and a lot of us speak Jersey-French, and we eat and drink our fill!*

*But we are British because of the antiquity of our links with the Crown. We identify with the King, the Home Secretary, the Privy Council, Cup Finals and Test Matches, tea, the Church of England, the Mailboat to Weymouth, the British Army barracked at Fort Regent, fish and chips, driving on the left, the Times and the Daily Mirror, Oxford and Cambridge.*

*Against that background the island divides into three religious camps: Anglican, Methodist and Roman Catholic. These different denominations are reflected in the social and political (with a small p) structures of the island.*

*It is easy to say, though obviously too simplistic, that if everyone spent more time working together instead of withdrawing into groups dictated by the trappings of belief and accidents of birth, the island might be a more unified place with which to face a German occupation. How am I, a teacher, expected to get the kids to live in harmony? How could the headmaster talk meaningfully about religion at assembly when attempts by the young to marry between denominations, all purporting to be Christian, are often met with long lasting hostility?*

*I am no longer a religious person but that does not stop me wanting to help shape things for good in the days ahead.*

# FIVE

*Monday 17 June, 1940*

Towards the end of the morning at the beginning of what became known as 'The Week,' Alice heard a subdued knock, which heralded the postman's arrival.

"Hello, Baptiste," she said cheerfully. "How's your leg today?"

"Bah," he snorted, "I haven't had time to think about it, everywhere I've been they're going on about the bloody Germans, there's a proper panic on you know."

"What are they all saying," asked Alice, "and d'you want a cup of tea?"

"People might start talking, love."

"That's better. I thought for a moment the old Baptiste had lost his sparkle. Anyway, I wouldn't have anything to do with a bloke with a gammy leg, you never know what might happen."

"That could be the beauty of it," said the postman.

"Tell me what's going on everywhere."

Baptiste placed his bag on the floor and sat down.

"Well, for a start, the Colonel's widow at the Hall is in a right old tiz. She burst into tears and grabbed my arm, you, when I arrived. She's decided to leave all right. Do you think you could go and see her?"

"Yes, of course, if you think it would do any good."

"Merci, ben des fais. Now what else? I've arrived in the middle of a few family rows and tears. Then there's my nephew, George, he wants to go and join up. Hilda, that's my sister, is in a helluva state."

"Oh dear, Baptiste, you, of all people mustn't start getting depressed or where will that leave the rest of us?"

"You're right, love, I'm sorry."

The fears and frictions encountered by the postman, were gaining ground, as the psychological pressures of the approaching danger weighed on every conversation and especially on the thoughts of individuals on their own, in fields, kitchens and other places of solitude.

Alice's motto was along the lines of 'no time like the present,' so she set off towards the Hall, stopping briefly to pass the time of day with Mrs Pring, standing in the doorway of her shop, and to commiserate when the shopkeeper said:

"Oh dear, oh dear, Alice, I don't know where it is going to end. People are buying all sorts of things and when I phoned town with my order, they said we had to be careful because they didn't know for how much longer the boats would keep coming."

As she pushed open the garden gate of the Hall, Alice realised what she was doing and wondered what she would say to the old lady, who scared her a little. She could hardly remember her name, Mrs Stride, because everyone referred to her as either the colonel's widow or the old lady. She had the aura of the aristocrat about her in spite of being the unassuming wife of the late boisterous military man who used to liven up the bar of the Royal with his rude army stories.

Alice needed both hands to lift the enormous brass knocker. The knock echoed through what sounded like an empty house and after a moment or two the old lady appeared.

"Er, hello, I'm Alice Birel. I live near the church. We've seen each other in the shop."

"I do recognise you, dear, I'm not quite that far gone yet. Your husband teaches at the school. Are you collecting for something?"

Alice was confused.

"Oh dear, sorry, no, it's Baptiste, the postman, well, he told me you were worried about the war situation and evacuating and I just wondered if I could help at all."

"That is very kind, come in, come in."

Alice followed the old lady past boxes and sheets over furniture to a couple of seats out in the garden. She said, almost in spite of herself: "Why do you want to go?"

"Because, my dear, I can imagine what life will be like here, for old people like me."

"What do you mean?"

"We will be the first to go won't we?"

"Go? I don't understand."

"Be disposed of dear or, if we are lucky, deported, which will probably be only prolonging the agony. If there is not much food and too many people - there's a Greek play along similar lines, I can't remember the name for the moment..."

"Don't be silly," interrupted Alice, then put her hand to her mouth. "Sorry, I shouldn't be talking to you like that, when we've only just met."

The old lady smiled.

They talked on through the making and drinking of tea but the strong-willed widow was not to be moved from her certainty about what would happen once the Germans had arrived.

"You see my dear, this man Hitler and his Nazi henchmen are not just silly fatheaded politicians like those who started the last war. They are fanatics who believe that those who are useless, deformed in some way or even ill, should be eliminated and that means old people and that means me. No, I must go. I admit I'm frightened of them, but I don't want to give them the pleasure of putting me away. Perhaps if my husband was alive! Now dear, enough of that. Look at my vase. Do you admire Art?"

"Yes I do," said Alice, "although I don't know too much about it. It's my husband's passion though."

"Well, look at this picture," said the old lady, holding the book steadily in front of Alice. "That marvellous vase of flowers... I adore Renoir, don't you, all those rich blues. He painted in Guernsey at one point you know. Well look at my vase now dear."

"It's exactly the same as the picture," said Alice, astonished.

"I did it yesterday, or was it the day before? My mind's in a bit of a fluster. Anyway I did it to remind myself that Art is greater than War. Much of the greatest Art has grown out of war, the Florence of the Renaissance struggling with its neighbours, the Franco-Prussian War and those marvellous schools of artists which grew out of the Great War."

"Isn't it terribly sad?" said Alice. "I could sit here and listen to you for hours talking about Art yet the war is driving you away."

"It is sad dear, but life is full of sadness, you know. You have to find ways to constantly strengthen your spirit to face it. In the times ahead, if you can bear to listen to a bit of advice from an old lady..."

Alice smiled encouragement.

"...try and focus your attention, your passion, on permanent things: love, aspiration, the beauty of nature, the strength of granite, the power of the sea."

Alice's eyes dampened in a welling of gratitude to this lady who seemed to be passing on some of her own strength. After a pause she cheered them both up a little by asking about Baptiste and the pond.

"My dear, I just didn't know what was happening. I thought perhaps a bomb had fallen. I was collecting some flowers when I heard a noise and just glimpsed his body in flight before the huge splash. He could have really hurt himself, you know. He said some words in Jersey-French which I imagine were very rude," she added with a smile.

As Alice walked back her mind was full of contradictory thoughts. She had been bolstered by the advice but much of the poor woman's fear had also communicated itself. Surely they wouldn't kill people so cold bloodedly? She had been worried about Jack, an able-bodied man but the old lady was worried because she was old and frail. What about Alice herself, young, strong and blonde? She felt a weakness in her legs. Her mind raced on in a turmoil. Should they leave after all? If the old lady was right, Alice's parents would be vulnerable too. She was desperate for Jack to come home.

~

At school the children were given freedom of the playground for half an hour to allow for a brief staff meeting before classes began. Jack and Andrew sat together, hoping the meeting was not going to be embarrassing. The Head, however, came in with a purposeful stride, placed his hands on the table and began.

"This is going to be a crucial time in all our lives. Above all, we'll have to do what is best for the children. Last week, as you know, I couldn't bring myself to believe that a German invasion was even a possibility and I spoke a little hastily. Since then I've been to a meeting in town where we were told all sorts of things, many of which have become questionable over the course of a single weekend. I'm afraid there is a lot of confusion between England and the Island authorities, not least over whether the islands are going to be defended or not. Talk of evacuation is growing; some say Guernsey has already decided to evacuate all its schoolchildren, utter folly in my view.

Anyway, I'm not ashamed to admit that recently I have felt a bit old and tired. No, no don't protest, you know it's true. If this sounds a bit philosophical, it's because I've been doing a lot of thinking and I have come to a few personal decisions. I am not going to leave the island. I'm going to run this school for as long as it remains possible to do so in the new situation and I intend to give a lead to parents and staff who ask for advice. There is a challenge to be faced with something more than usual. I simply ask for your help and co-operation."

When he stopped speaking, everyone wished to ask questions. Did he know more about any evacuation? Could teachers be forced to accompany the pupils? All agreed that the mass departure of a whole generation would be disastrous. Jack took some pleasure and strength from the spirit of defiance which seemed to grow.

They had, however, to return to the classrooms as the children were showing the first noisy signs of running amok. As they worked Jack looked keenly at each of the pupils, trying to assess their potential for living through an occupation. Would intelligence and good behaviour still be more valuable than cunning and deviousness say? If only they knew what the Germans were going to do.

At home for dinner, Alice told him of the anxieties which had been aroused by her visit to the Hall. Jack listened but could offer nothing certain. They discussed the old lady's views until Jack returned to school, a little tense and miserable, but eventually cheered by the prospect of cricket and an afternoon outside. A pity it was cloudy! Here was an idea to confuse the Germans, a cricket match with the fielders talking to each other in Jersey-French!

Children playing cricket are amusing, even if you don't like cricket or children. The ones who enjoy the game all want to bat and bowl at the same time. Those who don't like it sulk in fielding positions without a name and a ball struck into the air invariably heads in their direction, where, following a shuffling of feet and flapping of hands, it falls to the grass accompanied by abuse from everyone except the batsman involved.

The game over, bats and pads were carried back in a ramshackle way. Jack, forever musing on the oddity of words, wondered how carrying stumps askew, dropping pads and losing bails could be compared to the shackling of a ram, whatever, indeed, that was.

Andrew and Kate called him over: "Well Jack, decided to stay," said Andrew.

Jack's face lit with pleasure. "Great, marvellous. At least that's one thing settled. What decided it, although I could perhaps guess?"

Andrew passed a hand through his blond hair.

"You probably could. Me in England, Kate in Jersey, not best recipe for a love affair. Being parted happens to lots of people all the time but this would be for an unknown period in unknown circumstances, no letters probably, can't imagine a free flow of mail when the Hun's here can you?"

"That's a good point, you know I hadn't thought of that."

"Anyway," continued Andrew, "poor brain nearly worn out with thinking. Had to choose one way or the other. Written to parents, no turning back now."

Jack felt all the emotion and turmoil which lay behind Andrew's somewhat offhand assessment of his position.

"Well, congratulations and the strongest possible hope that you are doing the right thing. We seem to be spending a lot of time in the pub lately, it's a sign of the times, but this is something to celebrate. Come on, we'll collect Alice on the way."

They strode off down the road, Kate, seemingly smaller than usual between the two men. Jack talked about the ups and downs of the spirit, the erratic jerks of the soul which marked these peculiar days; the renewed strength of the headmaster at the staff meeting and concerns about the future for the young pupils.

"Talking about the kids," said Andrew, "don't seem too scared of the Jerries. Heard them at break threatening all sorts of ghastly things with slings and catapults and, meant to ask you, what are potatoes on bamboos?"

"The best thing is to show you," said Jack. "We should find what we want in Henry's field here."

He picked up a strong bamboo from near the hedge and speared it into a good sized potato from the pile of green or damaged ones left near the hedge. Then, with an action similar to the smash in tennis he hurtled the spud a considerable distance through the air. Andrew was delighted and they spent some time in a flinging contest in which distance was a clear winner over accuracy.

Jack laughed and said: "A German would have a nasty shock, if one of those clonked on to his helmet."

"Should wire the War Office," said Andrew. "Tell them we've got a secret weapon."

They came out of the field to a furore in the shop doorway. Women in disarray tugged and shrieked as Mrs Pring clutched and reclutched her hands, appealing for calm. She turned to Jack for help. The ladies were struggling over her last pack of sugar which contained six two-pound packets. Nothing had been delivered to the shop since the previous Thursday and whenever the besieged shopkeeper made enquiries she was told that the position was very difficult at the moment. The large bag burst open and the four ladies dived on the individual packets in an undignified scramble of fat thighs and suspenders before they dashed off clutching the bags to their breathless bosoms. One yelled: "I'll pay tomorrow" and the others did the same.

Mrs Pring was aghast. "They're like savages, Jack. Annie Laval asked me for sugar and I said it was getting scarce, so then they all wanted some. The more they argued the more they wanted it. I thought someone was going to get hurt. Is that a thing to do in front of young children? Ah but, if my Bill was alive, he'd have hit them with the broom, I'm sure."

Jack calmed her down and they eventually managed to get away. Alice was sitting, reading the Post, unaware that civilised behaviour had just broken down a few yards from her door.

"Didn't you hear the fracas, outside?" asked Jack.

"No"

"Four ladies, if that is the right word, were fighting for the last packets of sugar. A couple of them would have put the wind up Joe Louis, I reckon. But, let's forget about them, these two lovely people have decided to stay and brave the foe."

Alice was hardly able to contain her pleasure, all the more sweet at a time when misery and worry were threatening to gain a toehold. Instead of going to the pub, glasses were whisked from cupboards and the Dubonnet opened. It was a few minutes before Alice felt she had to tell them the news from the wireless, that the German army was advancing near the Loire, eager to seal off the Brittany ports to prevent possible British landings in that area. For the first of doubtless many occasions, they looked at the map of France to see exactly where the Germans were.

Alice asked: "Why don't you both stay to eat?"

Andrew tried to protest: "Eating here every day."

"Rubbish, this would only be your second time ever. Besides I want to talk to Kate, let's go into the kitchen."

"Did you hear about Baptiste on Saturday?" Jack asked Andrew. "He came off his bike and flew over the wall into the Hall pond. He scared the old lady out of her wits. You didn't see him limp into school today?"

"No"

"He claims to be the first casualty of the war."

"That's just like him," Andrew laughed then added seriously looking down at the floor. "Makes you wonder who the first casualty is going to be."

After a little silence Jack said: "So, you've made your decision, Andrew, it must be a great relief."

"Very, very difficult. Arguments on both sides. Love tugging against duty kind of stuff, but difficult to pin down what duty is in this instance."

"The stuff Nelson asked every man to do, you mean?" asked Jack pensively.

"More or less, but they didn't have much choice, did they? What does duty really mean when you get down to it? Putting some higher aspiration above personal considerations?" wondered Andrew.

"Something like that. I suppose if everyone put themselves first, there would never be a march forward of collective man, so to speak, no advance of civilisation."

Andrew mused then asked: "Do you think that a second major war in thirty years marks an advance in civilisation? If every German, for instance, put his own personal needs first..!"

"Perhaps you are right, but it would be too idealistic to think that could ever happen. In any case, the concept of duty changes with the society of the time. We did Corneille's play 'Horace' at college, very strong on love and duty, but our tutorial group found Horace's behaviour, though, no doubt, highly sound in classical days, downright comic."

Andrew asked several more questions, most of them rhetorical, but he looked as if his mind was elsewhere. It seemed to Jack that he was still seeking justification for staying on the island.

"Is it still a duty to die defending the homeland? Last war hundreds of thousands died defending a few miles of mud in a foreign field. Now French given up their capital without defending it to the death. It seems you only have to sacrifice yourself when you are winning, or at least not losing."

"Do you play chess, Andrew? There, it is normal and even expected that you will resign when you are clearly losing rather than waste the mental energy of both players by prolonging the game until the final checkmate."

"All hinges on the right moment to capitulate," agreed Andrew.

Jack continued: "There are, of course, many good reasons for continuing a fight which might be lost - stretches the enemy, prevents them having too easy a time in one quarter allowing them to concentrate on another and so on."

"If you told me," said Andrew, "that the Germans were going to attack England and the more men you could marshal to its defence the better, would go back tomorrow. As it is, don't want to leave Jersey and Kate just to end up uselessly in a barracks somewhere waiting for a diplomatic end to be sorted."

"Don't know about England. It is still far from clear whether Jersey is going to be fought for. Some blokes in the pub on Saturday told us that the soldiers have been recalled to England, yet apparently some more arrived yesterday and this morning. Saturday's Evening Post tells us that decisions have not been taken but tries to reassure us that the matter is in safe and competent hands. Yesterday I heard that the soldiers who have arrived have started digging defensive trenches in various places, around the airport for example. Nobody seems to know what is going on."

Andrew became agitated at the thought of trying to defend the island.

"If people taking decisions have slightest bit of sense, hope they do call the troops back to England. Carnage if they stay here and fight. Don't they know what bombers can do? Smash the town to pieces in no time. Look what happened in Guernica. Had a friend at college, a bit of a madman, went to Spain until he got shot in the leg. His descriptions of what planes can do, nightmarish. We've all seen the newsreels as well. Anyway what I was going to say, nothing to do with bombs, don't say anything to Kate whatever you do, but not totally sure that I am going to stay. May well be circumstances which will make me change my mind. Just can't bring myself round to telling her."

Jack was a little surprised but understood the torment Andrew was in.

"Can't go on talking about myself, frightful bore. What about old Stevens? Sprung a bit of a surprise on us this morning."

"Wonderful how he seems to have found renewed energy," agreed Jack.

Alice and Kate returned having talked mostly about Andrew's decision to stay, but Kate felt deep down that he could easily decide to leave at the last minute and couldn't make up her mind whether she would accompany him or not. If he were called up would she not be better off looking after her mother in Jersey than stuck on her own somewhere in England, perhaps with his parents whom she, of course, didn't know? Alice had shared her new worries about her own parents which had been triggered by her conversation with the old lady. If they went to England where could they go? Who would look after them?

Both conversations seem to stop for a moment so Alice said: "We've got some shrimps for tea. Jeanne took the kids down to Fliquet this afternoon and they were just giving themselves up, it appears."

"In that case," said Jack gleefully, "I'll open that bottle of Muscadet we brought back from St. Malo."

At the table, fingers flew into action. Heads were parted from shell and delicious pink and white meat was dipped into mayonnaise and popped into mouths, the dry white wine bringing out the taste. Andrew and Kate needed no urging to plunge their knives into the butter made by Alice's mother. The two remaining bountiful cows at Fliquet might well become life saving in the days ahead.

"Just look at the table," said Jack. "Shrimps are a natural harvest so to speak but otherwise there in front of us are the fruits of some of man's greatest achievements, domesticating the cow, harvesting wheat into loaves and bottling the grape and yet here we are back at war."

"Guns or butter," added Andrew, "was it Goering or Goebbels who said it? Never remember which is the fat one."

"You know," said Jack, his mouth nearly full, "my mind keeps springing poetry on to me, even though I'm not a great poetry reader. This afternoon while daydreaming a bit, umpiring at cricket, I saw myself walking fast along one of those long straight French roads with the Germans getting closer and closer behind me and this bit of Coleridge came to mind:

> 'Like one who on a lonesome road
> Doth walk in fear and dread
> And having once turned round, walks on
> And no more turns his head
> Because he knows that close behind
> The fearful fiend does tread.'

"But just when I reached that point," continued Jack with a smile, "I was assailed by a loud cry for lbw. Fortunately I never give anybody out lbw so I didn't have to worry about the decision. The bowler, of course, was terribly upset and looked at me like my aunt's spaniel."

"Poor kid," said Alice, "I bet the batsman should have been given out."

"Very probably," agreed Jack, "another example of a lost truth. Do you ever think there's a great book and film in the sky where the truth is recorded and we will eventually know whether the batsman should have been given out lbw, but the fallible human arbiter, overcome by thoughts of war and the poet Coleridge, created a lie by keeping his finger firmly in the down position? But wait a minute, Alice," continued Jack, "before you plead again on the bowler's behalf. "The players are just as responsible for this lie, if lie it is, because they appeal loudly and convincingly every time the ball hits the pads, however absurd the suggestion of lbw might be."

As Jack drew breath, Alice said:

"I fear we are in for a dose of philosophy. Andrew, you'd better nip round to the pub and warn them to expect another sermon tonight."

Andrew smiled but he was interested in what Jack was saying.

"You have strong feelings about truth then."

"Certainly strong in the George Washington or even religious sense, but not, perhaps, in any absolute sense. Take the likely German occupation, it may not be a one hundred per cent bad thing."

"But surely," interrupted Kate, "occupation by a foreign power, especially one with such clearly stated evil intent, must be bad."

Although his mouth was again full of shrimp, bread, butter and Muscadet, Jack did not want to be misunderstood.

"Of course, from virtually every stand point, it is dreadful and there is bound to be suffering and a terrible psychological shock, unacceptable feelings of bitterness and defeat. Of course none of this can be anything but bad. But people might, and I say might, begin to find themselves and find each other in a common cause against the enemy. Like today in the staffroom for example. I remember, too, when another English teacher, if you pardon the expression, Andrew, came to the school. It was before your time, Kate. He was a really unpleasant bloke, always whinging, criticising and wanting to change everything we were doing. Everybody, and I include the saintly Miss Cooley, soon got very fed up with him and angry words were often spoken behind his back. But Donald, who has a very shrewd head as you know, told me one day: 'Damn good thing that bloke is here; whenever things go wrong, we can have a bloody good go at him and we never bicker among ourselves anymore. Nobody even goes to moan to the Head if they know he's had a half hour battering from Phillipson.' And he was right."

"So, treat the Huns like a Phillipson and all will be hunky-dory," said Andrew with a smile."

"I doubt if it will be that simple," said Jack sheepishly, "but something along those lines."

"If only we had some idea what it was going to be like," sighed Kate.

"That makes it all the more important to look for something positive, some abstract ideals, even religious ones."

"Surely," said Andrew, "the morality and practice of religion must be a great help in times of trial?"

"It should be," replied Jack, "if people were Christians first and foremost, every day of the week and not just on Sunday mornings."

"That's a bit harsh, Jack."

"Maybe, but don't start me on Belheche whatever you do."

Alice thought it wise to step in at this point. "You must excuse Jack, he had a basinful of religion as a kid and, as he has got older, his views have soured a bit."

After the meal they talked of Reading and of Andrew's home and family. Kate seemed very quiet.

When they left, Alice asked: "Do you think Andrew is really going to stay?"

"I doubt it somehow, and so must you, otherwise you wouldn't have asked. His whole background is pulling him back to do his bit."

"I think Kate expects it too. It's pretty miserable for her. By the way," she added " I went round to Jeanne's this afternoon."

"Oh yes," said Jack, sensing a major question or problem in the air.

"After talking to the old lady this morning, I was worried about Papa and Maman."

"Yes, I know you were, but they are a bit different. She is English and lives on her own in a big spooky house. Your parents have got each other and us and Jeanne and the family."

"But are Jeanne and Henry going to stay, Jack? And us, for that matter? You haven't changed your mind about going, have you?" Alice asked a little desperately.

Jack caressed her hair: "Of course not, where would we go, in any case? I'm only in touch with a couple of people from my college days and I'm sure they wouldn't want a bunch of homeless people descending on them."

"You don't think Andrew thought we were trying to see if his family would help us?"

"Don't be daft, it didn't cross my mind for an instant."

"I'm glad," smiled Alice through tears in her eyes. "I don't want to go anywhere. I felt sick again this morning and I'm two weeks overdue."

"What!" said Jack, sitting bolt upright and staring at the Cézanne print above the fireplace. He didn't see it or anything else as he took the news in. He was thrilled at the idea of having a child but what a moment to choose! He hugged and kissed his wife all over her face.

"After so long," he mumbled. "Are you really sure?"

"I can't be certain, but I'll go to the doctor tomorrow."

"Is it OK to go to town?"

"Of course it is, silly, millions of pregnant women have travelled further than three miles to see their doctors before you know."

"That may be the case, but you are my wife. Have you told Jeanne?"

"No, of course not, I wanted you to be the first to know."

Jack could now feel his nerves rolling over and over in his stomach. Butterflies! It felt more like large birds. He couldn't keep his hands still, got up, wound the clock, picked up the Evening Post, put it down, moved his glass, picked it up, took a sip, passed a finger through his hair, put his hands in his pockets, took them out and thought: 'Bloody hell, just as the Germans are about to arrive, my wife announces she is probably pregnant. Oh God, what will things be like in a few months time; food, medical supplies?'

Alice was equally thrilled and worried, yet women had had babies in far worse conditions.

"If we did go to England," Jack said, "I might be called up and you would have a baby entirely amongst strangers. Here, at least, if I am locked up in a camp or something, you would have your mother and sister around."

"That's if Jeanne and Henry stay. He's in quite a state and doesn't stop talking about evacuating. He's virtually abandoned the tomatoes and has spent most of the day in the shed pricing his equipment, as if anybody is going to buy it now!"

"He didn't seem too bad on Friday," said Jack. "What's brought all this on?"

"They had a pretty tearful dinner, as you know, with Maman and Papa on Sunday, that's only yesterday," added Alice. "The days seem twice as long as usual at the moment. Jeanne told me they all more or less persuaded themselves that it would be better for the kids if she and Henry took them off to England. That's why Papa spoke with such feeling when we went round."

"But where does Henry think he is going to go? He's never even been to England and he certainly doesn't know anybody over there."

"Please talk to him again tomorrow. It's just panic, he hasn't thought it through properly. I feel awful, Jack but I've got to tell Maman we may be expecting."

"Of course you have, what's the problem?"

"The problem is that she will definitely want to stay if we do and if anything happened to them, it would be my fault for making them stay."

"You heard Papa say quite categorically that they've decided to stay and it's because they want to."

"Perhaps, but they shouldn't have to sacrifice any more for us."

"You are just being a bit oversensitive, love. Put yourself in your mother's position. She's never been to England either. Imagine how worried sick about you she would be over there, having no news, because you won't be able to write every day you know. There probably won't be any mail at all to England once the Germans are here."

"That's true," said Alice, wiping her eyes. "I hadn't thought of that. It's all so unreal."

"Go to bed. I'm just going to write a bit. "

*Journal Extract*
*What a time to choose!*
*... It's no use. I know I promised myself and my reader (will there be more than one?) that I would try to discipline myself to write every day. Technically, as I am in my third sentence, I am actually writing now but I can't go on for long or make much sense. After seven years of trying, it looks as if we may have conceived a child. Does this change anything? I know my immediate reaction was to agree with Alice that she would be better off staying here with her family rather than have her baby among strangers but will it be safe? Will there be the medical supplies which she might need? More questions and I thought there were enough already. I just can't write any more, I'm too jumpy. Let's hope that I can get some sleep.*

# SIX

*Tuesday 18 June, 1940*

Jack stabbed at breakfast like a man in a trance, walking from kettle to pot, from bread to butter, conscious only of splashing his pyjamas when he turned the tap on too enthusiastically, his mind an extension of his restless dreams and feelings of joy and numbness.

His clumsy nervousness followed him into the bathroom where he, not surprisingly, nicked himself shaving. He ate toast and drank his mug of luke-warm tea. Was there a point where it became luke-cold? Not wanting to wake Alice and unable to sit still, he left the house for school earlier than usual. As he walked past the farm, sounds from the outbuildings guided Jack to where Henry was rummaging amongst boxes and tools. He made an attempt to cheer him up.

"Well, Henry mon vier bougre, you'd better get out into the field fast, you can see the side shoots growing from here."

"Ah, it's you Jack, I dunno what I'm doing. I'm worried sick and Jeanne just keeps going on at me."

"But what's brought all this on? You were OK on Friday."

Henry said "Ah but," followed by a long silence. He was a maddeningly slow speaker even for a Jerseyman.

"I've been thinking too much out there in the field. Then Jeanne and her mother were crying like hell on Sunday. If it was only me I wouldn't care but I want the kids to be safe, Jack."

"Come on, Henry, damn it, it won't be that bad."

"How do you know, how does anybody know, what it's going to be like? It's all right for you, you haven't got any kids, you."

"Not at the moment." Jack paused. Henry did not seem to understand. "Alice may be expecting."

"Expecting what?"

"A kid, of course, you bloody twerp."

"What," yelped Henry, nearly knocking over the barrel next to him.

"A funny old time, isn't it?"

"I'll say, eh ben merde, and there was me worried. By cri, having a baby, now, but what are you going to do Jack?"

"I thought it was usual to congratulate people," admonished Jack, "We'll just let nature take its course."

"But surely you're not going to stay here?" bleated Henry. "What about medical treatment and so on. Will there be anything left by then?"

Jack didn't want Henry to know that the thought had occurred to him too, nor did he want to let himself worry too much about it. Alice seemed confident enough.

"I haven't had much time to think, but there's no reason why we shouldn't stay. Why don't you stay too to give us a hand?" He thought it best to leave Henry with that thought.

"Cheerio, must be off."

Henry just had time to say that he was going to town to see if he could ship some spuds.

Jack still had the pained face of Henry in his mind when young Fred tapped him on the shoulder.

"Hello, Fred, coming to gloat over the thrashing you gave me at bar billiards the other night?"

"I probably get more practice than you, Mr Birel. Can I talk to you for a minute?"

"If you're happy to walk in the direction of school again," smiled Jack. "What's on your mind?"

"Well, I've been going to town quite a bit these last few days and meeting some mates. Most of them were in the Stag last night and all they talked about was packing their bags and going to England so that they can join the army."

"But you're not eighteen are you?"

"I know, but I still want to go. What do a few months mean? I'm bigger, stronger and fitter than most of them, anyway."

"That's true."

"Some of the lads are in the Militia. Unless they are ordered to stay here and fight they will go and join up. I feel stupid, me, about just staying here and doing nothing. If the war lasts longer than six months, they'll have to do without all the blokes of my age if we stay cooped up here."

"But those lads are older than you, Fred, and they have done some training."

"I can train when I get there, can't I?" The boy was now on the edge of tears. "My father doesn't care two hoots what I do, but my mother keeps crying every time I say I want to leave."

"You seem quite sure that you want to join up."

"Yes I'm sure. I'd rather be in the army than sitting on my backside here with the Germans. My mother's the only problem." He looked questioningly at Jack. "You couldn't..?"

"Talk to her or something?"

Fred's face lit up. He was a completely different person. "Would you, Mr Birel, please?"

"I don't promise great results, my boy. There is nothing I can say to your mother that alters the fact that her son wants to leave home to go and fight in a war and that she might never see him again. You do realise all that don't you?"

"Yes, yes," said Fred excitedly, "I've thought of nothing else for days."

"Will she be home at about half past four?"

"Usually! Unless she's at the shop."

"Has she got a good right hook?" asked Jack and explained to the puzzled Fred about the behaviour of the shoppers the previous day.

"I don't need to be there do I? I'd like to go to town to see what's happening."

"Perhaps it will be better if you are not there. My brother-in-law is going to town, you could get a lift with him."

There was no respite from thoughts of occupation as he met the headmaster near the school gate.

"Good morning Jack. Things seem to have started. At least ten families have taken their children off to the boat this morning. Apparently when you get to the Railway Office now, a policeman sends you to the Town Hall to register that you want to be evacuated. It's all a bit chaotic and the States are going to discuss today or tomorrow how the whole business is going to be organised sensibly."

"The States are going to organise it sensibly?" laughed Jack. "That's a good one! But are there really that many people wanting to leave?" he added incredulously.

"Hundreds, I've heard, the queues are getting longer all the time."

"Where will they all go when they get to England?" asked Jack.

"That's the problem, nothing has been organised yet. Judge Dorey has gone to London to negotiate with the War Office; he's coming back tonight I think. But, I nearly forgot the whole point of what I want to tell you. I've just had a phone call, it will be in tonight's 'Post', all schools are to close until further notice so that families can get together to decide what to do. Nobody has said anything official about children yet, but Guernsey, as we feared, has decided to evacuate them all. Can you imagine that?"

At that moment Andrew arrived with the look of a man who has slept fitfully, if at all. On hearing the last few words of the headmaster, he asked them if they knew that women and children were being evacuated from town to the country parishes. Jack and the Head were amazed.

"Poor woman with three howling kids arrived on the farm where I'm staying. They said German planes had passed over town. Hard to believe or we would have seen them, surely. Also, the business about soldiers coming to defend the islands taken a new twist."

"How?" asked the Head a little anxiously.

"Yacht Club asked by Governor's office, following request by the Admiralty, to send as many boats as possible to St Malo to evacuate some of our troops from there. Mini Dunkirk by all accounts. Seems like part of the British Expeditionary Force had to retreat all the way to St Malo because their route to Dunkirk was cut off. They've been on the road for days, losing a lot of equipment and suffering casualties from German attacks."

"You just don't know what to believe any more about whether the islands are going to be defended or not," said Mr Stevens. "Certainly it explains why a lot of people want to leave. Everything is so topsy turvy. In three phone calls from town this morning I've been told to do three different things. First I had to keep the children at school until tonight, then I had to send them home straightaway, then I had to do nothing until further notice."

"Bloody typical," said the voice of the postman who had just come up behind them. "This could be the last letter you'll get from England for a while, Mr Stevens, I'd keep the stamp if I were you, it might be valuable some day."

"Do you think it could be the last one, Baptiste?"

"They say that the boats are only going to be used for people now and that the mail services are being suspended. Another bloody silly idea! There won't be many people wanting to come here so they could at least bring the mail in this direction."

"How much room on the boat would the mail take in any case?" said Jack. "And where did you hear all this from?"

"The bloke who brings the letters out from town in the van. He was on the pier this morning. What a caper, you. Dozens of yachts and little boats have gone to St Malo to get our troops out and bring them here. "

"Andrew was just telling us," said Jack.

"Lots of boats are also expected to come tomorrow," continued Baptiste "to start taking people off to the mainland."

"No wonder there's all this panic about today," remarked Mr Stevens. "Well I, for one, am not going anywhere."

"Nor me," agreed Baptiste."Can you see me in England you?"

The others laughed at the thought of Baptiste delivering letters in Hemel Hempsted or St. John's Wood.

"By the way, Jack," the postman continued, "the old lady's gone from the Hall. I've just seen her stop at your place to give your wife a big vase of flowers."

The classroom came almost as a release for Jack, from thoughts of Alice's possible pregnancy, from Henry, from Fred and his mother and the poignancy of the old lady's departure.

~

Out at La Moye, Jim had been digging potatoes for over an hour. The two Pinel sisters were shaking the stalks and picking behind him with less than their customary sparkle. They usually giggled at his silly jokes but this morning neither of them spoke much and they looked vacant. Seated on the hedge with their first cup of tea, Gladys Pinel told Jim that they had decided to go off to England and be nurses or something useful.

"That is a brave thing to do," said Jim, "but why are you so miserable about it?"

"Because of dad. He doesn't want us to go. He gave Phyllis a black eye when she told him this morning. Look at it. He wants us to slave after him just like our mother did, but we've had enough, us."

Phyllis interrupted, almost in tears: "He drinks all the time. He's got one barrel of cider in the shed and another at the back of the stable and he's always sneaking off to one or the other. When he's had a few, he's just like an animal. I can't stand it any more."

Although Jim understood her sentiments he was surprised at the venom with which she spoke.

"But that's not all," said Gladys, with a rare cross look on her face. "When we went to see Mr Dacourt last night to get paid for our work and to tell him we were going to England, he said that because he won't be able to sell his spuds, what with the Germans coming, then he's only going to pay us half of what he owes us and he doesn't know when."

"What! the old bugger!" said Jim, "that's bloody typical of the bloke."

"He told us all the farmers were going to do that."

"Is that right?" said Jim, bunching his fist with unaccustomed ferocity. "My wife is working in the tomatoes at this minute, in this heat. I'm damned if we are going to flog our guts out for next to nothing. We'll knock off now and go and see Dacourt at the farm. If he won't pay you in full, his spuds can bloody well rot and him as well, as far as I am concerned."

After some searching, they found the farmer moving his cows to another tether over by the disused railway line. Jim wasted no time on sophisticated opening gambits.

"What's all this tripe about only paying these girls half their money? And what about me, for that matter?" he added.

"Ah but," said the farmer, backing away a little behind one of the cows, "I'm not going to make anything, me, if the Germans come."

Jim took a step nearer. "What's that got to do with it? They've done their work."

"Yes I know," mumbled Dacourt, "but that's how it goes, eh, it's the war."

"It's the war!" shouted Jim, "that's a bloody good one. Thanks to Adolph bloody Hitler, we've got to work for you for peanuts while you potter about moving your underfed cows around and drinking cider with your cronies. When you did so well with your spuds last year, you didn't pay the girls double money did you? They get paid for their work not according to how much profit you make."

The girls stiffened as it looked for a moment as if Dacourt was about to hit Jim with his mallet. Jim, was only just managing to keep his hands at his sides.

The farmer shouted aggressively: "Don't come round here and insult me. I've been to the Parish Hall and it's all right for me to do what I'm doing."

"I'm dead sure you've been down there," retorted Jim, "anything to keep your arse tight-shut, so that not even a farthing falls out. I'm going there now because several of them owe my wife some money, then we'll see whether you pay these girls in full or not."

Jim couldn't remember feeling so angry. He seemed to have lost control of his veins and pulses as he gazed at the round-faced, bald, pathetic little man. Phyllis burst into tears. It was too much like home.

Some semblance of calm had returned by the time Jim strode into the yard of one of the Parish officials who was also his landlord. He was climbing into his battered rust-ridden lorry on his way to a special meeting of the States about Evacuation.

"Good morning, Mr Rostand," began Jim, with disarming calm.

"Good morning Jim, how are you, and your good lady?"

"She's fit and well and working in your field. Now what's this I'm told about you advising farmers to pay only half wages to people?"

"I haven't been advising farmers as you put it."

"Well why does Dacourt say you have?"

"Well, he has spoken to me and one or two others."

"And you told them that."

"Something like that, yes."

Jim paused for a moment and put his foot on the tyre of the lorry, gently stroking his chin between thumb and forefinger: "And what about Jennifer?"

"Well the same, it's the same for everybody," said Rostand with a shrug.

"The same," said Jim, giving each word full stress. "The same. She's in that field all day long and I still have to help out in the evenings and at weekends and you've decided, without even having the guts to tell the people involved, that you intend to pay just half wages."

"But I won't be able to sell my toms," replied Rostand.

"Damn your toms. Like I told Dacourt, last year when you made a bloody fortune, I don't remember you offering my wife a penny more for her efforts. I don't see how your sales come into it."

"Be reasonable, Jim, it's this year and we've got to live."

"We've got to live! Be bloody reasonable! How do you expect us to live, then?" Jim was now shouting again. "If you don't pay my wife in full and if Dacourt doesn't pay the Pinel girls in full, today, then for a start I'm not paying another penny of your rent. You can take me to court if you like and I will tell them the sort of bloke you are who only pays half wages. Then there's the Farmer's Union and the Evening Post."

"Come on Jim, don't be so hot headed." Rostand looked uneasy but Jim was not to be stopped, he no longer minded what he said. "What are we fighting Hitler for, if people like you can behave like this? All I want is for my wife to get a fair day's pay for a fair day's work, and it's low enough at that."

"Look Jim, I didn't think there would be such a fuss about this. Come round tonight and we'll talk about it again."

"I'm sorry, Mr Rostand, it's not tonight I want to know, it's now. I suppose you want another afternoon out of my wife at half-price?"

"Don't be silly. It's just one of those things. We've all got to make sacrifices at a time like this. Everything I give to your wife will be a loss to me. Think of it like that. We must give and take. Dacourt's the same and he's got three people to pay, him."

"Give and take. That's a bloody good one. I'm not standing around here arguing with you any more. I'm going to start by ringing the Post from the telephone box over there."

The farmer was silent for a moment or two then he switched off the engine. "How much do I owe you?"

"I don't know," said Jim, "but I don't want the money now, just your word that when you pay it, it will be in full."

"All right, all right, merde, I've heard enough about this."

"And hang on, I haven't finished yet," said Jim. "You'll phone Dacourt and tell him to pay the girls Pinel in full today, because they are going off to the war tomorrow."

Rostand became, if anything, more agitated and began to splutter. "I've heard enough from you. To come and shout at me like that. You sound like a bloody communist. Anybody would think we couldn't live without your work. I've got an important sitting to go to and I'm forced to stand here and listen to your nonsense. Hilda!" he yelled into the house. "Get Dacourt on the phone." He slammed the lorry door and ran scowling into the kitchen shouting back, "I'll have to think seriously about abandoning those toms now."

Jim knew that things would not end there, but he was ready to accept it. No more work was preferable to gratuitous half-pay for work already done. His wife could always find something else and who knew what the war would bring in any case? He smiled as he heard the angry Rostand shouting abuse at Dacourt down the phone for having dragged him into it.

Jim slipped out of the farmyard and walked back along the edge of the railway line, wondering what would happen to it when the Germans were there. Back in the hot shimmering field the girls were sitting on barrels, holding five pound notes in their hands.

"Thank you," said Gladys, kissing Jim on the cheek. "Old grumpy has just paid us in full and told us there is no more work, but we don't care, obviously, we're off to catch the first boat we can."

To Jim's surprise they lifted a pile of rotting stalks near the barrels and picked up ready-packed suitcases.

"If you see our old man," said Phyllis, "you might as well tell him we've gone, if he's sober enough to hear you."

In turn they kissed Jim on the cheek and he watched them dance across the uneven ground to the old railway station now used as a bus stop. There didn't seem much point in his staying alone, so he covered the barrels with fresh stalks and began walking along the little flower-strewn path by the golf course towards the tomatoes where Jennifer was busy tying, unaware of the little dramas going on not far from her.

Henry drove to town with his usual scant regard for the Highway Code, made less obvious today by the equally unpredictable movements of a heavy volume of traffic going in the same direction. Fred, next to him, was young enough to find the ride amusing yet, nevertheless, was glad to be freed from the lorry at the bottom of La Motte Street.

~

Henry drove on past Howard Davis Park and down Colomberie and Hill Street to the jam at the Weighbridge, his mind still far from the steering wheel. He parked near the closed offices of the potato shippers. The weighing and buying area in the centre of the square was deserted. Elsewhere, people thronged the road to the quay and a biggish crowd was gathered outside the Yacht Hotel. Henry stood, hands on hips, staring at the file of passengers in the distance clambering on to the mailboat. Fortunately for his peace of mind, he couldn't see their faces.

The agent from the shippers tapped him on the shoulder and asked with a smile:

"You haven't brought any spuds down, Henry, have you?"

"I thought I might as well try," replied Henry.

The agent shook his head from side to side. "We've stopped shipping them now, mate, all the boats are going to be used for people. There isn't half going to be a clearout tomorrow."

"That's true is it?" asked Henry, "are you going, you ?"

"You're dead right I am," replied the agent. "I've registered down at the Town Hall, you've got to go there now, not the Railway Offices."

"But how do you know all this about tomorrow?" asked an increasingly worried Henry.

"Have you come in from the jungle mate? Everybody in town is talking about it. The blokes from the Railways have been told that the boats are coming overnight and Judge Dorey has phoned after his meetings with the Home Office in England to get everything prepared."

"So you don't want my spuds," Henry managed to joke.

"I tell you what, I'll take a couple of pounds home to cook and eat cold on the boat tomorrow."

"What a bloody cheek! Righto, take what you want, mon vi, they're no use to me, I've got a field full back home. Where are you going to go?"

"I'll start by going to the merchants in Covent Garden. I've done them good service over here, I'm sure they'll help me out."

"It's OK for you, you're not married, eh."

"No fear, you can keep that game for me"

"What about the people who don't know anybody over there?"

"That's what the Jurat went over for. They must have sorted something out, although I wouldn't be surprised if it's a bloody great cock up. You know what politicians are like. Well, I'm off to pack my stuff. Thanks for the spuds."

They shook hands and Henry again felt pangs of worry in his stomach. He knew even less now what to do. Boats coming, hundreds of islanders heading for the harbour. Surely Jeanne must see she should look after her children rather than her parents? It was all right, perhaps now in June, but if the Jerries were still there in mid winter the population would probably freeze to death. Surely the kids would be better off in England? Until what age was call up? Was he too old at thirty eight? Suppose none of his close relatives left the island and the war finished quickly and the Germans never came, he would look pretty silly when he came back. But if he stayed and the whole thing dragged on into more and more hardship, he would bitterly regret not going.

He found himself in the Yacht asking for a beer. The atmosphere bustled with people milling in and out, lots of mothers and girlfriends, crying. News from the Town Hall described the queue stretching into King Street on one side and past General Don's statue up the Parade on the other. Bits of conversation came to him, truth and fiction muddled together:

... hundreds of dogs and cats being put to sleep at the animal shelter; a little girl distraught at such a loss; a middle-aged woman desperately asking for a young man with ginger hair and a tartan rucksack; they just took your name and address now; the police were all leaving; there were crowds of boats at anchor in St Ouen's Bay; you had to pay double for your ticket; you didn't have to pay for your ticket at all; you were only allowed one tiny bag; a special ambulance ship was coming for the sick and old; the hospital was going to be evacuated; the Governor and the Bailiff had already left on a special plane; the soldiers who'd just arrived were going back and the island was going to be abandoned...

Rumours got wilder and wilder. The talk going round and round in his head did little to bolster Henry's wavering morale. The confused individual rarely finds solace in the mass confusion of others. Without finishing his beer he walked out into the sun, up to the Town Church, through New Cut and into King Street towards the Town Hall. The crowd extended out of sight. A photographer from the Evening Post was taking pictures from all angles and many people covered their faces. How many were simply leaving their old lives behind? Old scores, debts and marital strife lost in the mayhem of the departing boat! Henry usually disliked crowds, especially when he was depressed but the drive for him to register was such that he joined the back of the long line, some almost silent, others exchanging opinions and jabbering about their latest piece of information. He had smoked his last eight Silk Cuts since arriving in town.

Time crawled wearily by. Many newcomers joined the queue. Others left. Minor dramas took place as a wife, mother, father, brother found a husband, son, daughter, sister or friend and pleaded, cajoled or bullied them to come home. More words miscarried from mouth to ear:

... they had stopped registering; it was just as easy to walk up to the boat and get on instead of registering; only families with children would be allowed to go; only men of military age; all the boats for the next day would be used for the soldiers now leaving the island; the boats were being bombed in the channel; people were being left on the quay at Southampton with no arrangements made for them... It was difficult to judge how much was true.

~

Earlier, when Fred was released from the cab of Henry's lorry, he walked up La Motte Street and made for the Stag's Head where a number of his Militia mates were already gathered.

"We're off any day now," they told him as he came in through the door.

"All of you?" asked Fred a little taken aback.

"Yes, we've got priority, look." They showed their tickets and passes, boat and train all the way to Aldershot. "Just wait till we get those uniforms on, the girls will be flocking round."

"And the booze is cheap in the canteen," added another.

"What about the fighting?" asked Fred.

None of the lads seemed too worried about it. One said "Hitler'll never invade England, but if he does we'll be there to sort him out."

The landlord, of barrel chest and glittering eye, laughed sarcastically. "If you're so bloody good at kicking Hitler about, why don't you stay here and stop him coming?"

The less boisterous and more reflective member of the group said quietly:

"I'd like to, but there's no chance is there? We were told down at the army office that the War Cabinet has decided not to defend the islands. The troops are going to be pulled out today or tomorrow."

"That's a fact, is it?" asked the landlord, "because in here this last week, I've heard that those soldiers are going to do everything from invade France, fight a last-ditch battle on Sark and retreat to America. People have gone off their ruddy heads."

"We'll that's what we were told by the officer at the Recruiting Office, so you can take it or leave it."

"Mind you, I'm not surprised," added the landlord, resting his considerable abdominal volume against the bar counter. "I never believed the soldiers were going to stay anyway but that just about settles it for the Germans coming, ruddy squareheads."

"Are you going to leave, you?" one of the group asked him.

"No ruddy fear. They won't eat me. I'm too old and tough. I reckon things will be OK once they settle down a bit."

"What will you do then?"

"I'll keep the pub going you silly twerp."

"What about if the Germans come in?" asked the reflective one.

"What about it?"

"Will you serve them or what?"

"Of course I will," said the landlord loudly. "If they've got money in their hand and a machine gun at my throat."

"That's flippin marvellous, isn't it?" said the boisterous one. "Here we are, us, going to spill blood and you'll be standing there dishing out pints to the Jerries and cracking jokes, I suppose."

"Don't be so big for your boots, you little pipsqueak. You haven't polished a button yet and anybody'd think you were a ruddy VC. We can't leave the island empty just to please you. If they come here we'll have to do as we're told, just like you in the army. To hear you talk it's going to be a picnic here so why are all these people queuing up to clear off?"

Fred preferred to stand apart for a few moments, sipping his beer in confused frustration. Was it worth going, even if Mr Birel persuaded his mother to give her blessing? Would he go anyway without it? A pity he couldn't travel with his mates who were now officially volunteer recruits. How would he spend the time in England, one hundred and eighty days to be precise, waiting until he was eighteen? Could he get away with lying about his age? What about Percy? He worked at Lloyds bank and wanted to leave too. He wasn't eighteen either..

"I'll be back," he called to his mates, but they heard nothing in their determination not to leave a single pint in the pub for the Germans.

On his way from the Stag to the bank, Fred bore witness to many of the dramas of the day - the desperate request for a cigarette, the urgent questioning from a distraught mother looking for her son just like him, queues at the baker's, the long queue at the Town Hall and three further queues within entwining distance, emerging from the banks on the corners of Broad Street. Two policemen walked up and down, easing people back on to the pavements. Fred asked what was going on.

"It's the same at all the banks, my boy. Look over there. All these people want to draw their money out to take away with them. They might put restrictions on tomorrow when the real rush comes or they'll have none left."

"Merde, I hadn't thought of that," said Fred, realizing that his total assets were not even worth troubling the bankers with. More frustration at his complete dependence on his parents!

"Are you off, too?" asked the policeman.

"I don't know. I wanted to see a friend who works in the bank, to find out if he is going."

"Not much chance of getting in unless you join the queue or come back to the side door when he finishes work."

Fred kicked the pavement, angry at his naivety and helplessness; saddened too by couples arguing and children crying. His twisted feelings tightened even more at the sight of a pretty girl sitting alone on a brand new suitcase. He wanted to talk to her, pass some of the time with her in the queue, ask her to take a message in to Percy but knowing full well that he would not be able to screw up the courage to speak. He stood bursting with inadequacy and shyness until fate intervened on his behalf. Suddenly. without a word, the girl toppled sideways as she fainted into the surprised legs of the people next to her. Fred rushed forward, helped to pick her up and, in a few moments was standing silent but content, holding a glass of water for her as she recovered on a chair in the bank. He felt himself blush when the policeman winked at him..

~

Across the town Alice was in the doctor's waiting room. All the way in on the bus she had fought back the tears which so many thoughts conspired to bring on, not least the departure of the old lady. She had been sitting at home playing patience and feeling quietly sick when there was an almost inaudible knock on the door. The old lady stood there, beautifully turned out in a long yellow and green dress and a large ribboned hat. She was holding her 'Renoir' vase and, when Alice opened the door, she thrust it into her hands and whispered:

"Take it my dear and look at it and throw the flowers away before they fade too much. Keep the vase to remember at least one happy moment. I must go now or I shall cry. Goodbye."

She turned and walked with difficulty to the waiting taxi and never looked back. Alice had put the vase on the kitchen table and burst into tears just as Baptiste arrived. She excused herself and ran upstairs leaving the postman bewildered. From that moment she had not been able to get the old lady out of her mind. What would happen to her? How could she ever find again the peace and beauty of her own house? Who would look after her? Why, oh why did she have to go?

The doctor's surgery was not far from the bus terminus at Snow Hill. The atmosphere of the room depressed her; the taut, pale faces of the other patients, the claustrophobia and dark gloominess on a bright summer's day. Words and pictures seemed to merge into images that her conscious mind could not give meaning to. Would the doctors stay on the island? Did they fear being used by the Germans to do away with the old and infirm? Would they allow new Jersey children to be born? She wanted to scream at the horror of her own ridiculous thoughts.

~

After further uncertain and contradictory phone calls from town, the headmaster shut the school at one o'clock instructing the children at a final assembly to tell their parents to look every day at the Evening Post for a notice saying if and when the schools would be reopening before the start of the proper summer holidays.

Jack felt odd at the sudden release from his labours but, in the context of impending fatherhood and occupation, there was little left to surprise. The unusual was rapidly becoming the norm. After checking that Alice hadn't returned, he called at the shop, crowded and humming with animated conversation. Throughout the morning rumour had erupted from the area around the pier and Town Hall and the lava of truth, half-truth and the imaginary had intermingled, first enveloping the town, before finding conduits to the country parishes. The few phones, drivers of delivery vans and returning shoppers had all contributed to the island-wide confusion. The worst, as always, was the first to be readily believed and passed on. Minds no longer concerned themselves with what the Germans might or might not do, but on whether, as a result of an enormous conspiracy of fate, one would find oneself alone on the island when they arrived. The ultimate nightmare was of running down the pier as the last boat pulled out of the harbour.

Jack waited for his cigarettes and the more he heard the more he sensed that those who were now talking of leaving were not doing so as a result of well-argued reasoning or even because they were scared, but simply because others were said to be leaving. Once evacuation was seen to be happening on a large scale, people would evacuate for no other reason. Although the talk was irritating, Jack felt disinclined to start moralising in the shop. What right had he to say anything? So, for the moment he just laughed and visibly shook his head from side to side at the more outrageous things being expressed:

...the harbour was so full of boats they were jammed together and none could leave,; husbands, wives and children had to travel on separate boats in case they were bombed; England had been invaded so there was nowhere to go anyway...

As he came out of the shop he met Mary, the barmaid from the Royal, coming in.

"Hello Jack," she said a little surprised, "you're having a long dinner hour."

"The school's closed."

"Why, what's happened?"

"Orders from the Education Office," said Jack. "They didn't say why but we imagine it's to give families some time to sort themselves out about evacuating."

"People are beginning to panic a bit," she said, shaking her head sadly. "The driver from the brewery says there's a helluva queue down at the Town Hall, but he reckons it's a waste of time queuing because with so many people turning up at the boat, nobody'll be able to check whether you are registered or not."

Jack agreed that it was likely to end up as first come first served.

"By the way," she added, almost in a whisper, "it wouldn't surprise me if Henry went, I spoke to him yesterday and he made it sound as if the world was coming to an end."

"I know, I know," replied Jack with a helpless gesture, as he said goodbye. Before going indoors to make a sandwich, he exchanged a few words with Adolphe, resting on his shovel behind the cemetery wall.

"Eh ben mon vier bougre, it looks as if you've got a job on."

"Ah by cri yes, I've got two, I'm digging one with each hand you."

"It's Alan Legrand's father isn't it?"

"Yes, and a retired Englishman from R r ozel."

Peter Legrand had been seventy five. He had lived all this time, seen his island through years of change, of social movement, only to die just before perhaps the most significant moment in its history. These thoughts of death distressed Jack as his mind could not help associating them with the war and the Germans arriving. It would be miraculous if nobody got killed. Somewhere, at this moment, at work, at leisure, in a house, pub, street or shop, someone was marked to be the first to die at Nazi hands. Those who evacuated would escape at least that particular brush with fate.

Jack recalled vividly a story in which a servant had told his master that he had just seen Death looking at him and that he was riding away to Sumatra to escape. That afternoon the Master was surprised to see Death in the market place and he asked him what he was doing there and Death said that he was about to leave because he had an appointment with the Master's servant in Sumatra.

These thoughts reminded Jack that, as a child, on first noticing the measles spots on his stomach, he had run and run across the fields stopping every now and then to see if he had left the spots behind. He had never seen his parents as distressed as when they found him sobbing in the cow stable. At least the war would bring them no more worries. Could they be sitting up there looking down on all this? Perhaps in heaven you saw the antics of humanity as comedy whereas in hell you observed them as tragedy.

Yet life was full of good moments and it was the duty of everyone to find and savour them and pass them on to others. It was a fitting thought to have on Baptiste's arrival.

"Well, what's new?" asked Jack.

"Nothing very clever, mon vi, I've heard that the bloody States, tu parles d'une bande de feunmyi, a load of manure," he added for Mary's benefit, who had just joined them from the shop, "they're considering closing the pubs early."

Mary said that Jacko would be furious. She turned to Jack:

"Why do you think they want to close the pubs?"

"The only thing I can think of is that they don't want people to get boozed and into an even bigger panic than they are already."

"W w what w w orries m me," said Adolphe, "is w w what I'm g going to do if I s suddenly get s sober."

The others collapsed with laughter and reverted to further discussion about the closing of the pubs, this latest intrusion in their lives. Baptiste also informed them of several houses which had hurriedly written notices pinned to the door saying something like: 'Gone to England, no deliveries please.'

"Some have even left bloody addresses for forwarding mail. Do they think I've got time to write them all down, although I managed it at one house because they had left an envelope marked 'Postman' with the English address and a fiver inside."

"You don't get many like that," said Mary. "You're doing well, what with your Derby win the other day."

There was still no sign of Alice when Jack had eaten his cheese sandwich so he decided to get the visit to Fred's mother out of the way. It was going to be difficult. He had no right, in any case, to interfere in such an important private family decision, yet he knew he owed it to Fred, as his former pupil, and to the mother, herself, to be clear about the dangers to her son whether he went or stayed.

"You can't just come here and tell me what to do, Mr Birel."

"I don't want to tell you what to do. It's just that boys of Fred's age sometimes find it difficult to talk to their parents about really important things."

"Whether he talks or not, I know what he wants to do. I was only sixteen, you know, when my brother was taken to the last war. I read most of his letters, but some were so bad, my father wouldn't let me see them."

Jack didn't know what to say. "I'm sorry. I didn't realise."

"I've lost my brother to war," Fred's mother continued," and I've seen the last twenty years of what he was supposed to have died for, and I'm not going to let my son do the same thing."

Jack had only one other point to make. He took a sip of tea and a bite of chocolate cake. He was overcome with a sad helplessness. Eventually he said: "I understand you, Mrs Le Gros, but can you just consider one thing? I know that if Fred joins up in England, anything might happen to him but have you thought about the dangers if he stays here?"

Mrs Le Gros just stared at him without speaking. Jack took another sip of tea. It was too weak for his taste and he was uncomfortable in his chair. He heard himself continuing: "Even if he stays at home and behaves himself, young men of his age are likely to be very vulnerable if there's any trouble. You must have read of the things the Germans have done in Czechoslovakia and so on."

Still she didn't speak and Jack went on:

"He might become frustrated along with others and they may do something which will have serious consequences."

He couldn't face developing this theme further. At last Mrs Le Gros said something and Jack saw she had remained silent because of the intensity of her emotion. There were no tears but her voice was very broken.

"I'm willing to take the risk to keep him home where he belongs. Thank you for coming, Mr Birel, but if my son is to die, I want to bury him."

Jack apologised, thanked her for the tea and cake and quickly let himself out. The sun was still shining but banks of cloud were building up.

~

In town, the doctor, whose grey hair, smiling face and gentleness of touch always reassured Alice, told her that there could be little doubt that she was pregnant. She left his surgery in a dream, dabbing her eyes again and again with a little light blue handkerchief, fast becoming saturated. Her exceptional welling of inner joy was such that she noticed little of the to-ing and fro-ing in the town that day, making her a poor witness of the alleged conditions of panic which prevailed. Her one thought was to get back and tell Jack the news, but not before buying shared favourite gastronomic goodies - a bottle of dry Brut Champagne, some coquilles St. Jacques, a piece of fillet steak and two large éclairs.

Jack ran and grabbed her as she got off the three o'clock bus. A quick question to confirm her condition then he spun round like a young man from Verona long-parted from his Juliet. Had Alice been lighter and not pregnant, he might well have thrown her high in the air. He ran the gamut of noises you hear from the big wheel at a funfair.

"Why aren't you at school?" was all Alice could say.

Jack told her in mid-dance and Alice added:

"We had better go indoors before Mrs Crouton thinks we've gone mad. I just spotted her behind the lace curtain."

"But we have gone mad," said Jack, executing on the wall near the bus stop an intricate routine which Fred Astaire would have been proud to add to his repertoire.

"Have you eaten?" asked Alice when they got indoors.

"I just managed a sandwich after chatting to Baptiste. He told us he had found out from somewhere that the pubs are going to close. Then I went to see Mrs Le Gros."

"How did that go?"

"About as bad as I feared. I didn't know her brother had died in the Great War, did you?."

"Of course! I'd forgotten. It was Ivor Quenneville. That was her name before she got married. Did she mention him?"

"Yes, she told me that having lost a brother to war she was not prepared to lose a son as well."

On hearing this, Alice could barely speak. Eventually she said: "Imagine if that little person inside me wanted to go and fight in a war, what would we think? We'd better go in or Mrs C will really think we are mad - dancing one minute and crying the next."

They made a cup of tea and gradually regained their equilibrium, getting on with little jobs and hugging each other constantly. Then Alice said, revealing the contents of her shopping basket.

"Shall we have this now?"

As he gazed at the table, Jack's psyche made a second leap. In spite of the war, the Germans and the evacuation, they ate in contentment and toasted each other in Champagne before collapsing on the couch.

Later in the afternoon, arm in arm, and picking wildflowers on the way, they crossed the field to the farm. Jeanne was alone with the children and anxious that Henry had not returned from town.

"I don't know what's happened to him. He usually always comes home for dinner. He's such a stickler for eating at one o'clock. It's beginning to get on top of me all this. He paces up and down there in his shed, then he comes into the house and starts on his nonsense about us evacuating then he goes out again. At night he's not sleeping; he just can't keep still for a minute."

Alice did not want to thrust her own exciting news at her sister but then thought that it might, help a little to take her mind off the vagaries of her husband's behaviour. Jeanne apologised several times that her fretting about Henry had made her forget Alice was going to the doctor.

"He went on and on," she said, "worrying about how worrying it was going to be for you having a baby now of all times. He even seemed happy that he had found somebody with more to worry about than him."

She brushed strands of her hair back and began to smile. "Have you told Maman yet?"

"No," replied Alice, "that's one of the things I wanted to see you about first. What did they really decide to do when they were here on Sunday?"

"To stay put of course, didn't they tell you?" said Jeanne, surprised. "It was Henry again. He managed to half-persuade them into thinking that the kids wouldn't be safe here. I started crying because I was tired of hearing about it all morning. The man's enough to turn anybody silly when he starts."

Alice was relieved. There could no longer be any possible doubt that her parents wanted to stay on the island whatever happened. She put an arm around her sister's shoulder:

"Good, I would hate them to feel they mustn't go only because I'm having a baby."

"So, you're definitely not going?" said Jeanne

"No."

"Well, please tell Henry that. If he knows that you are staying, in your condition, it might help sort him out a bit. There's his lorry, thank goodness. Can you speak to him for a few minutes?"

Henry was a long time coming in. He looked tired, grunted a greeting and sat heavily in an armchair quite prepared not to speak unless every word was painfully extracted from him.

"Well?" said Jeanne.

"Well what?" he replied.

"Oh for goodness sake, stop behaving like a little boy. Jack sees enough of them at school. What have you seen? What have you done? You told me you were going to see what was happening."

"Things are happening all right."

Another painful silence.

"What, for example?" Jeanne was only just keeping her control.

"There are lots of boats arriving tomorrow and thousands are registering at the Town Hall."

"So what did you do?"

"I took the spuds to the pier but they didn't want them. Then I had a drink at the Yacht. There were a lot of people there. Then I walked into town."

"And you went to the Town Hall"

A grunted 'yes.'

"And you joined the queue."

A nod.

"And you stayed there most of the day."

"Yes."

"And you registered."

"Well, obviously, after waiting that long," Henry said angrily.

"Why?" Jeanne's voice was breaking.

"Because," Henry said in a heavy, monotone and depressed voice, "we decided that we would probably go."

"You decided, more like," Jeanne shouted. "You so confused everybody and upset them that we didn't know where we were any more."

Jack having sat embarrassed through this exchange picked up a glass and disappeared into the kitchen scullery to get some water or anything else he could find.

"You know Alice is pregnant," he heard Jeanne continue through the door.

"Of course I know. I told you myself she suspected it. "

"Well, aren't you happy for her? Now that it is confirmed, you haven't said a thing about it."

"Because you haven't stopped since I got in."

He turned to Alice. "I'm sorry, it's marvellous news. I hope everything goes well. I've told Jack to take you to England as soon as possible."

Jeanne screeched: "England! England! that's all you ever think about. They've already told you they are not going. Papa and Maman aren't going, your father isn't going, your brother isn't going. I can't see why you.." and she burst into tears and ran out of the room.

Henry didn't know whether to get up or stay. Alice made him a sign to remain where he was and went up after Jeanne. Jojo came in from outside and said "Where's mummy?" Henry mumbled that she would be down in a minute.

Jack picked up the boy and bounced him on his knee.

"Nothing I do is right," said Henry.

They stayed until Henry and Jeanne were actually speaking to each other, albeit in a strained manner. Jack promised to return the next day and accompany Henry to town, as his brother-in-law was still determined to spend time where the source of wild rumour was at it fiercest.

An hour later, summoned by Jack, Alice's parents arrived and parked at the customary forty degrees to the pavement. Jack had not told them on the phone the reason for calling them and the old couple looked concerned. The pleasure of the announcement was all Alice's. Papa's moonlike face lit up with joy. They stood in the kitchen talking excitedly, an exaggeration of normal conversation between Alice and her mother when both spoke at once and only half-listened. This helped to explain the garbled accounts they often gave of what the other had said. Eventually they made their way to the lounge where the bottle was opened. Questions, plans and recommendations criss-crossed the low coffee table, made by Alice's father from the upper half of a stable door. The atmosphere was so different from the sad blessing of Papa on Sunday when he had, for a moment, believed his whole family was on the point of leaving him forever.

"I just can't get over it, I'm so happy for you, Jack"

"It certainly feels dreamlike. Let me fill your glass."

"I haven't had champagne since your wedding, I don't think."

"That's a good one!" interjected Maman. "You had some when you went to Barneville last year."

"That was in France," twinkled the old man. "That doesn't count, it's just like having a cup of tea over there."

"Well, you tell some good ones, you," laughed his wife.

"Do you think I should have any more?" asked Alice.

"I doubt it love, there's not much left," replied Jack ducking.

"Have you told Jeanne?" asked Maman.

"Yes, but things aren't too good there at the moment. Henry is beginning to drive her mad."

"He had already started on Sunday," said Papa shaking his head. "He was trying to persuade us all to evacuate. What a picture he painted of what life would be like here!"

"I promised to go with him to town tomorrow," said Jack. "He just can't stay at home."

"You won't be at Peter Le Grand's funeral, then?"

"It's tomorrow, is it?"

"Half past ten."

"I suppose we could go there first, though I don't think a funeral is quite what Henry needs."

"You're right." Papa paused reflectively. "I was sorry to hear Peter was dead. He used to farm at Greencliff where your uncle was before he got married. We helped each other out with different things, but he's not been the same since his wife died."

When the old couple had gone and Alice was curled up on the couch listening to music on the wireless, Jack turned to his journal.

*Journal Extract*

*... First I must get a few things down from yesterday. A little more about religion. Mr Stevens, the headteacher, seems a completely different person from the somewhat bumbling and blinkered one who made such a mess of his assembly the other day. He spent some time in church, he said, which gave him a huge spiritual uplift. There is no doubt about it. He is a genuine, honest person who doesn't parade religious twaddle. I think he understands my argument too. Leaving the evil of Nazism to one side for a moment, mothers, wives and children, and indeed the men pressed into uniform themselves, on both sides in this war, will be praying to the same God to spare their loved ones.*

*Then, there's Andrew. He's decided to stay. We had another interesting discussion about duty. Deep down I think he feels a very strong pull to go and join up in order to 'do his duty' as he sees it and still feels guilty about putting love first. We'll just have to see what he actually does. Actions, they say, speak louder than words, something which will apply to all of us in the times ahead.*

*... I must think some more about what one can do positively and purposefully when the Germans are here. I see I've written 'when' not 'if'. What constitutes the patriotic duty of the occupee? I think I've invented a new word there.*

*Hopefully we can all do something constructive in this war, taking a leaf out of the old lady's book. Alice told me all about how she recreated in real flowers a 'Renoir' painting. It is the best inspiration so far, a million miles away from the behaviour of the frenetic shoppers. It's in pride of place on the mantelpiece. I must get Alice to draw it so that we have a permanent reminder.*

*... What about today! I've been going round in a bit of a dream, parcelling 'Germans' in one part of my brain and 'baby' in another,and sometimes bringing both briefly together. It has been confirmed by the doctor, that a young Birel, all being well, should be with us in about eight months time. Alice is delighted, obviously, and seems amazingly calm about it. I'm going to have to be careful not to burden my anxieties on her. I'm not as scared as I thought I would be but parenthood is a frightening business at the best of times when you haven't been through it before; that's without the Germans.*

*... I want to go to Peter Le Grand's funeral tomorrow. As one life passes on, another is on the way, a natural cycle which has gone on through time. I owe it to his son Alan, who I think will be a great source of strength to the community when times get difficult - good humour, common sense and no nonsense. What splendid qualities those are! Especially when you consider the fracas over the sugar in Mrs Pring's shop this afternoon. It seems that parents can sometimes behave far worse than their children. It does not bode well for any testing times ahead.*

*What are we going to do about my brother-in-law, Henry? He is getting more and more depressed and agitated because he just doesn't know what to do for the best. But how could he spend all day in a queue to register for evacuation? He must know that Jeanne will never agree to leave and he can't possibly take the children on his own; he wouldn't cope for five minutes. Why is he giving himself so much heartache?*

*..Then there's Fred. I promised, perhaps a little rashly, that I'd talk to his mother who is distraught about his possibly leaving. I'd completely forgotten her brother was killed in the Great War. It just goes to show that everyone has their own way of looking at things and that whatever actions are taken, someone is going to get hurt. Who is to say what is right? Maybe Henry too, is right? Perhaps we are not being fair to him.*

*This wait for the Germans has gone on for several days now. The longer it goes on, the more anxieties are turned over in the mind and the more likely it is that people will crack and rush off to England. I feel now that our own minds are made up to stay but there seems to be one niggling doubt after another - the prospect of fighting on our doorstep and the pregnancy, to name but two, as they say.*

# SEVEN

*Wednesday 19 June, 1940*

Jack tried to keep the joy of the pregnancy in the forefront of his mind to counterbalance starting the day with a funeral. He washed slowly and shaved with special care. He had to hunt hard for the black tie he had last worn at his father's funeral. It was impossible not to dwell on sad thoughts.

Papa arrived on time, wearing a suit of faded black, ill-fitting, yet perfectly acceptable for the occasion. How odd, thought Jack, that weddings and funerals see men in congregations at their most ungainly, trying to fit into suits of their younger shapes.

They walked briskly to the church porch, shaking hands with the other mourners. Jack lost himself deliberately in the contemplation of the architecture of St. Martin's Church and the stone which had lasted hundreds of years. It dated back to the 11th century but was thoroughly restored in Cromwellian times. A particular feature was the extraordinary number of buttresses needed at various periods to keep the building up. Many had been constructed from tombstones. On most of them the information about the deceased could only be gleaned by reading sideways or upside down. Jack could almost see long-lost congregations mirrored in the smoothly polished granite.

Once thoughts are awakened in a church, every subtle ornament, cross or smell directs them to some aspect of after-life. Even the most hardened unbeliever or determined agnostic feels uncomfortable trapped in a pew, waiting for a coffin to be brought slowly to the bier. If there was no God, what was it all for? What had been the point of Peter Le Grand's life? Or Jack's own for that matter, or that of his unborn child?

He looked slowly around him at the serious faces, each masking different worries, each seeking answers to similar questions. They felt a common sadness that Le Grand was dead but the most sobering thoughts were on their own mortality, particularly at this time of war approaching at an ever-increasing pace. Jack was glad not to have reminded Henry of the funeral. Goodness knows what this atmosphere would have done to him.

The noise of the hearse's arrival echoed down the stones of the church; the banging of doors, the crisp words of the bearers as they struggled to get the coffin easily on to shoulders. Then the vicar led the procession slowly up the aisle. During the service Jack couldn't help wondering how often this experience might be repeated as a direct result of the German invasion.

After paying his respects to Alan and his family at the graveside, Jack left Papa talking to his contemporaries and sought out young Fred, who was chatting to Adolphe behind one of the buttresses. For once the sight of the gravedigger swaying gently with the trees failed to provide any comic relief.

"Well Fred, I'm afraid I didn't get very far talking to your mother yesterday."

"I know, she told me last night, but thank you all the same."

"While I was talking to her, I couldn't help feeling that she was right."

"You mean that I shouldn't go," said Fred in dismay.

"I think you are both right. How can I say that a young man is wrong to want to escape from the island to give himself a chance to fight and how can I say to his mother that she is wrong not wanting her only son, who is too young in any case, to go off and be killed, as her brother had been, in 'some foreign field.' Only you and she, Fred, can come to your own decisions."

"There isn't an answer is there?" said Fred with some feeling. "Anyway I went to the bank yesterday and saw Percy. There were long queues of people by the way, trying to get their money out. It's going to be worse today. Percy's mother is a bit like mine. He said Alan Le Grand had been encouraging him but he didn't like to ask him for help at the moment with his father dying."

Jack said he hoped things would work out and wished him luck, adding that he would like to say goodbye, if Fred did eventually go. He left the graveyard, a change of tie, a quick snack, a brief exchange with Alice then Jack walked up to the farm. Henry was pacing up and down his well-worn worry path.

"Ah, there you are," he said, "I've been waiting here for ages. Can't you get up now that you are on holiday?"

"I've been to Peter Le Grand's funeral," said Jack

"Ah, that's who it was. I saw the hearse go past. I don't feel much like funerals, me, unless it's mine."

"Don't be so bloody daft."

The drive to town was memorable. Twice Henry strayed over to the right of the road, once on a dangerous bend near Poplar. Jack said: "The Germans aren't here yet, you know, Henry."

"What do you mean?"

"We still have to drive on the left."

"D'you think they are going to drive on the right then?"

"Bound to, I reckon."

"I hadn't thought of that. It's going to be funny driving on the wrong side like that."

"But not half as funny as doing it now," laughed Jack. He thought it was a good moment to add:

"Why don't you stay and see how it goes?"

"Don't you start as well," replied Henry mournfully but with a resigned shrug as if the crisis of the previous evening had helped calm his nerves a little.

Farmers did not park lorries, they just left them lying about around the Weighbridge. Jack and Henry were having a coffee and bacon roll near the town church when a young chap in shirt sleeves ran up to the door and shouted excitedly that Judge Dorey was about to address the States on the outcome of his trip to England. Drinks were left on tables and window ledges. Jack and Henry dashed into the Royal Square, jostled by people arriving from all directions. The States Chamber and stairs were already packed and the crowd assembled on the steps outside and down into the road. Everyone pressed forward in almost total silence, hoping the news would filter into the street. Cars stopped on the steep part of Halkett Place and drivers shouted questions through their windows. Murmurings were heard coming down the stairs and a tall man near the door took it upon himself to pass on what he could catch to the crowd behind him.

"The Chiefs of Staff decided on the 11th, I think, to defend the islands which is why soldiers and equipment were sent here. On the 15th they reversed their decision to spare devastation of the islands and last Saturday the War Cabinet agreed that the islands should be demilitarised."

A spontaneous hubbub broke the silence. Now it was official that there would be no fighting ...They can just walk in; .. .that settles it; ...why the hell bother to send soldiers in the first place..? there's no point in staying here now...

Henry observed that the soldiers were probably leaving already and that it was the end of everything. Jack found it difficult not to get cross. He pointed out to Henry that the main thing he had been working himself up about, had been the prospect of a battle."For God's sake," he added, "don't be such a bloody tchu."

The tall man near the door, wedged even taller by the tightening crowd, managed to raise his arm again. Everyone fell silent.

"The War Cabinet has decided to evacuate the islands, for those who want to go, and they are sending ships for this to be done."

Loud murmurs now! More people were arriving and pushing. Jack hardly heard the next few words. "Women and children are to be evacuated first, then the men of military age and finally anyone else."

"Who else is left?" somebody shouted.

"Older blokes," somebody else shouted back.

"Where does that put us?" asked Henry.

"We must be of military age," said Jack, "I think it's up to forty."

"Did he say we had to go or just that we could go?" somebody shouted again.

"I'm only telling you what I hear," complained the man at the door.

A newcomer, just a few yards from where he was standing, was informed by one of the crowd, to Jack's incredulity, that the whole island was going to be evacuated. Another said that all men over forty would have to stay. Other comments were silenced by a further announcement from the door that the States would foot the bill of people too poor to pay for their passage. The other details would be discussed in committee. The Jurat sat down to applause and grateful thanks for the mission he had undertaken.

Slowly the stunned crowd dispersed and the two men decided to abandon their coffees and that the pier was the next most likely place of interest. Their steps in that direction were halted at an open window by the now familiar voice on the wireless of Alvar Liddell reading the news. The Germans had reached both Rennes and Cherbourg. The capture of the port at the northern end of the Cotentin could only make evacuation more risky. Henry was not slow to appreciate this and kept repeating his fears to Jack as families, mothers pulling children, men on their own dashed past them in an ungainly race towards the harbour.

The first real panic had gripped the town. Evacuation was now official with the full approval of the War Cabinet and therefore, Churchill himself. It became the obvious course of action. Wilder and wilder statements sped from mouth to mouth:

... there were cars lined up in Halkett Place ready to rush the States' members to special planes at the airport; ..their families were already there; ...none of the Crown Officers, the Bailiff, the Attorney General or Solicitor General had been in the States that afternoon because they were already in England in a secret house; ...they had waited to tell the population about evacuation when it was too late because the Germans would be able to stop the boats; ...there was an agreement with the Germans that no more boats would leave after tomorrow; ...German spies had landed from a dinghy at Bonne Nuit and were spreading rumours among the population to increase the panic...

Even Henry smiled when he heard this last remark and Jack said: "As if they needed the Germans to spread panic! Listen to them!"

Henry reluctantly agreed but still held firm to the idea that women, children and men of military age would have to leave. Jack gave up repeating that nobody would be forced to do anything and that instructions would be in the 'Evening Post.'

At the harbour the difficult weather conditions became obvious. Quite a large crowd had assembled near lots of little boats, recently arrived back from St Malo. A few had been requisitioned in the French port, but most had gone across from Jersey during the previous two days. They had been forced to brave strong winds and heavy seas in order to leave before the Germans arrived. Most of the soldiers had now disembarked and were sitting on knapsacks, smoking and looking bored. Lorries with seats used for church outings arrived and the crowd gave a kind of muted cheer as the first soldiers were driven away.

Jack asked a private for more information and had great difficulty understanding his Yorkshire accent, in spite of his three years in England. He just managed to make out that the soldiers had been forced to leave St Malo in a hurry. None of them had known where they were going and they were surprised to find themselves in Jersey. They certainly didn't know whether they were expected to stay and help defend the island.

Further down the pier, several yachts and motor boats were tying up with more soldiers and some civilians speaking French. Many had clearly been very sick. A farmer from St Martin's came up to Jack and said: "We had a bit of a to-do last night. Our next door neighbour came in and told us her husband had gone. We didn't know what she meant at first, but she explained that somebody had told her they'd seen him get on a boat yesterday afternoon and she didn't know a thing about it. They kept having rows but what a way to get a 'divorce', you!"

"Hell," said Jack, "that's a bit much. Poor woman. I wonder if any of these are doing the same thing."

"I wouldn't ask if I was you. You might find out things you'd prefer not to know," added the farmer. "It couldn't be easier could it? You've just got to tell your fancy bit to be on the boat, tell your wife you're going to buy some fags and off you go. Nobody in England is going to check who's with who when all this lot arrive."

Railway Company officials shouted that a boat was due in and out later that evening and that all the others would be leaving the next day. The evacuation was scheduled to last three days unless the Germans intervened.

Jack and Henry returned home to relate these developments, in their different ways, to their wives. Like the rest of the island they read every word of the Evening Post. The paper informed them that, from the next day, evacuees had to report in three queues at the Town Hall, women and children, men of military age and others. The population was exhorted not to panic and the paper stressed several times that it was in no way obligatory for anyone to go.

The British Government was willing to evacuate the islands and accepted to look after the refugees in England but the fewer who went, the lesser the burden on the already considerably burdened people of the mother country.

Jack, after reading the Post for the second time in the kitchen of their little cosy house, suddenly announced to Alice that he fancied a cup of Bovril.

"I thought it was only pregnant women who were supposed to have cravings."

"Well, there you are," said Jack, "as I told Andrew the other day, 'tu n'as pas acuou veu la grosse bete qui t'mangera.'"

"What does that mean again?"

"You should jolly well know that by now. Just because you went to school in France and speak 'good' French! Your father says it all the time. You haven't yet seen the big beast that's going to eat you."

"How you managed to get to that from a cup of Bovril, I'll never know."

Both of them knew, as they bantered that more serious matters were lurking below the surface. Unusually Jack was the first to bring them up.

"It looks as if proper evacuation is going to start tomorrow. The Post says it could take three days but now that the Germans are in Cherbourg, anything could happen. A lot will depend on whether they've moved ships there or not. I don't think they have."

"So, what are you saying?" asked Alice, a little anxiously.

"What I am saying is that this might be the last night before we have to decide one way or another whether we are staying or not."

"I thought we had decided."

"We have, but I want you to be absolutely sure, now that you know you are pregnant. I want to stay, but I get a little panicky sometimes at the magnitude of it all. An afternoon with Henry doesn't help, but, in a way, I understand him and feel very sorry for him."

Alice was silent for what seemed like a long time, but Jack couldn't break the silence. Eventually she said: "I don't want to go. This is my island and my identity. Even if I was on the boat, I'd get off again."

"I thought and hoped that you'd feel like that. I feel the same. So let's go to bed and seal our decision."

*Journal extract.*
*Time is running out*

*..I couldn't write anything before going to bed. Now I can't sleep so I shall try to write a few words.*

*Sad to start the day with a funeral. The poems I studied at school are much more apt than when I learned them. St. Martin's could so easily fit the description of the country churchyard of Gray's Elegy and Peter Le Grand has, for much of his life 'followed the lowing herd slowly o'er the lea' and he now lies 'beneath those rugged elms' where 'the rude forefathers of the hamlet sleep.'*

*Went to town with Henry today. Stood outside the States chamber listening to a chap passing word down the steps of what was going on inside. It still amazes me how people can pass on the opposite of what they have just clearly heard. But we do know now that the decision to have an official evacuation has been taken.*

*..Seeing those soldiers come ashore after their journey from St Malo really brings it all home. Most of them were as young as Fred and pretty green around the gills. They certainly didn't look as if they could defend anything. What with them and the troops from England who've been arriving the last few days, there is probably more military presence on the island than there has been for a long time. Tomorrow, if we are to believe what was said in the States, they will all leave and we will be left to face whatever happens.*

*There has been a dramatic development as regards the Royal Jersey Militia. Apparently it had to be disbanded to comply with the British view of demilitarisation but, encouraged by their Commanding Officer, Lieutenant Colonel Vatcher, they all volunteered to go to England together to join up in the Royal Hampshire Regiment. The States gave permission for the Militia to be reformed on that basis.*

*It's not surprising that Fred and Percy are anxious to join up too. Let's hope they all get back safely and also all the evacuees on the boats which are being sent over by the British government.*

*..There can't be many days left in which to escape, if that is the word, now that the Germans are in Cherbourg, although probably only army personnel at the moment. There might be U boats in the area though.*

*..Alice is more determined than ever not to go, so, unless we are all ordered off the island, which doesn't seem likely, we are here for the duration.*

# EIGHT

*Thursday 20 June, 1940*

Thursday proved to be for everyone the longest and most dramatic day. Jack awoke to determined banging on the front door at seven thirty. Heart pounding, he went downstairs knowing it could only be bad news. His first thought was that Henry was on his way to the boat but when he opened the door, a distressed Mrs Le Gros said without preamble: "Where's Fred, has he been here?"

Jack's heart sank as he shook his head.

"Well, he's gone. I hope you're satisfied. He would never have gone if you hadn't encouraged him. I've got to get to the boat to stop him. How am I going to go?"

Jack had no idea what to say, faced with such a confrontation only minutes from sleep. Mrs Le Gros was too upset for any kind of discussion. She just kept repeating that she had to get down to the harbour.

Jack invited her in and Alice made a cup of tea while he dressed hurriedly and ran up the road to see if Henry would take them in his lorry. The scene in the farm kitchen was little improvement on the one he had just left. Jeanne and Henry were facing each other like two boxers. She was holding the children to her in the melodramatic manner favoured by many Victorian painters. She was shouting. "We are not going, so you can do what you like."

Jack did his best to describe his predicament with Mrs Le Gros. Jeanne told him through tears not to ask Henry to go down to the boat because he was quite capable of jumping on it and leaving them. At this Henry finally broke down.

"But it's because of you all that I want to go. I'd never leave on my own, can't you see that? It's the kids I'm worried about. Well don't blame me if anything happens to them now."

He wiped his eyes and put his arm around Jeanne, who heaved a sigh of many things but managed to keep quiet. Henry walked straight out to the lorry and started the engine. Jeanne whispered urgently: "Please keep an eye on him all the same, Jack."

They stopped near the cemetery where Alice had her arm around Mrs Le Gros. The distraught mother climbed up the high step into the lorry and sat next to Jack. Few words were exchanged the whole way to town. Even at this hour, there were traffic jams. Henry was forced to park halfway down Colomberie and they had to continue on foot, Mrs Le Gros trying to run with a hobbling gait and sobbing the whole time. All along Hill Street and down Halkett Place, cars were abandoned everywhere; lorries and vans jammed out of sight round the market. People were running in and out of the vehicles towards the Town Hall or pier and the church clock was only chiming eight thirty.

At the harbour the scene was even more incredible. It looked as if the whole population was there. Boats of all shapes and sizes, including cargo boats and colliers, were berthed all the way around the Albert Pier and evacuees were crowding onto them. Jack and Henry soon lost Mrs Le Gros and each other but, from the start, their search for Fred was hopeless. It would be impossible to get on to every boat, search it then get off again. Unless the lad was still on the pier or decided to show himself, there was no way they would find him.

Jack found himself near a boat called the SS Malines which was being guarded by two young soldiers holding rifles. A docker told him that it had arrived at about seven o'clock to take all the troops on the island back to England. As they spoke, lorries, filled with soldiers, drew up one behind the other very fast. Given the news about the fall of Cherbourg, the military clearly intended to leave with the least possible delay. Those who had arrived the previous day from St Malo were immediately recognisable and still looked the worse for wear. Jack heard one soldier comment to his mate "Let's hope none of their planes come over while we're still in the harbour."

Two or three more soldiers were detailed to keep onlookers back from the boat. There were no cheers or applause. Arguments broke out among the islanders between those who saw the soldiers' departure as necessary and wise and those who preferred the bravado of feeling let down and abandoned. A sergeant gave an order and the men began marching towards the gangway to mixed shouts from the crowd, although the cries of 'Good Luck' and 'Smash the bastards over there' were winning the day. The men walked unsmilingly aboard.

In no time, it seemed, the SS Malines was pulling away. As it headed for the harbour mouth the crowd watched in silence, shaken by the significance of it all. Even though the departure of the troops was not unexpected, Jack's heart was heavy at the realisation that the way was now completely open for the Germans to come and capture the island

Then, as if prompted by that mysterious force which inspires large crowds to act on cue, the people on the pier began to wave handkerchiefs and cheer as the boat turned out to sea. After a few moments hesitation, the soldiers began to wave back. It was difficult not to shed tears. Jack wiped his eyes unashamedly as he joined his fellow islanders running towards the end of the harbour to watch the stern of the boat draw round the breakwater behind Elizabeth Castle. It was not yet possible to start dreaming of the day when, perhaps the same boat, would bring British soldiers back.

The suddenness leading up to this departure and the sight of the leaving boat created a psychological pull on the onlookers. Jack could hear the words ' leaving,' 'settles it,' 'not staying now.' He himself had to shake off pangs of doubt.

After a further half hour of being elbowed, jostled and pushed, Jack spotted the still distraught Mrs Le Gros near the gangway of the largest boat. A policeman had taken her on board but to no avail. No crew members knew who had come on board or when. Their whole attention was concentrated on trying to make sure the boats were not dangerously overloaded. Bewildered men, women and children sat everywhere, on the stairs and on the floor. They had the minimum amount of baggage and many were crying. One had a sewing machine, another some garden tools.

"You can leave the lady with us," Jack told the policeman as Henry suddenly appeared.

"Oh dear," sighed the tall copper, "I must have taken at least twenty people on the boat looking for somebody."

Jack felt a heavy numbness. All around him there seemed to be only sadness, misery and fear. Many of those now pushing their way up gangways were engaged in the same dispiriting search for somebody dear to them. A child started howling nearby. What a time to get lost! Henry went off again to look for Fred, leaving Jack with the equally impossible task of trying to comfort his mother. The silence between them grew and grew until it was almost head bursting. Henry returned, shrugging his shoulders in failure and naming several acquaintances he had seen getting on to another boat, fellow farmers from St Martin amongst them. One had shouted that he had let his cows loose before leaving and that Henry could have them if he wanted.

"To be honest, Jack," Henry added, "I still feel worried about what is going to happen to us, but I'm glad I'm not going in all this panic."

"That's a relief," said Jack. "We are not going to forget these scenes in a hurry."

They continued to take turns to look for Fred until the first boat started to move. All idea of time was lost. The boat, crowded along every handrail, made several lurches as if reluctant to get under way. By now Mrs Le Gros was so distressed that Jack wanted to get her to a doctor or the hospital. The policeman, a source of strength to all around him, told them of a special First Aid Unit near the abattoir at the end of the pier. Even then, it needed sustained persuasion and cajoling to get Fred's mother to walk the few hundred yards to lie down on a camp bed and try to relax.

Jack remembered he had promised to phone Alice and Jeanne. He managed to persuade Mrs Le Gros that her husband ought to come and join her. He waved aside her repeated opinion that he would be more a hindrance than a help, which was why she had not wanted him there in the first place.

Jack had to queue at the phone box near the abattoir then had great difficulty getting through. The lines were jammed, not least because many telephone operators had joined members of every other job, service or profession in the rush for the boats.

After a seemingly interminable wait, Mary answered the phone at the Royal and agreed to distribute the various messages. Jack also told Mary to warn Mr Le Gros that he would probably have a longish walk from wherever the bus managed to reach because of the abandoned cars. Mary had not been up long and all this panic came as a great surprise to her.

"Please let Alice know that we are OK but that some of the scenes here are really heartbreaking," added Jack, "and tell Jeanne that Henry looks as if he has lost his appetite for going."

~

Mary quickly put on a blouse and skirt and went out to convey the messages. Her first surprise were the cows walking about the yard of the pub sniffing at the empty beer crates. She heard shouting from the road where the Constable was calling a farmer a coward and a 'salaud' for abandoning all his cows and leaving for England. After further loud arguing the man agreed not to go unless the Constable himself were to decide to leave.

Returning from Mr Le Gros, she recognised Andrew, the teacher from England, looking thoroughly dejected, talking to Alice at her door. The news of the departing soldiers had pressed hard on his battered conscience and decided him to leave as well. Kate had felt unable to accompany him so they had parted in the hope they might last out whatever time the war took and then meet again. Andrew was clearly embarrassed at having changed his mind with apparent suddenness but he had known, deep in himself, that he would probably not stay when duty called him so strongly to join up and fight.

"Hardest decision I ever took or want to take," he said to Alice. "Hope I see Jack on the pier, helped me a lot to sort myself out. If I don't see him, tell him thanks for everything. Goodbye, Alice, good luck with the little chap or chapesse. Can't have too many Birels around if you ask me."

He ran across the road, carrying a small airforce grey suitcase and jumped on to the bus, ahead of Mr Le Gros still struggling to get his jacket on. The first thing the conductor said was: "I doubt if we'll manage to get as far as Snow Hill."

~

On the pier Jack sent Henry to find cups of tea. After a long delay he returned.

"There are queues for everything. I got some sausage sandwiches while I was about it."

They ate and drank with gusto and tried to persuade Mrs Le Gros to do the same but she shook her head stubbornly at every suggestion. Now Henry stayed behind while Jack took the cups back and went for a little walk in the town. To his amazement the scenes were even more chaotic than on the pier. Queues from the Town Hall door stretched out of sight in every direction. A policeman told him that about fifteen thousand people were trying to leave.

King Street was still jammed with empty cars, many with their doors wide open. Some shops were completely empty, not a shop assistant to be seen. One was locked and boarded up, two had 'closed for an indefinite period' scrawled on pieces of card and hung on the door. Others seemed open as usual. Jack scribbled his impressions then turned back to the Weighbridge hoping that the bus had finally brought Mr Le Gros.

The little man was indeed sitting with his wife, enabling her to regain some strength by criticizing his every attempt to suggest or intervene. Only the most rusty, unappetizing boat remained in the harbour and the restless crowd was being urged to return later in the evening or the next day when there would be more boats. Angry voices continued to demand a place on the last vessel, claiming they had registered at the Town Hall a week before whereas many people, now well on their way in the channel, had just turned up and rushed on board when control broke down. It required strong action by several policemen to drive everyone back.

Jack and Henry, relieved of their responsibility vis-a-vis Mrs Le Gros, strode to the Royal Square where they were able to stand quite a way up the stairs leading to the States Chamber. An open door allowed them to hear the proceedings inside. Today it was Jack's turn to pass on information to the growing crowd, again overflowing well into the Square.

The session opened solemnly with a strong condemnation of those farmers who were simply turning out their livestock and abandoning their farms. Jack heard the Constable of his own parish recount his altercation with a farmer as he was leaving to come to the Chamber.

A question was asked about how Britain would be repaid the costs of evacuation and the reply stressed that it was the clear duty of the islands to find this money. The figures of those who had registered the previous day were read out. 4861 wished to travel free, 3480 were willing and able to pay. Of these 434 were men between the ages of 20 and 33. It was clear, however, that these official figures were way short of what was actually happening, and that the three categories of evacuees described the day before were not being enforced at all.

At this point Jurat Dorey, the island emissary to England, rose to make an impassioned speech in which, carried away by his own rhetoric, he tried to differentiate between young Jerseymen going to join the forces and others who were simply escaping. There was no comparison, he said, between 'young men of old Norman stock leaving the island with a mission to fulfil and the other rats and rabbits who were cluttering up the ships and who were simply going to be a burden to Britain.' His words were carried to the Square to be greeted with large howls. Taking strength from the Jurat's approach, other States' members made further outspoken criticism of those who were panicking and mindlessly leaving the services of the island in disarray. The anger and shouting grew in the Square; several scuffles broke out and there was considerable movement in the ranks of the people packed on the stairs just below Jack.

In the Chamber two decisions were then taken. The banks would open for just three hours on Monday, Tuesday, Wednesday and Friday and the pubs were ordered to close at two o'clock that afternoon because of the panicky conditions which prevailed. The Constables of the twelve parishes and their Honorary Police were empowered to put this into effect.

By now, news had reached the States' members of the vast and restless crowd in the Square outside and it was announced that the Bailiff and another Jurat, Judge Pinel, would come out and address them.

"We'd better try and make our way back into the Square or we won't hear anything," said Henry.

"They'll speak from the balcony of the Club at the far end, unless they climb on the roof," suggested Jack.

"That might stop a few of them buggering off," observed the man next to Jack.

Nothing more could be heard in the Chamber and people on the stairs began to turn and exert pressure on those below until, eventually, Jack and Henry emerged into the sunlight. The lucky ones, positioned near the Peirson or Cosy Corner could call for sustenance through the open windows, though only until two o'clock, if the newly-created decree came into immediate effect. Young men had climbed on to the plinth in the centre of the square and were holding hands with George II, looking slightly more absurd than usual in his Roman toga. Henry and Jack edged forward with difficulty along the high steps at the side of the States' building until they found a niche near the plaque dedicated to Wace, the first real Jersey writer of note, from the 12th century.

As if inspired by the Anglo-Norman poet, Jack scribbled in the little French squared notebook he now kept permanently in his pocket - quick sketches of anxious faces, the hubbub of conversation, the angry raised voice, the occasional hearty jester, the restless children, the assortment of bags and suitcases, the general atmosphere of tension.

For most people, it was the first really big crowd they had seen. There may have been more present as spectators at some Murattis, the annual inter-island football match against Guernsey, but they had been spread out around the ground and, Jack smiled at the thought, sitting in stands. Today the throng, if that was the word, was packed into a single square hemmed in by buildings. He wondered what was happening in Guernsey and the smaller islands. He had only been to Guernsey twice, once to play football, himself and once to watch the Muratti.

Shortly before noon the Bailiff of Jersey, Alexander Coutanche, a tall man with a friendly face and drooping cheeks, yet with a strong determined jaw and mouth, appeared at the Committee Rooms window to spontaneous and loud cheers. He began by saying that he would stand on a chair so that those below might see that he had not gone - an opening greeted with further cheering and applause.

He acknowledged that there was grave anxiety amongst the population.

"He's right there, eh Henry." Jack nudged his brother-in-law.

Raising his voice the Bailiff said that it had been stated that some of the authorities had left the island. He paused and looked to all parts of the Square.

"That is not correct," he stressed slowly and firmly. "I know a lot of you want to leave. You must act according to your consciences, but as for those rumours of a general pack-up of the powers that be, I can assure you that as far as I am concerned, I am staying and my wife is staying at my side. I have sworn to guard your rights as Bailiff and I shall do so." He paused again then asked the crowd to join him in singing 'God Save the King' the words ringing out in defiance from all those present.

Jack was fascinated by the change in behaviour of the crowd. Many of them had contributed to the morning's panic and a good number must have registered to leave the island, but they were now cheering with fervour the man who was urging them to stay. Human nature being what it was, thought Jack, the Bailiff could not have made a speech to stem panic until panic had actually started. The day before, his words would not have had the same effect.

Judge Pinel took his place on the balcony, taking a much harder line with those who wanted to leave.

"He's looking as fierce as usual," Jack said to Henry, "I wouldn't want to stand on his toes."

The Judge said that earlier that morning he had been grieved to see Jersey men and women fleeing from their island in panic. "It was the duty of every one," he said stressing each syllable "to stay at their posts and not throw an extra burden on the mother country." Then referring to the intensifying bombing of British cities, he finished by saying that it would be safer in Jersey than on the mainland.

From the conversations Jack heard around him, these short speeches had, without doubt, a marked effect. Others, though, remained unswerving in their determination to catch the next boat and views supporting immediate departure were still being forcibly expressed. Nevertheless the overall atmosphere had shifted from near-despair to restrained hope.

Jack and Henry started back towards the lorry, surprised as they crossed the town to see the number of cars which had moved or were moving. Many of the owners of seemingly abandoned vehicles had not left after all. Near the Forum cinema Jack said: "Let's see what's on. You never know, there mightn't be any more films once the Germans come, unless they try to show us some of theirs."

Henry read the title: 'Another Thin Man' with William Powell and Myrna Loy.

"That sounds promising," said Jack, "shall we go tonight to help take our minds off things?"

"What about the kids?"

"Take them to Fliquet. It will help the old couple to have something else to think about too."

"What about if the Germans land at Fliquet while the kids are there?" asked Henry, his mind still never too far from worry and fret.

Jack shook his shoulders in mild exasperation. "Let's go back by the coast," he suggested.

They drove along the back of Howard Davis Park, through Georgetown, and round by the FB fields.

"Look, Henry," said Jack, "there are people playing golf and tennis as if nothing was happening."

"You're right there, Jack. I wouldn't have noticed anything strange. These people are not panicking, them. You'd never think we'd just seen crowds running about like silly buggers in town."

"The tennis players are neatly dressed in white too. It's a pity the Bailiff can't see them, it might cheer him up a bit."Then he said suddenly: "Stop here a minute near this phone box."

"Who are you going to phone? Not the Bailiff, surely?"

"No, the 'Evening Post.' They may like to know that while people were panicking at the harbour, others were playing tennis and golf as if everything was normal."

Jack came back looking pleased.

"What did they say?" asked Henry.

"They said it was a really good idea and that they would put it in the paper."

They followed the coast from Greve d'Azette, past Green Island, the Martello Tower at Le Hocq and around by La Rocque, where the expanse of stark, moonlike rocks reminded them that it was a big tide and Jack suggested they go low-water fishing the next day.

"I should be getting back to my toms," said Henry.

"They can wait another day. You'll only start thinking all your 'niolîn' again."

They were heartened to see more golfers on the picturesque course at Grouville, sand dunes undulating to the beach with the impressive Mont Orgueil Castle in the background. Jack remarked that he would love to play golf properly.

"I've been down here once or twice in the holidays with the Scotsman who teaches at Trinity. I wonder if he's gone back home."

"I've never played, me," said Henry dismissively. "Bloody waste of time walking after a little pimple like that."

"Quiet, Henry, you've just committed a sacrilege."

"What are you talking about?"

"That's where Harry Vardon was born, in that little cottage, there, mon vi."

"Who's Harry Vardon?" asked Henry.

Jack shook his head in mock despair, though not surprise. In sporting matters the ignorance of his brother-in-law knew no bounds. Jack had taken him to a Muratti once and all he did throughout the match was stand behind the crowd about three deep, with his back to the pitch, talking about potatoes with other farmers. His only comment on the game was to ask who was playing in red and white, and now. Who's Harry Vardon?

"Harry Vardon was one of the greatest golfers who ever lived. He won the British Open six times."

"What's the British Open?" asked Henry.

Jack did not bother to reply.

As they swept round the bend behind the castle, thoughts of the defeated France returned to Jack. There, visible and clear, was the coast of Normandy, a wide strip of sand exposed at low tide, behind which invisible German tanks, lorries, cars and motor cycles would be moving about. If Cherbourg had fallen the previous day, they must also be in Carteret.

"Eh ben, Henry, do you think they are looking at us through binoculars?"

"Who?"

"The Germans of course."

"Where? "said Henry, nearly letting go of the wheel.

"From Carteret."

"Bloody hell, I thought you'd seen them down the road. I was just thinking about them, too. Suppose they took a pot shot at us to see how far their guns fire."

On reaching St Martin's Church unscathed, Jack raced indoors to give Alice the news from town but she outnewsed him with Andrew's departure. Part of Jack was stunned. The other part had expected the possibility but it was still difficult to come to terms with the fact that someone you had got close to could just disappear from your life as easily as that. So many thoughts came at once; the man's courage and sense of duty, the emotional strain behind his choice, the pain Kate must feel. He was sad not to have said goodbye.

"You didn't see him on the pier?" he heard Alice ask.

"But you've got no idea how many people there were, coming and going and shouting and crying."

He told her of Mrs Le Gros, of the policeman, of the boats and the staring eyed panic. He finished by saying: "Henry was quite moved, I think, by the sight of so many people just abandoning everything they have."

"Talking of abandoning things, there are cows wandering all over the place around here."

A few minutes later when Jack had realized to his amazement that it was only dinnertime on this momentous day, there was a knock at the door which made him nervous. Knocks these days heralded unwelcome news. To his surprise, he found Jacques Galtier, the Constable of St Martin standing there.

"You're back from the States," was all Jack could think of saying.

"Yes, and I've got a helluva job on. I've had to notify all the pubs to shut at two o'clock. That went down well at the Royal I can tell you!" One of my Constable Officer's is sick and another one hasn't got back from town yet, but in any case I need more help than that, so I just wondered if there was any chance..."

"Of course, but not, I hope, telling the pubs to shut!"

"No, I've managed to phone them all, there aren't that many. Some of them will be pretty angry, that's for sure. The big job is seeing to the houses that have been abandoned and locking them if possible, rounding up and sorting out any animals wandering around and taking charge of any valuables or perishables in the abandoned houses we can get into."

"It does sound like a pretty big job, you're right."

"You're telling me; as if I haven't got enough to do. So I thought that you and Mr Stevens might be able to help us since the schools are closed."

"All right, I'll do my bit. Why don't you ask Henry as well? Every little thing we can get him to do will help."

"I heard he wasn't too good."

"He's perked up a bit today, funnily enough."

"He can go round with Edmund Le Gris. They might cheer each other up."

A bit later in the cluttered little room at the Parish Hall, Edmund Le Gris, pipe flapping, was asking Galtier question after question about how they were going to set about their task. Jack felt himself back in the classroom...must we draw a margin, sir...on which side do I put the date...can I write in pencil sir?

Eventually Edmund stumbled upon a question which actually was fundamental to the job in hand. "How are we going to know where the abandoned houses are?"

"That's what's been puzzling me too," said the Constable, lifting his cap and scratching his bald patch. "Nobody said anything about that in the States this morning."

Jack suggested they ask Baptiste. "He must have seen some empty houses on his round."

"That's a good idea, mon vi," said Galtier, relieved. "We can try his house since the pub is closed. By cri, he won't be too happy about that," a remark he knew to be an understatement.

Baptiste was indeed home and, as anticipated, far from happy. Before they had time to tell him why they had come, he launched into a tirade of Jersey-French which summarised his views on the pubs closing at two and on the parentage of all the States' members before saying:

"So you expect people to stay in Jersey only if they are not drunk? Well me, I've a bloody good mind to bugger off sober if the pubs are going to be closed. Even Hitler wouldn't come up with a hair-brained scheme like that."

Galtier thought he had found a lull in which to ask Baptiste's help but the postman got into his stride again on the second major disappointment of the day. The Jockey Club in England had decided that there would be no more racing until further notice.

"If we can't drink and have a bet," ranted Baptiste, "what the hell is there left to do?"

He seemed oblivious of the fact that the Constable, as a staunch Methodist, did neither as a matter of principle. Jack, amused at the postman's rhetorical question, and hoping to relieve the tension, said: "Not at your age, anyway."

"Ah you reckon?" replied Baptiste. "I'd show you a thing or two yet. You'd be surprised what I see on my rounds sometimes."

Here at last was the opening. The Constable asked Baptiste if he could make a list of houses which had been left empty. This he did quickly and thoroughly, providing twenty-seven names and promising to get his colleagues from other parts of the parish to do the same. At last they could all get started, Henry and Edmund towards Rozel and the Constable and Jack past the shut Royal towards Faldouet and Gorey.

At the first farm, they found all the cows in the stable with a pile of hay, oats and turnips in the mangers in front of them.

"I s'pose he thought somebody'd come before they ran out of food. Write down how many cows there are, Jack, while I take some of this out, otherwise they are going to get bloated."

"Are you going to organise people to go round feeding the cattle?" asked Jack.

"I'll have to do something. We can't afford to let them die. We'll need all the milk we can get when the Jerries are here."

The farmhouse itself was locked but, through the kitchen window, they could see that everything was spick and span.

"Write down we haven't got the key and let's go," said Galtier.

The next little bungalow was very different, door wide open and the dirty dishes left in the sink. Jack noted the need for organising washer-uppers to prevent places starting to smell and attract flies.

"We'll have to have a meeting at the Parish Hall to sort all this out," said the Constable. Jack winced under his breath. He had been to enough meetings like that already.

Some houses were in the keep of helpful neighbours who had the keys but, at the second farm they visited, the cows had been turned loose and were sniffing and messing all over the yard. Two Alsatian dogs were tied on long chains to the shed. Galtier was furious.

"If this so-and-so comes back, he'd better never come and see me for help. Phone the Animal Shelter from the house, Jack. Do you know, we were told in the States this morning that 2,200 dogs and 3,000 cats have been destroyed. Let's hope we don't have to start eating them before long."

"Ah come on," rallied Jack, "things won't get that bad."

"Don't be too sure. Just look at that!"

They had walked into the house where the table had been left with three half-eaten meals, bits of sausage and fried eggs congealed with fat on the plates. Full, nearly full and nearly empty cups of tea stood on the stained napkin which served as a tablecloth.

"Anybody'd think that some force from outer space had whisked them away."

They were to see two more partially-eaten meals left on tables. How could people take the trouble to cook, sit down to eat, and then leave before they finished? Such was the nature of panic.

At one house the neighbour came round and invited them in for a cup of tea.

"Have you heard the terrible news?" she asked. "A poor man's been killed at the airport. He was chopped by a propeller, how awful!" She thrust a handkerchief to her mouth.

Jack was reminded of when his brother Jim worked at the airport. He had saved a chap from walking into a propeller. The elderly man had thanked him hundreds of times and wouldn't let go of his hands for minutes. These grisly thoughts did little to encourage Jack and the Constable to do justice to the lady's scones.

At home Alice answered a knock to find the headmaster raising his hat before speaking. He looked flustered and slightly bemused and said there wasn't much time to lose. Alice asked him in.

"I hope you haven't come to say that school is starting again tomorrow."

"No, no, nothing like that, Mrs Birel. Is Jack here?"

"Afraid not, he's helping the Constable. They've gone round the parish sorting out the empty houses."

"Ah, so that's what he wanted. My wife said he'd been to the house. Anyway your sister-in-law has just telephoned me from La Moye. She wanted to get hold of Mr Birel. She was understandably, distressed."

"What's happened ?" asked Alice with growing concern.

"Nobody's ill or hurt or anything, don't worry about that, but somebody out there, appears to be under the impression..." he paused and stood thinking for a moment, "but it can't be true otherwise they would be doing the same thing here."

"What is it please?" asked Alice with some impatience.

"Sorry. Lorries have been sent around the parish there collecting all the men of military age to transport them to this evening's boat. Apparently your husband's brother was fetched from a field, a bag was hurriedly packed and he left on one of the lorries."

"What?" exclaimed Alice, her voice close to a shriek.

"Your sister-in-law told me she had telephoned a friend in another parish who has a husband the same age as Jim, and they knew nothing about it so she telephoned me to see what the situation was here in St Martin's, whether your husband had also been taken down to the boat."

Alice, in her anxiety, tried to bypass the Headmaster's carefully constructed delivery.

"But how could such a thing have happened?"

"After the meeting in the States, there have been so many rumours. I rather fear the parish officials may have been confused or stirred by what Jurat Dorey said in the States this morning. I was there but I assure you that there was no mention of anyone being obliged to go anywhere. I tried to explain this to your sister-in-law. The immediate point is - can we stop her husband from leaving on the boat?"

Alice mentally wrung her hands. Neither Jack nor Henry were there. She was not supposed to cycle in her condition. She could ask Jeanne to go straightaway by bike down to the harbour and phone her parents to come and take her in the car. She asked the Head if his wife would be happy to look after Jeanne's children. He readily agreed on her behalf. She thanked him and walked quickly to her sister's.

~

Meanwhile Jim, sitting quietly on the uncomfortable bench in the back of the lorry, was unaware of all this activity on his behalf. He began to reflect on his situation. Feeling guilty about having left his potatoes undug the day before, he had decided, in spite of the departure of his two helpers, to dig and pick as much as he could on his own. He had told Jennifer, however, that on no account was she to go back to work in the tomatoes. The day already felt long and he felt minded to open his flask of tea when he spotted his wife running down the field, unstoppable in spite of the entanglement of her feet in tufts and stalks. She had come straight from the shop where Mrs Mourant, in tears, had told her she had been asked to inform as many people as possible that all men of military age had to leave on the next boat and that parish lorries were being organised to take them down to the harbour.

Jim had walked home with his wife and eaten several biscuits without being conscious of it. Jennifer just managed to pack a few basics for him before one of the lorries, with several men sitting on benches in the back, arrived. No time to talk or think. He had kissed his wife, who burst into tears, then climbed up to join the others and was driven away. After a silent half mile or so, he had questioned the others on what exactly was happening. He was told that Judge Dorey in the States had said that all men of old Norman stock and military age had to leave. "From the whole island?" asked Jim.

"Must be."

Jim did not think for a moment that such an operation would be mounted if it had not been decreed by the States so he assumed that Jack, Bert, his brother-in-law from Trinity, and other school and Militia friends would also be on their way to the boat.

The lorry stopped on the pier where a couple of recently arrived cargo boats were docked. The driver lowered the backboard and the twelve men, as if in a dream, clambered down with a little jump and stood in a bunch near the Railways Office. The tallest, who happened to have the piece of paper given to him at the Parish Hall, showed it to a man in uniform who was happy to stamp it. Jim asked the harbour policeman if the groups from the other parishes had already gone on board. Looking puzzled by the question the policeman answered:

"I've not seen any groups, only individuals or families. There are still people here as you can see but it's not as bad as this morning. I've never seen anything like it. There must have been ten thousand embarked."

Not knowing quite what to do, the men from St Brelade's went on board the nearest boat but Jim decided to wait for his brother at the bottom of the gangway. One or two people he knew passed him with a nod as they walked up carrying bags, several holding the hands of young children who were crying in bewilderment. The sea seemed to have a more intense tang of salt and seaweed, the fat gulls screeched as they dive-bombed a cardboard box thrown from a porthole, ropes creaked and the water lapped onto the steps. Only now, did Jim fully realise what he was doing. He was being forced to leave his wife, his home, his island with no time to think or protest. He felt a sickness deep in his stomach and an overwhelming sense of loneliness. The clanking of chains, the throbbing of engines and the shouts of busy-looking men suggested that the boats would be leaving quite soon. Still there was no sign of Jim's relatives or contingents from other parishes. He was too upset to feel puzzled. He just sat on a capstan and gazed into the water, seeing his face broken up by the rippling little waves.

~

Back at La Moye, after phoning Mr Stevens and hoping the message would get through to Jack, Jennifer had clambered on her bike and began to pedal furiously towards town. Her mind vacillated between fears that she would never see her husband again and vicious thoughts about those responsible for taking him away. How could they have made such a serious mistake? The breeze in her face kept the tears back as she pedalled along the seemingly interminable Route Orange to the Red Houses. On this occasion, she took little notice of the majestic beauty of this tree-lined avenue. Her whole being was wrapped in the thought that she must prevent her husband from leaving the island. If she was unable to do so, she would get on the next boat, just as she was, and follow him. At last came the long twisting descent to St. Aubin's. From the little picturesque old harbour where she and Jim had spent much of their courting days, there was still the long sweep of the bay to cycle round to the main harbour in town – a good three miles.

~

At St Martin's Jeanne had left straightaway on her bike having entrusted the children to a delighted Mrs Stevens. About twenty minutes later Alice's mother had arrived to collect her and Mr Stevens from the bus stop near the church. All their pulses were pounding in a race against time.

~

Feeling miserable and numb as he waited, Jim stood up and was about to go on board when he heard his name called. He turned, but failing to recognise Jeanne under her headscarf, he wondered where the cry had come from. To his surprise she came up to him and said breathlessly:

"You don't have to go!"

"What!"

"It's all been a mistake," she added, "none of the others are going."

Jim sought confirmation from the policeman who replied: "I wondered what you meant when you asked me about other parish groups. I've not heard anything about it."

Jim had barely taken in the policeman's answer when Alice, too, came running up and hugged him with delight. She had run all the way from the Weighbridge where Maman could get no further with the car. She was pale and out of breath and Jim made her sit on a chair he fetched from a little office tucked away in the bulwarks. Mr Stevens, himself breathless with trying to keep up with Alice, rested for a moment against the harbour wall and gave a thanksgiving prayer. Jim then shouted to some of the lads leaning over the handrail of the boat and the message was passed on to the group from St Brelade's that they didn't have to go. Immediately most of them disembarked, threatening to do unspeakable things to those responsible when they got back home.

When Jennifer cycled up soon after and showered him with grateful tears, Jim was too happy and relieved to waste any more anger on a silly official who couldn't listen properly to what was being said in the States' Chamber.

~

While all this was happening, Jack and Henry met at the Parish Hall, having returned within a few minutes of each other. Their experiences had been similar. Both were astonished and eager to tell the stories of the strange behaviour of individuals in crisis. Henry had seen dozens of letters stuffed down a toilet and half-flushed away, a bath overflowing down the stairs and a copy of a will left on a table, asking whoever found it to act as executor in the event of the person's reported death in England. Jack and the Constable had spent half an hour in one house trying to calm a man whose wife had left a note saying she was gone. Elsewhere, they had seen an open safe with pound notes still in it, a mattress ripped open with feathers everywhere and a bungalow with all the light bulbs removed.

On returning home Jack was surprised not to find Alice and even more surprised when Henry arrived to say that Jeanne was not there either and that she had left a note saying that the children were being looked after by Mrs Stevens at the school.

"I've just been up there to fetch them but they were playing with some toys and were quite happy to stay there. I couldn't understand what Mrs Stevens was on about," said Henry. "She says they've all gone to the harbour to stop your brother leaving because he's been taken down to the boat or something."

"She must have got that wrong," said Jack, "you know how flustered she gets."

"Well, that's what she said."

"Well it doesn't make much sense."

Not long after when Maman's car drew up, one wheel parked on the pavement, Alice came in bubbling with the story.

"It was nice of Mrs Stevens to look after the kids, I didn't know what to do so I phoned Maman, I thought the more of us went the better."

"But I won," said Jeanne, her face smiling and shining with pleasure. "You didn't know I was a champion cyclist, did you, Henry? Oh and Jim is coming back on my bike with Jennifer."

She took her husband by the arm and Jack was delighted to see the happy contrast with the dispirited woman he had seen earlier that morning.

A bitty and confused conversation continued for a little while before Jack and Henry eventually understood what had happened and how near Jim had been to being whisked off on the boat.

Half an hour later, a clatter of handlebars on the outer wall announced the arrival of Jim and Jennifer, who had been invited by Alice to stay with them overnight. The ride back had given them time to restore calm and savour their good fortune. Drinks were poured to toast Jim being plucked from the pier in the nick of time by three lady admirers.

"I've never been pursued by so many girls at once!" said Jim, enjoying the attention. "Do you know of any houses or better still, farms, to let around here?" he asked. "Once I've told my landlord what I think of him I doubt if he'll be too keen on my staying in the parish cottage any more."

Amazingly Henry offered a positive reply. "When the evacuation is over, there will be a pick of houses. What a business, you!"

The Evening Post thudded, as usual, against the door and they gathered excitedly to see the pictures of the pier and town. Two tragedies were also given prominence. First, the death of the man at the airport. Bystanders had called out but nobody had been near enough to stop him walking into a propeller. The other was the attempted suicide by a man in the north of the island who was so worried about the state of things that he had drunk some Jeyes fluid. The paper said that he was 'comfortable.'

These events and the pictures of the chaos on the pier were upsetting but relieved briefly when Jack spotted a little paragraph which said that while all the panic was on, people were still playing golf and tennis as if nothing had happened.

"I phoned to tell them that!" he said excitedly. Henry had to confirm it was so.

It was not long before the conversation returned to Jim's extraordinary experience. After he had gone off on the lorry, Jennifer had not known what to do and had convinced herself that she, too, would be leaving at a moment's notice to follow him, so she had burnt all her letters, including a few from her husband.

"What did you do that for?" asked Jim.

"I don't know," she replied and began to cry tears of relief.

Henry mentioned the letters he had seen stuffed down a toilet. Jack observed that lots of people seemed to be doing inexplicable things.

Excitement stirs the appetite and their thoughts turned to tea. As if by providence, Paul Vigot, the fisherman from Rozel, the little harbour nestling down the road on the north coast, appeared at the door with a basket of mackerel.

"Eh ben, Paul, you couldn't have come at a better time," said Jack.

"That's good. You talk about I've had a catch today, you. They're just giving themselves up. I've never known anything like it."

"Let's hope you'll be able to carry on fishing, then."

"Why shouldn't I," asked the puzzled fisherman.

"The Germans."

"Why should they bother about that?" asked Vigot.

"I don't know but they won't want people leaving an occupied place by boat, will they?"

"But where can I go in my boat? If I wanted to go anywhere, I'd go now," he said with the simple logic of the ordinary man.

"That's true but they might not think like you. You're not worried, out at sea, that they might take pot shots at you from the French coast?"

"Ah bah, tchi niolîn," said the fisherman, shaking his head.

They ate heartily. There is nothing to beat mackerel just out of the sea and fried in butter. Then Alice was packed off to bed, tired after the exertions of the day. In the spare room Jim and Jennifer celebrated their reunion in the fullest sense of the word.

It was too late for Jack to start on his journal, other than to list a few aide-memoires. He forced himself to get up next morning while everyone else, mentally and physically exhausted from the previous day, had a bit of a lie-in.

*Journal extract*
*The real panic*

*I'm writing this early on Friday morning. I can hear birds singing. Yesterday was the most incredible day of intense drama which touched thousands of people. Evacuation has marked a turning point from which there is no way back.*

*Things started early with Mrs Le Gros knocking at our door because she discovered Fred had left to catch one of the boats to England. He'd said goodbye to no one it seems. Henry and I took his mother down to the harbour. I suppose we half thought it would be just a case of finding him on the boat and leaving her to persuade him, or not, to come back home. What we didn't expect was the number of boats and the number of people heaving on to them. Apart from one or two football matches I went to at White Hart Lane when I was at college, I've never seen so many people in one place. All the talk of women and children first just didn't happen. Maybe it was obvious that families would want to stay together. No sign of young Fred anywhere. It was a hopeless task from the start. I feel for Mrs Le Gros. Her son's departure is a kind of bereavement and I feel some responsibility. But he had to make his own decision.*

*... Henry amazingly was very good. In a curious way I think the panic decided him to stay.*

*... We watched a boat called the SS Malines load up with equipment and soldiers. They did not hang around. At first the watching crowd was very subdued as if they couldn't believe what was happening but once the boat was under way through the harbour mouth, they did start to cheer. All British military personnel have now gone. Let's hope the Germans have been informed so that they don't attack the island thinking soldiers are here to defend it.*

*...I shall never forget the scenes at the harbour or in town, abandoned cars, shops boarded up, people losing control or reason, but that doesn't excuse Jurat Dorey talking about rats and rabbits. No wonder people in*

*the Royal Square were angry when his words were reported to them. Yet thousands are leaving. In the square I found myself next to the plaque to Wace. His poetry was a kind of journal too but I doubt if mine will last 800 years!*

*...The Jurat did have a point about the island being left depleted. He specifically mentioned telephone operators. I can vouch for that. I was ages trying to get through to the Royal. Is the law of averages strong enough to prevent, say, every plumber from leaving the island? The evacuation over, there could be all kinds of imbalances left in its wake, of men to women, of teachers to pupils, of managers to workers, of rich to poor, of the more adventurous to the more passive, of potential resister to potential collaborator, of law abiding citizen to looter or black marketeer.*

*..I wonder how many changed their minds today about going or staying; quite a lot I think and Jim said there were only a few boarding the last boat while he was there later in the afternoon. The departure of the soldiers seemed to suck people after them, but, later, the speeches, especially by the Bailiff, would have influenced some to stay. I noted down the sort of things people were saying..it mightn't be so bad..he's a good bloke, Coutanche..as long as he stays..sort things out with the Jerries..I was going to go, me but eh...will it really be safer over there?..might as well stay.*

*..They say a picture is worth a thousand words or something like that. I understand what that means. An artist or photographer would capture so much more meaningfully, the looks on the pained faces of people down at the harbour or in the Royal Square. So many people feeling obliged to do what deep in their hearts they did not want to do. Nevertheless many around here in St Martin's have not even considered leaving.*

*..I thought we would be returning to a bit of calm and quiet at home but it was not to be. The Constable appeared and asked us to help with sorting out the abandoned properties. What a job that's going to be! We saw some extraordinary things, meals left uneaten, animals turned loose in some places, others tied up in stables, some houses locked up, others left with everything open. Chaos and misery everywhere.*

*..Going off around the parish with our Constable at St Martin meant that I missed what, for us as a family, was the drama of the day. Thanks to a 'foutaise' in St Brelade's, Jim, my brother might already be in England by now....*

Jack proceeded to give a detailed account of the 'incident' as Jim, Jennifer and Alice had described it during the course of the evening.

*... It is such a strange thing to have happened. More than strange. How easy it is to be swept along by events, to do what you are told by those in authority. In Jim's position, I would probably have done the same. Thank goodness he didn't go on board. He could so easily have waited inside somewhere, the boat might have left at any time and that would have been that. I wonder if, having arrived in England and discovered the truth there, he would have been able to come back? I doubt it somehow.*

*And the amazing thing is that Jim said two of the twelve from his lorry did not choose to get off the boat once he had shouted to them that it was all a mistake. They had had no time to prepare for departure yet they chose to go anyway. What made them stay on board when the decision that they should leave the island had not been theirs? Weariness? A sense of resignation? Relief that a decision had been made for them? To start a new life in England because of a twist of fate and one that they were free to undo - it's yet another example of the bizarre way people are behaving. We are all still pretty stunned by the whole affair.*

*Whatever is today going to bring?*

# NINE

*Friday 21 June, 1940*

Consumed in their particular drama of the previous day Jennifer, Alice and Jim had missed much of the frantic activity around the town. So, at breakfast, the lure of visiting a St Helier in disarray gripped the conversation. Many would be attracted to the town for a complexity of reasons; a powerful wish to be at the heart of things, curiosity driven to excess, the singularity of the events and perhaps, deep down, the irrational fear that whilst one sat blissfully munching toast, the whole of the rest of the island might be filing onto boats.

Baptiste walked in as they prepared to leave for town.

"I haven't got any letters. They've stopped sending out bills. Nobody's going to pay them in any case."

"So you've come to see me, instead, have you Baptiste?" smiled Alice.

"But you should have told me all these other people were here," he winked.

"By the way, did you know I was expecting?"

"Well, ah by goodness me, bougre, well, merde, you deserve a big kiss for that," chuckled Baptiste, which he proceeded to deliver.

"But I nearly forgot why I came, you," he continued. "The Constable wants another meeting tonight about all these empty houses and what to do. It's going to turn 'salope' all this."

"What d'you mean?" asked Jack.

"You know Denis Le Breuilly. They were already on the boat when they changed their minds about going. Well when they got back home last night, all the food was gone from their bloody larder, you."

"No!" the others replied, almost in unison.

"Too true," said Baptiste, pleased with the effect.

"Do they know who did it?"

"Not yet," said the postman, "but I'd string up buggers like that, me."

"I hope nobody thinks we've gone," said Jim. "Did you lock the door?" he asked his wife.

"I don't know what I did," replied Jennifer, "the state I was in. Anyway, I'd rather have you than a few tins of ham," she added, clutching his arm.

"If people are stealing already, what's it going to be like when the going gets really tough?" Jack reflected sadly.

"That's just it," said Baptiste, "I'd boil the buggers in oil."

"So far we've got the panicker, the abandonner of animals and the petty thief," mused Jack.

"Petty thief, mon tchu, if you'll excuse me, ladies, it's bloody looting," said Baptiste with feeling, "People get shot for that in wartime."

After the departure of the postman, Jack offered to ride Jennifer's bike to town. The two brothers cycled off leaving their wives to catch the bus. Past Five Oaks, they let themselves freewheel along by the Cottage Homes, wondering what would happen to all the elderly people housed in the pretty individual cottages with their own little gardens. Along past St Saviour's Church where Lillie Langtry was buried, round a couple of bends and the entrance to Government House came into view. Several cars were sweeping in and two others were parked near the guardhouse. Jack's curiosity was aroused and he stopped to ask one of the chauffeurs what was happening.

"The Governor's off today."

"What?" said Jack. "When?"

"About twelve, I think."

"Why?"

"Well, stands to reason, he's the head of the armed forces here, so he can't stay if the army's gone and the island's demilitarised."

Jack had spoken to Major General Harrison at a teacher's function not long before. He was a popular man, often seen taking his dogs for walks. As the direct representative of the King, he couldn't stay and be taken prisoner. This meant that the political ties with the mainland were about to be cut.

The bus overtook them near the Maternity Hospital, a reminder to Jack that in a few months, quite probably under the Nazi flag, his own child would be born. He still couldn't quite believe it.

In the Peirson where they met up, Jack told the pub clients about the Governor leaving. Alice and Jennifer wanted to see him go, and long before twelve, they were mingling with the crowds on the Albert Pier, fewer and slightly more orderly than the previous day.

"Ten boats have gone this morning, some pretty small mind you, completely packed out," one of the crane drivers told Jack, "and there's these four and another one tonight."

"Where are all the boats from?" asked Jack.

"Cargo boats, most of them. Some are pretty filthy I can tell you. It can't be much of a crossing. Those who got on the 'Isle of Sark' were lucky."

"How's the Governor going?" asked Jack.

"Oh, he's all right, don't worry. There's a Naval Auxiliary Vessel come specially."

"Where is it? I can't see it."

"It's anchored out in the bay. A launch will be sent to the harbour to pick him up."

They climbed the steps to the top promenade of the sea wall. They could see the vessel at anchor near Elizabeth Castle, where, in 1603, Sir Walter Raleigh had been one of the Governor's illustrious predecessors. The craft looked trim and fast.

"Surely, it could easily come into the harbour," remarked Jim.

A man next to him, in a slightly pompous voice, said:

"Small naval vessels never go into harbours if they can avoid it. They become too vulnerable a target."

"Oh, I'm terribly sorry, I wasn't aware," said Jim, in an accent learnt from the BBC.

Precisely at noon, a convoy nosed its way through the peering crowd. The Bailiff and several States' members had come, in their official capacity, to bid farewell to the King's representative, perhaps also to show themselves to the population as proof they hadn't left surreptitiously by plane. The Lieutenant Governor, to give him his proper title, and Lady Harrison, got out of the car with the Union Jack on the front. They stood to attention whilst a band which seemed to have appeared from nowhere, played the National Anthem. The Lieutenant Governor saluted, shook hands with the island dignitaries, waved to the crowd and walked briskly down the steps into the launch. There were cries of 'Good luck sir' and the vessel sped towards the harbour mouth.

At the Airport the last civilian plane scheduled to leave the island waited until news was confirmed of the Governor's departure by boat in case enemy intervention necessitated a change of plan.

"This is history," said Jack. "It's difficult to realise it. Let's hope he or his successor gets back soon."

Back in Conway Street they stared in amazement at the long, weary queues stretching out of every bank; rows of tired, bored, scared people slowly disappearing inside revolving doors. One of the many policemen keeping order said that the rush on the banks was so bad there was now a maximum withdrawal limit of £25 and even that might soon get cut down.

"We'll have to start making our own money at this rate," said the policeman.

"The Germans will probably make us use theirs," suggested Jack.

"How's that going to work?" asked Jim.

"I imagine you just go to a bank with your pounds and change them into whatever the Germans use, just like we get francs when we go to France."

The inquisitive steps of the ladies had carried them to the Town Church where the bells announced a wedding.

"What a time to get married!" said Jim. "If they go away on honeymoon, they probably won't be able to come back. They won't be going to Paris, that's for sure."

Jennifer and Alice were thrilled that such a happy event could still be taking place. The men made predictable comments along the lines of 'as if the Germans coming wasn't bad enough.' They left their wives chatting with the guests and made their way across the now nearly empty square to the Peirson. As they approached, they heard the wireless through the open window announcing that the Germans had captured Brest.

As if to reinforce this message, the noise of engines suddenly rent the air.

"Look," said Jim, pointing towards the harbour, "that must be a German plane."

"It's not going to bomb the Governor's boat is it?"

" I don't think so, it looks a bit small, I think it's a reconnaissance plane."

They hurried back to the church to collect their wives, knowing that the plane would have shaken Alice, in particular. Near the church porch everyone was looking up, many with hands to their mouths. Alice was pale and relieved to clutch Jack as he arrived.

"Look, it's coming over again," somebody shouted.

It was nearer this time and people ducked and screamed. The bride dropped her bouquet and began to sob. There followed a long nervous silence as nobody seemed sure quite what to do next. It took a little while for a calm to settle.

"This is something they'll always remember when they look at the wedding photos," said Jim. "I wonder if anyone got a snap of the plane. They'll need a few bottles of champagne at the reception to get over it."

"I think we need a drink, too," suggested Jack. "Let's go down to the Yacht, there may be more happening on the pier."

The brothers were just in time to see and hear another large crowd cheering near one of the potato boats, the SS Hoder. Every member of the Royal Jersey Militia, 11 officers and 193 other ranks, led by Lieutenant Colonel Vacher, had volunteered to join the Royal Hampshire Regiment. Proudly, yet sadly, they marched to the boat. The onlookers, many of them the families of the young men, watched with a mixture of pride and tears. Jack felt a lump in his throat.

When the boat left the crowd repeated the farewell given to the British soldiers the previous day by running to the end of the pier and waving and cheering until the stern disappeared around the back of Elizabeth Castle.

When Jack bought the round at the Yacht, the publican said gruffly:

"With Cherbourg and Brest gone, it's only a matter of time before the Jerries get here,"

"You're probably right. Anyway let's hope the Governor makes it to England OK" said Jack.

"He's gone, has he?" remarked the publican. "Like I always say, he's only a man like the rest of us."

"Agreed, but he is a symbol."

"I don't believe in symbols, me. When you see all those bloody twerps in the States we're supposed to listen to..."

Jack made a small attempt to point out that this was hardly the same.

"The Governor is like the King. Just imagine the blow to England's morale if the King got killed."

"You reckon, you? Well as far as I'm concerned the King is just another bloke like you and me. If he walked in here now, I'd offer him a pint but I wouldn't go scraping about on my hands and knees."

Jack saw little point in pursuing the argument. Whether one was a confirmed monarchist or not, it was obvious to him that if the King was killed by military action, it would have a far greater impact on the hearts and minds of the British people than if a man in the street was killed. The same applied to Churchill. What a difference since he took over!

They made their way to a table by the window, next to a sad looking man muttering drunkenly to himself. When Alice and Jennifer sat down he perked up a little, realizing he might have a sympathetic audience.

"Just seen the missus and nipper on to the boat, gone."

They looked at him in surprise.

"Gone," he repeated.

"Why haven't you gone, too?" asked Jim.

"Not me, no, not me, got my farm and my old folks."

They didn't know quite what to say.

"Hope they're all right. Gone on the boat."

"I'm sure they'll be all right," said Jennifer, sympathetically.

The man got up suddenly, spilt the remainder of his beer and lurched towards the door.

"Must go home."

"Is that true what he was saying?" Jack asked the publican.

"Oh yes, quite a lot of blokes have done that. Most of them get sloshed after they've been to the boat. There were two in here yesterday. I had a job to get them out at two o'clock. Their wives and kids were off on the boat and the two men, sitting just where you are, were crying in each other's glasses."

"I'll tell you something better than that," said a middle-aged man with a goatee beard, perched on a bar stool, drinking whisky. "A neighbour of mine, quite a nice chap, plays a lot of tennis, left with his wife and kids yesterday morning, went to England and came back on his own today."

"What happens when you arrive over there?" asked Jennifer

"He told me," said the goatee, "that they all walked from the boat to a theatre and were given sandwiches and tea before getting on special buses to the station where trains were waiting to take them north."

"So, how will these husbands know where their wives are?"

"They must have the addresses over there."

"But, how awful," said Jennifer. "They won't be able to write once the Germans are here."

After a bit of time in the shops that were still open, they parted towards their separate homes agreeing to meet for tea the following Sunday unless anything happened in the meantime. Before going to the meeting at the Parish Hall, Jack read the Evening Post.

"It says here that things have been a bit different in Guernsey," he told Alice. Listen to this:

"'No queues, no panic, arrangements working smoothly. Nearly all children of school age have left, another 6000 people expected to leave.' The poor bloody teachers must have had to go with them. What a performance! Let's hope they don't decide to do that here. A class outing to Grève de Lecq is bad enough."

He continued reading. "'Everything was orderly – places of

entertainment have been closed since Tuesday.' That's typical of Guernsey, I bet the pubs shut earlier than us too. 'Evacuation started when the notice was issued by the Bailiff. All children of school age registered at schools. Mothers wishing to accompany them went to the rectory and other people to the Constable's Office. Four ships left Wednesday and another four on Thursday. It says in big black type: 'GUERNSEY IS TAKING THE SITUATION CALMLY'! And all that went off in an orderly fashion!" said Jack. "Don't make me laugh."

"Since it's written there!" said Alice, "Trust you to think that nobody's capable of doing anything."

"Just a minute, I don't think everybody is incapable, but I saw what happened here yesterday with so many people getting on to boats, I can't imagine that Guernsey was any different."

"Well good for them," said Alice. "Fancy evacuating all the kids, though! Suppose the war goes on for years and they grow up and don't want to come back. What sort of place will Guernsey be with a whole generation missing and nobody to breed the one after that?"

As Jack expected, the meeting at the Parish Hall was long and futile. The Constable knew no more than he did the day before and kept repeating: "After the special session of the States tomorrow we'll know what to do." The theft of food from houses had shaken him and he spoke about setting up night patrols of volunteers, an idea that didn't go down particularly well. The only useful outcome of the gathering was that it enabled Jack to speak to Alan Le Grand.

"How are you Alan?"

"All right, but what a waste of time, that was, merde."

"You're right. I'm sorry about your father, I haven't seen you since the funeral."

"Thank you, but, you know, since my mother died, he's been 'foutu'."

They started walking towards Alan's lorry.

"It's a bit obvious to say that you're still here," said Jack.

"What, not evacuated you mean?"

"Yes."

"We were thinking of going you know, then the old man died."

"You could still go, couldn't you?" suggested Jack.

"I suppose I could but it wouldn't seem right to bury him then go off and leave him behind."

"But he wouldn't know."

"He wouldn't have known either if I'd buried him in the garden instead of giving him a proper funeral."

"That's true but all those who have gone must have left someone behind in a graveyard."

"Perhaps, but they haven't just put them there. The flowers haven't even faded. Anyway, that's how I feel."

"Fair enough. Percy's gone I gather," said Jack.

"Yes, he went off with Fred Le Gros," Alan replied. "They didn't tell anyone, the little sods. Percy's mother was wild, you. She said I encouraged him to go."

"Which you did, if I remember, in the pub the evening your father died, it seems so long ago."

"Too bloody true! What kind of life are blokes of seventeen going to have here? It will be dangerous, for a start, bound to be."

"That's what I tried to tell Fred's mother," said Jack, musing on his own intervention.

"They could easily do something they think is a big joke and end up getting shot against a wall. They're nasty bloody sods, the Nazis when they get going."

"I hope things don't get that bad, Alan, but it could be dangerous, right enough."

They walked on a few more yards in silence then Jack asked Alan why he had considered leaving.

"I just couldn't stand the idea of being cooped up here with those silly arses stamping around. I'm still worried I might do something daft myself, let alone the youngsters."

Jack paused a moment as if wondering whether to mention it or not, then said:

"What would you think about forming a group of people?"

"What, to retreat to the woods at Le Scez and fight to the death with bows and arrows?"

"Not quite," Jack laughed nervously. "Look, why don't you come in for a minute?"

"Just for a minute, though. Bonsoir, comment allez-vous madame?" he said bowing towards Alice.

After the sitting and pouring skirmishes, Alan said: "Now, what's all this about a group?"

"I've been thinking," began Jack," it's going to be difficult just, you know, living with the Germans. There's already panic and stealing. All sorts of things might happen when they actually get here."

"That's for certain!"

"So I wondered if a group might get together which could help unify attitudes, stop people being stupid, help people in trouble. I haven't thought it all out yet."

Alan finished his drink and looked pensive: "It sounds a bit vague all that."

"I know. It's just that I want to do something, not just sit and watch with good intentions."

"Look, I'll think it over," said Alan. "There might be something in it, but I must go, I'll see you tomorrow."

"Where?"

"At the Parish Hall, of course. You can bet your boots that once the Constable has been to his famous meeting of the States, he'll be calling us to meetings every five minutes. Night patrols! That was a bloody good one, guarding the property of people who have pushed off. He's lost his pedals, as the French say."

After he left Alice asked: "What's all this about forming a group? You haven't said anything about it to me."

"I've only just started thinking about it," said Jack defensively.

"You're not planning to do anything stupid are you, attacking Germans or anything like that?"

"No, of course not! Don't be ridiculous, that would be just suicide. Alan's right, my ideas are a bit vague but I think we must try and help people behave decently towards each other. As I told Alan, we've already got hoarders and looters. Things could easily get a lot worse when people like Belheche start causing trouble."

"I more or less see what you're getting at but we've got to wait and see surely. Promise me that you won't do anything hot-headed."

"Now, you're being daft, but, yes I promise."

Sitting before his notebook, Jack spent a long time going over things in his mind. He jotted notes on a piece of paper before writing in his diary proper, almost as if he was doing an exam. He wanted to bring coherence to the many themes which were beginning to intertwine.

*Journal extract*
*After evacuation*

*In the face of subtle and more direct pressures, many people have acted contrary to their original intent. Some changes of mind have happened because of the rapidly changing events, a collective bandwagon. Others have realised that their first option was not, after all, the best. Many have been influenced by stronger-minded relatives or friends, or have simply acted suddenly and sometimes, mindlessly.*

*..Two more 'happenings' today in addition to the continuing evacuation - the departure of the Governor and the German plane over the harbour, both very significant.*

*..Why do I keep returning to the idea of wanting to do something? Is it because I haven't 'done' the big one, the evacuation?*

*Those I've talked to have more or less told me the same thing – that they cannot see how anything can be done in the abstract, in advance. They say my ideas are a bit vague, and, of course they are. I must avoid romanticising.*

*..Nevertheless I feel helpless and frustrated. Whenever I talk about it, I never seem to get anywhere. How can you make people behave better towards each other in war than they do in peace? This is the mess some philosophers call the 'human condition' I suppose. So far I have only thought about people behaving in selfish, uncharitable and nasty ways towards each other but there could be more serious and worrying developments.*

*In normal times we have laws, a justice system to enforce them and a police system to prevent them being broken and to pursue those who break them. It has taken several hundred years to reach that point and we know where we are. Law, justice and policing form the bedrock of civilized society and of protecting people. However, when an enemy occupier seizes power and takes over the established order, everything changes. Most people, in all likelihood, will condone acts of lawbreaking and hostility towards the Germans but will such support remain if reprisals are out of all proportion to the crimes? Does some degree of moral responsibility for subsequent suffering also rest with those who commit acts, knowing that reprisal is inevitable?*

*In the meantime, I wonder if it wouldn't be best for the Germans to arrive soon so that we can all return to some kind of normalcy, although goodness knows what normal will mean when they are here.*

# TEN

*Saturday 22 June, 1940*

Today the special session of the States beckoned Jack, the observer and diarist. The spluttering bus to town was as crowded as on the previous Saturday, in spite of the intervening evacuation. Conversation babbled ..who had gone ..when they had gone ..who had given what to whom ..the Constable coming to the empty houses ..the stealing of food ..the Bailiff's speech … the Evening Post and, occasionally, direct mention of the Germans.

Jack was early enough to squeeze into a prized seat inside the States'

Chamber. Most of the other bus passengers had come to shop, to stock up with necessities. 'Should we be doing the same?' he now asked himself. 'Food, soap, medical supplies?'

In the States the members were called to order and discussed, first, the question of the abandoned houses. Jack took notes all the more when he saw that none of the Constables were taking any.

After the minimum of debate, a prepared proposal was accepted, authorising the Constables to enter all non-occupied and abandoned premises and to remove all provisions found there. If perishable, they were to be disposed of at the Constable's discretion.

That's going to worry him, thought Jack. We'll be up half the night discussing that one.

If not perishable, they were to be placed in the hands of the Food Controller. If spirituous liquor, to be given to the Principal Agent of Impot.

A Constable of one of the country parishes in the north of the island, St Mary or St John, raised the point that some people had been to see him before leaving for the mainland and had asked him to auction their goods and keep the money on their behalf. Opinions were strongly expressed against such an idea. There was quite enough already for everyone to do. Those who had left had abandoned everything and that was that.

'They want to have their cake and eat it,' a Jurat remarked predictably.

'No, they want to auction it,' another said in a loud aside to a few desultory ho ho's.

There followed a question seeking to establish the precise status of the island. One of the Crown Officers declared that Jersey was not a neutral state, even though the Lieutenant Governor had left, and therefore the Union Jack should continue to be flown.

From around the Chamber many emotional words were spoken, pointing out the vulnerability of the island and the increased need for Air Raid Precautions. Then after a brisk, heated exchange about the liberty of the individual to walk the roads at night in a free community, a curfew was imposed, beginning that evening, from 10pm until 5am. Jack could not understand what such a curfew was meant to achieve.

The next item was the contentious one of the pubs closing early. Many Constables spoke of the unpopularity and the anger caused by the very early closing imposed in the previous two days. It had been called a Hitlerian ruling, enough to make loyal subjects question the wisdom of staying. It was agreed that two o'clock had been an exceptional measure. Drinking was a big problem on the island and, in these critical times, people might turn even more readily to alcohol and act in ways detrimental to themselves, their families and Jersey as a whole. The new pub closure time was fixed at 7.30 p.m.

It was then decided to form an 'Island Defence Cabinet' because once the Germans were there, it would not be possible for the whole States' Assembly to keep meeting regularly.

'If they're allowed to meet at all," thought Jack, grimly.

The last brief item, the need for petrol economy, was strongly endorsed.

"Now, they'll all get into their cars and drive home," thought Jack.

Outside, the first rain for some days was falling steadily. Damp shoppers were sheltering in shop doorways and under the large portico entrance of the Public Library. Here and there an umbrella on legs walked briskly by. This change in the weather was fitting; wet, grey and dreary like the melancholy lull in the island's wait and matching the uniforms of the impending invaders.

Jack just caught the two o'clock bus and had to stand squashed against wet coats and soaked hair, his feet wedged in by heavy baskets. His discomfort lasted as far as Five Oaks when seats emptied as many people left the bus and dashed off in every direction trying to get indoors before they were drenched.

It was still pouring when they reached St Martin and Jack ran full tilt into the Royal, the nearest dry place. For once he was the first with news. Even Baptiste had not heard that the pubs would now be closing at seven thirty.

"M m merde," commented Adolphe. "W what am m I m I going to do, me?"

"You want to get yourself a girlfriend," suggested Baptiste.

The others found it difficult not to smile. There he sat, a gravedigger, hunched over yet another brown boiler, his shirt unchanged for at least a week, ground clogged to his boots and trousers, unshaven, a threadbare beret wedged on his head and one yellow tooth. His appeal to the opposite sex could best be described as limited.

Naturally Jacko the publican, was very angry that his Saturday night trade was going to end abruptly at the time it usually began.

"I don't see the point," he kept saying. "What's it for? What bloody difference will it make if people are in the pub when the Germans arrive?"

Mary came in from the kitchen and turned on the news just as the brothers Bigou arrived reeking of rum. The French Cabinet was in Bordeaux studying the peace terms laid down by the Germans.

"What else can they do?" said Baptiste rhetorically. "They're 'foutu.'"

As usual the elder Bigou knew everything and had to make himself heard.

"That's what they've put Pétain in charge for," he said.

"Who's Pétain?" asked Mary.

Jack had almost forgotten, in the local events of the last few days, that the Great War Marshall had been recalled to replace Reynaud at the head of the French Government. Bigou 'la bouche,' as Baptiste called him, began telling Mary who Pétain was. The man he actually described was Foch but Jack felt it was a dangerous name to start pronouncing in the present company so, for Mary's benefit he restricted his explanation:

"Pétain was the saviour of France at Verdun."

"He must be old, then," she said.

"About eighty, I think," said Jack.

"That's stupid," she said. "Haven't they got anybody younger?"

"Well," speculated Jack, "as a national hero, it won't seem so bad if he's the one who suggests that they should accept a humiliating armistice."

"Churchill's nearly bloody seventy," said big-mouth Bigou, "no wonder we're up the spout."

"He's doing very well so far," said Mary

"Just wait till the Germans attack England," said Bigou with more than a hint of sarcasm in his voice. That was enough for Jacko. "Look," he said, leaning with menace across the bar, "I've just about had my fill of your bullshit."

"Right," said Bigou, "we'll go then, there are other places to drink."

"I know, and you've obviously found a few already."

The brothers were impressed enough by Jacko's size, to content themselves with muttering as they went out.

"I'll be glad to see the back of them," added Jacko, "those sort of buggers get everybody down. It wouldn't surprise me if they end up like that with the Germans," he said linking his two little fingers together.

"They make my skin creep," said Mary, "especially the little one. He hardly says anything, just looks at you with bloodshot eyes and grins every time his brother speaks."

A further news item reported that the 1910 class in England had to report and register.

"Hell, they're calling up my brother's age group already," said Jack.

"In what year were you born, you?" asked Jacko.

"1907."

"Me," said Baptiste proudly," I was born the last year of the last century, the same year as the siege of Mafeking. Good job my parents had more sense than old Mrs Courage. They called their son Mafeking. Well, you know him."

"I wondered where he'd got that funny name," smiled Mary.

"I rem mem member Queen Victoria when she w was a little girl," said

Adolphe.

"Encore du niolîn," said Baptiste as they all laughed.

Jack recounted more details of the States' sitting and left them in loud confused argument about abandoned houses, auctions and curfews.

"See you at the meeting tonight," he added to Baptiste as he left.

Alice had been in the garden until driven indoors by the rain.

"It will do everything good," said Jack. "Henry'll be pleased, if anything can please him at the moment, but he'll have to go some to keep up with the side shoots on the toms."

"He was in the field until it started to rain," said Alice.

"That's good, I'll call in tonight on my way to the meeting."

"You haven't got to go out again, have you?" Alice pouted.

"Yes I must, love, but we'll have to be back by ten, that's when the curfew is going to start."

"The curfew, what do you mean?"

"It's from the French 'couvre feu.'"

"Yes, all right clever clogs, but what does it mean?"

"It means you can't go outside after a certain time."

"What happens if you do?"

"You get shot."

"Who by?"

"The Centenier"

"Don't be silly."

"I don't know," laughed Jack, "but you might get shot once the Germans are here if they impose one."

"The Centenier has got more than his work cut out at the shop, without worrying about a curfew" said Alice. "There's been more trouble and Mrs Pring had to call him."

"What happened?"

"Old mother Le Brun started it. She wanted to buy all the packets of tea that were left and Mrs Pring refused. Mrs Le Brun then started calling her all sorts of names and insisted on having the tea. Another lady pulled Mrs Le B by the hair and a bottle of vinegar got broken. What a mess and smell everywhere!"

"And poor old Claude had to come and keep them apart! Mrs Le Brun could eat him on toast. There'll have to be official rationing soon. It's not fair to put all the burden on the shopkeepers," added Jack.

The arrival of the Evening Post kept their thoughts on the events becoming more and more surreal. To his surprise, the report of the States' sitting Jack had witnessed was pretty accurate. He turned to the rest of the Post.

"You talk about there are some funny announcements here. Here's one from Reis Bakery:

'Though London is his home town and all his relatives are around there, Mr Reis is staying put. He feels sure that with rational thought, behaviour and discipline, it is the best thing to do.'

"You're making it up," said Alice, laughing.

"Come and see then. I can't believe it myself and I'm looking at it."

"Well, honestly," said Alice, "why can't he just say his shop is staying open instead of all that fuss?"

"He says we've just got to phone him if we are in trouble with bread supplies. Here's another one, listen: 'Foster's Radio. Although we are an English firm and our staff are 30% BRITISH (in capitals) the whole of our staff is staying.' I think we should put in an announcement, don't you love?" continued Jack. "The Birel family are 50% Jersey, 25% Norman 24% Breton, and 1% undecided. With rational discipline and good behaviour they are staying in their little home to await the arrival of Birel the Younger."

Alice giggled and put her arms around her husband.

"Do you really believe it?"

"Only just," replied Jack. "We must go to the doctor on Monday, to get a list of things we might want for the birth."

"What, already?"

"They may be in short supply, love."

"Don't make such a fuss."

"I'm not making a fuss at all. Now, don't argue."

"Yes sir, terribly sorry sir, I didn't realise you missed school so much."

Jack chose to ignore her.

"The wedding we saw at the Town Church," he added, looking back at the paper, "did the happy couple sprint off down Mulcaster Street towards the harbour? Anyway, it looks as if they held the reception without the bride and groom."

"Why?"

He read: "'Mr and Mrs J. E. Baker wish to thank all friends on behalf of their daughter and husband for the beautiful gifts received. Owing to existing conditions, they had to leave for Guernsey on an earlier boat.' That's a good way to describe it: 'existing conditions.' I must remember that," said Jack. "I wonder what a philosopher would make of it."

Alice came back to look over his shoulder, then pointed to the page. "Look, there's a message for you from the Dean, there at the bottom of the page. It's business as usual in the churches tomorrow."

"I should jolly well hope so," said Jack. "Can you imagine a notice saying: 'owing to the existing conditions, there will be no services tomorrow as all the vicars have taken up new stipends or whatever in the south of England.' I've a good mind to go and hear what they have to say."

"Don't you dare, you old hypocrite."

"Just listen to this," Jack stirred angrily in his seat. "This is what the Dean says about those who haven't rushed off in panic. 'It is those whose faith has stayed in God who are level-headed, clear-visioned and sober-minded and who act with courage, endurance and fortitude.' What was I saying just the other night? Doesn't it make you want to spit! How would he know, even if it was true, that those who've stayed are level-headed, clear-visioned and sober minded? Is he including Adolphe, for example? And Belheche ? And me for that matter, the agnostic. I haven't rushed off anywhere. How dare he make a moral right about staying or going ? According to him there couldn't have been any believers running down to the harbour on Wednesday morning. Don't make me laugh, Dean, I could name you half a dozen churchgoers I saw with my own eyes, clambering on to boats and, in one or two instances, barging frailer people out of the way."

Jack was warming to his theme and beginning to pace about.

"And what about those Gallos who left their dogs chained up, their cows shut in the stable without food and who pushed off in a panic leaving their own food half-eaten. They are at church every Sunday, them."

"For goodness sake, Jack, he's only trying to keep everybody calm, except you, of course. Religion won't do anybody any harm at a time like this."

"That's beside the point. What gets me is his smug assumption that only the churchgoers are staying for some righteous reason and that those who are leaving are the heathens and the godless. It's just not bloody true and I've a good mind to go round and tell him."

Alice knew there was little point in arguing, especially as she believed him to be right. He poured himself a beer and went back to the 'Post.'

"On page three we are told about those who have gone, the whole staff of Robinson's. What do they do? And Tanguy's dairy are apologising for not delivering milk for two days. Lucky for us Henry's cows haven't evacuated. Here's a story that's sad in one sense but uplifting in another. A woman is going to carry on her husband's butcher's shop because he has left to join the army."

"Who is it? We must get some meat there," said Alice.

"Thomas, in the New Market. Monday, when you go to the doctor."

"Honestly, fuss, fuss, fuss, you're worse than a child."

Jack ignored her and continued reading in a posh voice.

"The Royales Bridge Club will resume their sessions at the Forum every afternoon until further notice. What about us: 'The Fliquet Nap Club, owing to the curfew, will rattle the first kitty at 7.30.'"

"How long did you stay in the pub?" asked Alice.

"I was only sheltering from the rain and that was four hours ago. Look, here's something about food, but it's not going to help Mrs Pring much in her battle with the Amazons of St. Martins. 'In view of the existing conditions' there they are again, how long does an existing condition last?"

"Go on reading, for goodness sake," pressed Alice.

"'Shopkeepers are not allowed to supply any articles of food in excess of customers' normal requirements, signed A Le Gresley. Food Controller.' So, Mrs Pring's still going to have to make all the decisions herself. He took up an acting stance. "Does Mrs Le Brun, nearly off the scales, require more food than the slim and svelte but expanding Mrs Birel? Merde, merde, merde, listen to this: 'Public Instruction Committee: Staff and pupils of all colleges and schools under the above committee are requested to meet in their respective schools for the purpose of registration of staffs and scholars on Monday next, June 24th 1940 at 10am.' Bang goes our extra bit of holiday, just as I was beginning to enjoy it. Enough to make you want the Germans to come."

Alice frowned.

"Just a joke, my love! Look at the time, I must be off. Here's a strange ironic story. Three Irishmen found guilty of something or other have chosen fifteen days in prison rather than be deported from the island. On the same day we learn that 10,000 have deported themselves of their own accord."

He looked out of the window.

"There goes Baptiste on his bike. I didn't expect him until half past seven at the earliest"

"Why not?" asked Alice

"The pubs aren't closing until then. He's going to be in a bad mood."

At the meeting, the Constable lived up to every expectation. He was flustered out of his mind by the need to categorize provisions. Baptiste referring to them as rotten fruit, tins of grub and bottles of booze did little to calm his agitation. He was further preoccupied with the question of whether to have each lorry go round to one third of the houses to collect everything or have the three lorries go to all the houses to collect one category of provision each. Jack had to hold himself in check as all the Constable's Honorary Police were there and he, along with Henry, Baptiste and Alan were merely volunteer helpers. After grumblings, pipe chewing and much shaking of heads, the decision was taken, reversed then retaken to use as many lorries as possible to collect everything together as they went along.

"But what are we going to put all the things in?" bleated Galtier, the Constable.

Alan replied peevishly, fed up with the endless shilly shallying, that they were bound to find something at each house or farm to put the stuff in. He threatened that if they didn't start soon he was off home.

"It's all right to moan," moaned Galtier, "but I'm responsible for it, me."

They were about to leave after a final shrug when the Constable added:

"But what are we going to do with the perishables?"

Baptiste suggested that they eat their way through them as they went around. Galtier turned on him to vent his mounting frustration.

Baptiste listened for a moment then he stood up, placed a hand on Galtier's shoulder and told him, roughly in this order, what he thought of the new closing time, the Constable's contribution to the closing time, the dictatorship of closing time, the belief that even Hitler wouldn't go that far and that Hitler would certainly know what to do with bloody perishables. Jack and Alan led him away before he began on the Constable's pedigree.

"And what," he added as a parting shot, "are we going to do with wine and beer because it's not spirituous liquor?"

"Well you're not going to have it for a start," shouted Galtier. Fortunately the arrival of the headmaster brought back some semblance of order.

It was agreed that the needy of the parish, large families and old people living on their own should receive whatever unrotten perishables were collected.

"Have we got to draw up a list or what?" asked the Constable with renewed anxiety.

The headmaster agreed to do that and suggested that Galtier sit down with him and a cup of tea, to supply the names of the old and needy.

"But there's so much to do," the Constable kept repeating.

"All the more reason for getting started," chided the Head. As the four helpers went out, a Centenier gave them some spare Constable's Officer's badges in case they were challenged anywhere.

At each house they separated items and scribbled the addresses on boxes. There were certainly some surprises to be had. Twelve bottles of unopened whisky lined the shelf of the bedroom cupboard of a well-known, non-drinking, chapel-goer. An empty bottle lay on the floor tangled with old socks and the bedspread. It was impossible not to laugh, cruel though it seemed to Jack. But he was determined to keep quiet about what he saw.

"We are snooping uninvited into people's lives," he said to Alan.

"You're right," said Alan, "we shouldn't go around gossiping about what we find," his hearty laugh ringing out again as he contemplated the contents of the cupboard.

"What is life all about," asked Jack rhetorically, "to make a bloke so full of guilt and half-baked ideas that he has to drink in secret in his bedroom?"

"You're the teacher. You'll have to do something about it."

"If only it was that easy."

Jack thought it a good moment to bring the subject round to their brief chat of the previous day. They climbed into the lorry and moved on to the next house.

"I like the idea," said Alan, "but I'm not too clear what we can actually do."

"Well, we've just made a start by agreeing to keep quiet about what we see in all these houses, then we can check that people remain fair and unselfish; something the law can't usually enforce."

"I see what you mean," replied Alan. "Hang on, is this the place? We'd better pull off the road, it's a bit tight getting in there. But what do we actually do? I'm a practical sort of bloke. Do we make up a set of rules saying this is how the self-appointed Guardians of the Peace want you to behave and then paste everybody's head in who doesn't do it?"

Jack smiled a little painfully as they walked into the house.

"I'm embarrassed every time I talk about it. The last thing I want to do is set myself up, or anybody else for that matter, as vigilantes or guardians of anything."

"But it does sound like that, doesn't it," said Alan.

"I suppose so. Let's sit down a minute. The perishables can only get a bit more perished. What worries me is this. The Germans are likely to be tough and brutal with some people. One danger is for those people to find somebody weaker and be tough and brutal with them. Another danger is that if the Germans are controlling everything, especially the food supply, then the only access to it will be dealing with the Germans directly and all that that might lead to. But then again, if people have to find food for themselves, it might be even worse. Whichever way you look at it, it could easily end up as the survival of the fittest, the devious, the cunning and the evil."

"You're probably right," said Alan, deep in thought.

"I'm not an idealist or bloody hero or anything," continued Jack, "but when you look at a crowd of kids in a classroom you see how unequal everything is and how helpless some people are. Really, what I want to do is see that the least fit don't lose out and that the crooks and bastards are stopped from taking over with the encouragement of the Germans."

"I go all the way with you, there," agreed Alan, "but we don't manage to do that very well in normal times, mon pauvre bougre. However good your intentions, people will mistrust groups set up unofficially like that. I reckon what might be more effective, would be a 'quiet visit' by Jacko and Baptiste."

"Around here, perhaps!" said Jack. "What upsets me," he added with resignation, "is that we can't do much to prepare before the Germans get here. Ah bah, let's drink this bottle of beer since the Constable hasn't decided what to do with non-spirituous liquor."

"Good idea," said Alan. "Look at this, it's amazing what some people read. He must have bought this in Paris. I couldn't believe it when I went there on my honeymoon. What do they call those boxes on the walls along the Seine?"

"Bouquinistes. So you went to Paris too?"

"That's the ones. Anyway I didn't need a manual then I can tell you."

After two more houses, they returned with their booty to the Parish Hall.

"We'd better get home before the curfew to show the good example," said the Constable, flapping slightly less than before.

Alice was reading the Post when Jack got in and they went over his conversation with Alan.

"What does he think?"

"The same as everybody, that we can't actually do anything before the Germans come."

*Journal extract*
*I managed to get into the public gallery of the States today and realised that it is the first time I've been there. Most of the debate was about what to do with abandoned property, foodstuffs and possessions. How much effort should be put into this is an interesting moral question.*

*They also discussed Air Raid Precautions which is worrying. Surely, if the islands are not going to be defended, there should be no danger of air raids?*

*Then they imposed a curfew although nobody seems to know why or what it is meant to achieve. People are unlikely to object to not being allowed out before 5am (I certainly won't) but having to be in before 10 pm seems a bit early, even if the pubs are going to be shut.*

*Things livened up a bit when they got on to closing the pubs early. Many Constables, have been very upset at being compared to Hitler on this matter and tried to speak up against the idea, but the members voted for 7.30pm*

*..It looks as if the French Cabinet has accepted the terms of the Armistice and put Pétain in charge. I wonder if many French people will answer the call a General de Gaulle made from London the day before yesterday. I heard a rumour in town that a plane refuelled at the airport on Tuesday on its way from France to England carrying somebody important. Some people thought it might be Churchill on his way back from trying to persuade Reynaud, the French Prime Minister, to keep fighting, but that would have been far too risky. Imagine if the German's had got wind of it.*

*..The trouble at the shops is getting worse.*

*..There are some strange things in the Evening Post. Some people apologising for not being able to provide normal service because staff have evacuated, others positively boasting that they are still here and that it is business as usual.*

*Also, the Dean has the nerve to describe the people who have stayed as 'those whose faith has stayed in God who are level-headed, clear-visioned and sober-minded and who act with courage, endurance and fortitude.' Talk about getting carried away with rhetorical claptrap! Can't he see that there is no right or wrong about this? People have been lying awake night after night worrying about what to do. Buckets of tears have been shed. What right has he got to point an accusing finger at those who have gone? He's as bad as Judge Dorey with his rats and rabbits and young men of old Norman stock. Let's hope that none of them come to regret the behaviour of some of these so-called clear-visioned and sober-minded people in the days ahead!*

*..What price my own modest efforts at finding a moral position for the days ahead if the 'official guardians' of what constitutes morality are capable of writing such blinkered balderdash in the Post?*

# ELEVEN

*Sunday 23 June, 1940*

The church bells woke Jack up late. He had slept particularly soundly, worn out by the physical activity of lugging boxes onto the lorry. He was again tempted to go to church, if only to collect information for his journal. But would that be hypocrisy? Was hypocrisy doing what you didn't want to do because of what people might think or equally of not doing what you wanted to do for the same reason?

'So, aren't I being hypocritical by not going to church because people might think I was being a hypocrite if I did? Voltaire couldn't beat that. I'd better not start on that one with Alice, though.'

"Remind me to collar the headmaster when he comes out of church," he told her. "I'm going to write up as much of my journal as I can. We'll have to go to Jim's quite early if we want to be back by ten tonight."

"Damn the curfew!" said Alice with feeling.

"I told the Constable I couldn't help with collecting tins of food and bottles of gin today."

An hour later, Jack was pleased with his work. The words seemed to come of their own accord. Not too much chewing of pen, scratching of head or screwing up of paper and he had done enough to be near the church when the ancient worm-pitted doors creaked open to release the congregation. The first person he met and couldn't avoid was his neighbour, Mr Belheche, the solicitor's clerk, oozing, in Jack's eyes, with righteousness.

"Good morning, Mr Birel, I didn't see you in church."

"I wasn't there," said Jack

"Oh!" said Mr Belheche.

"I don't go to church, as you know," Jack added peevishly.

"Yes, but I thought, at this time of trial, you might find the need."

Jack counted to the proverbial ten.

"A very good attendance," Belheche added.

"Yes, I'm sure," said Jack, "although some were missing, I suppose."

"Not from the regular congregation. The rats and rabbits, to quote Jurat Dorey, have gone, but not many of them were churchgoers."

"I didn't see you at the boat the other morning," said Jack.

"I didn't go to the boat."

"I thought you must have done," added Jack sarcastically, "since you seem to know who was on it and whether they went regularly to church or not."

Belheche realised that Jack was now baiting him and before walking away, he said: "Some things are going to change when the Germans arrive."

Jack stared after him in disgust. He wanted mentally to wash his hands. 'Must be careful, though, not to start judging people before they actually do anything. If, for example, I saw Alice talking to a German soldier, I'd assume that there must be a very good reason, but if I saw Belheche doing it I would almost certainly assume he was fraternising in some way. This will be one of the dangers for everybody to avoid. The island is rife enough with rumour and jumping to conclusions at the best of times.'

He was woken from his reverie by a wasp crash landing on his nose and he flung a desperate hand at it. His nose was large enough without a lump on it as well. He plunged into thoughts of Cyrano de Bergerac: 'un pic, un cap, une péninsule' and Chaucer's warted Miller, as he always did when the mind focussed on noses. Recovering from his brush with the Nazi of nature, he spotted the headmaster about to suffer the far worse fate of being cornered against a tombstone by the large bulk of Mrs Le Brun squealing about why her son had to go in and register at school the following day when the headmaster knew perfectly well that he had not left the island. With commendable compassion and presence of mind, Jack stepped in and said: "Come quickly" to the headmaster and "Excuse me" to Mrs Le Brun.

"What on earth is the matter. Is your wife not well?" asked Mr Stevens as they navigated past the bicycles piled across the side entrance of the cemetery.

"She's fine," laughed Jack, "but I imagined you would want to be rescued from the dragon in red. I would like to talk to you, though, if you've got a moment or two."

"Well, thank you, she is a positive menace, that woman; not a very Christian thought I know, just out of church, mea culpa."

Jack laughed again and said: "This register business tomorrow, does it mean that we are back at school?"

"No, I don't think so, not tomorrow anyway. I think the authorities simply want to know what the position is. If the staff-student ratio has radically altered in some schools, they may ask for volunteers to teach in another school. But I doubt if we will go back properly before the Germans come. They will probably issue instructions of their own."

"Like what, for example?" asked Jack

"No idea, although I've tried to speculate a bit! They may insist on doing the teaching themselves or have somebody in the school keeping an eye on what is going on."

"You don't think they'll just let us carry on as before?"

"They might, but we will be in a very good position to influence, even incite our pupils and, although I am sure they wouldn't hesitate to do it, it would look bad for them if they had to start punishing children. According to the papers, they've told the French that they want a co-operative sort of occupation."

"I wanted to ask you about the law and moral responsibility and so on. Is it wrong to disobey the German rule of law do you think?"

"Morally, I would have thought not," replied Mr Stevens.

"But what about if the Germans carry out reprisals against innocent people, do not the perpetrators share some of the responsibility for what happens?"

"Certainly if they knew that reprisals were likely to occur."

"This could be one of the most serious issues we have to face," said Jack solemnly. "Did the sermon today give any clear lead as to how we should behave towards the occupier?"

"You should have come to listen for yourself," the head said admonishingly with a little smile.

"I wanted to but decided it would seem hypocritical to appear in church only when the going was rough. I disapprove of that sort of religion."

"You disapprove of all religion, though, don't you Jack?"

"Not if it's sincerely held or practised. Not if people acted in their lives as they imply they will on Sunday mornings."

"That's a bit of a cliché, Jack. People are fallible, that's the whole point behind original sin after all. You have to forgive the occasional lapse."

"The occasional lapse, of course, I forgive, and non-believers you know, have similar lapses. What I object to, call it a cliché if you like, is when a person's whole attitude to life and the way they treat other people is obviously at serious variance with their professed Christianity."

"It might be better if we didn't argue, Jack, in case things get too personalised. The sermon you ask about, was given by a rector from Gorey. He certainly didn't go into lawbreaking and reprisals. He simply urged us to go out and plant beans as a practical contribution to events and, on the spiritual plane, asked us to be ready to assume whatever God thought it best to call us to."

"What do you think we can be called to?" asked Jack. "That's what I'm trying to work out.."

"To give a lead and example to others for one thing!"

"That's just it. I've been wondering if a group of people could get together who might give precisely that kind of moral leadership."

"Apart from our elected and appointed leaders you mean? What sort of leadership do you have in mind?"

"To think through attitudes towards the occupiers, how to live with them and how to live with each other when they are here!"

"And on what basis are you going to make your moral judgements? On Christianity?"

"On Christian values, certainly, there's nothing wrong with them, but they can easily be practised without setting foot inside a church."

"I wouldn't disagree. In my dim distant days when I did some Latin I read Cicero's 'The Good Life.' I can't remember a great deal now but I think the three major premises were, identifying truth from fiction, restraining the passions and behaving with understanding in our association with other people."

"That would seem a good place to start," said Jack, his face brightening, as he tried again to set out his own tentative ideas and hopes.

The headmaster interrupted to take up one of the points Jack made about the black market.

"That is where you may need to show some of Cicero's understanding or, indeed, basic Christian charity. It is dangerous to label things too quickly as obviously wrong. When people are starving, they have to eat."

"But they don't have to sell themselves."

"It depends very much on what you mean by that. The danger, Jack, and I hope you don't mind my speaking frankly, is that any group of the kind you propose, will take as it's starting point, preconceived ideas, probably Christian ones, I agree, but as they are relevant to what we might call 'normal' times. Once the Germans are here, it will be another story and my mind turns immediately to the casting of the first stone. Do any of us know what we will do when things get really serious? At the moment, for all intents and purposes, nobody is lacking food in this island, so we have no idea how people are going to act when they are really hungry and their children are really hungry. We must talk this over more, Jack, but I have to go now I'm afraid."

Jack thanked him, but felt a little deflated. Perhaps he was in too much of a hurry. Everyone had more pressing matters to sort out in their minds first. One thing he could not accept would be any suggestion of 'every man for himself.' He had no doubt that the Head would agree with him on that.

When he got back in the house, Alice was not feeling well and reluctantly agreed with Jack's fussing that they had better put off their projected visit to Jim and Jennifer at La Moye.

"I'll have to phone Mrs Mourant at the shop to tell them we can't come, or failing that, Colonel What's-his-name across the road."

~

Jim and Jennifer were disappointed. Following Jim's near evacuation, they felt even more isolated than usual 'out west.' Also, they had hoped to discuss further with Jack the possibility of a house or preferably a farm becoming available somewhere in St Martin's. That morning Jim had given in his notice.

"Jack told Mrs Mourant he'd had a job to get through on the phone," Jim told Jennifer. "I'm not surprised, it says here in the Post that telephone operators have been at their posts for 18 to 19 hours at a stretch with only 60% staff. Anyway let's go to the pictures instead. Which one do you fancy?"

Jennifer chose 'Hollywood Stadium Mystery' at Wests Cinema, partly because she liked mysteries but mainly through an inexplicable aversion to William Powell in the other offering.

Everywhere the remaining islanders were looking for things to do in this hiatus of time, reviving old hobbies or starting new ones.

Alice's parents played Tablanette, their favourite card game for two, learned on one of many trips to the now-occupied Normandy peninsular.

Baptiste was razor fishing down at La Mare, below the Martello-type Conway tower. There were no tourists gathered around today, fascinated at seeing him put salt on little keyholes in the sand and wait for the black shell to slide out vertically, looking exactly like a cut-throat razor, not one of those new-fangled safety things from America. While the visitors were still laughing in surprise, Baptiste would pluck the rising razor between index and thumb, pause a moment then hold it up in triumph. He knew the catch wouldn't be marvellous today, the tide was barely low enough and the sky was overcast. They only came out in vast numbers when it was hot, sunny and windless. Still, he had enough for a feed, since the missus didn't touch any. It was all he could do to get her to cook them. He'd try and get a few shrimps for her from the rock pools nearby.

The headmaster was reviving a student interest in botany. He was out collecting wild flowers and plants from the fields opposite the school. He would press and classify them, something to do when the Germans were there. He felt quite excited - perhaps a book even on the flora of the island or classes for adults in school, if the Occupiers allowed gatherings of that kind.

That afternoon, cups of tea were proposed, made and consumed in vast quantities from Corbière to St Catherine's, from Grosnez to La Rocque; stamps were stuck in books, accounts were drawn up hopefully, letters were written, cuttings were taken from the Evening Post, a photograph of Winston Churchill was defiantly pinned to a wall, bread was made, cows were milked, a baby was born, several were conceived and church bells rang at six o'clock.

Sitting on a fallen tree near what they called 'our brook' in Le Pont, Jack was writing more in his journal and Alice alternated between knitting and reading. He looked at the sky through still wet leaves and felt inspired by Wordsworth to jot down a few lines:

One impulse from a vernal wood,
Will teach you more of man
Of moral evil and of good,
Than all the sages can.

Somewhere in Normandy, German Officers of moderate rank, were planning the invasion of the Channel Islands.

*Journal extracts*
*Waiting*
*... I've just heard the news on the wireless that France has accepted the terms of the armistice. The northern half of the country extending down the whole western coastline is to be occupied and the French fleet has to be surrendered. I think Churchill will do everything in his power to stop that happening because those ships, in German hands, would increase significantly their ability to mount an invasion across the Channel. ..Already England, desperate to maintain air superiority, is training hundreds of men to become pilots.*

*... Thanks to Mr Stevens I think I've got my thoughts a little clearer. I like his summary of Cicero's analysis of the 'good life'. Taking great care to differentiate truth from fiction, not to act precipitously or rush to judgement on others are pretty well what I had in mind.*

*... That said, I could have done without another confrontation with Belheche. He stretches one's tolerance and understanding to the limit. He is at the other end of the spectrum from Adolphe and Baptiste, totally humourless, pompous and self-righteous. How dangerous is he? Until now, most people more or less ignore him or just politely pass the time of day ( curious phrase...) But he seems to be almost welcoming the Germans. He hasn't said so in as many words, but keeps repeating that 'some people', and he certainly means Adolphe for one (he's never forgotten falling into that grave Adolphe had left uncovered), are going to get their come-uppance.*

*... It is worrying what people like Belheche might do when the Germans are here. The occupiers, if that is what we will call them, are bound to encourage informants and be on the lookout for locals willing to help them.*

*... Another Sunday over, a time for reflection and taking stock after the upheavals of the week. The waiting is starting to get to us. People are saying more and more things like: 'I wish they'd come so we know where we are.' Will it be as dreadful as some fear or not so bad, as others hope? If I am anything to go by, the same people are both dreading and hoping.*

*They could easily be here tomorrow.*

# TWELVE

*Monday 24 June, 1940*

It seemed more painful than usual to shake the limbs in the direction of work on Monday morning. Three days of drama, followed by a weekend lull, had dulled the senses. Colleagues might be gone, supplies were shorter and the Germans could be arriving at any moment. The buses were fuller, the car population answering the call for petrol economy, if only because of rumours of police checks on the roads leading into town.

Jack just made it to school for ten. Although there were fewer children, there seemed to be more; a menagerie of chattering, chirping, squealing and shouting and the same mix of truth, fiction and uncertainty he'd heard in town.

"...has gone just like that; ...the headmaster has gone too; ...none of the staff are here; ...the Germans have landed at Gorey; ...Fritzes my dad calls them; ...we ought to fight them; ...there won't be many,most of them have to stay in France; ...gran's gone; ...we won't have to come to school again this year; ...all the children have left Guernsey; ...I don't care; ...are you scared? ..we keep visiting relations; ...mum is crying all the time; ...the Germans don't play cricket; ...no more sweets or ice cream; ...shut your face; ...they'll stay in all the hotels; ...dad's mad about the pubs closing; ...went out after curfew; ...you'll get shot, you will; ...what's a curfew? ..you can see them with a telescope; ...big planes; ...why are we here today?..goose stepping; ...swasticas ...can't have sugar in my tea any more; ...keeps going to town; ...saw the boat Thursday; ...he hasn't gone, you liar..."

It took several loud blasts from the whistle to bring silence. The children filed into the little hall. The headmaster, by his presence dispelling the rumour that he had gone, spoke well. He said he knew they were excited to see each other and he had left them for half an hour in the yard to chat and get things out of their system. They would be going home soon. Now they had to listen very carefully. He told them why they had been called in that day and gave them several examples of how rumour and panic had affected people during the previous week. They must be very careful not to repeat things unless they knew them to be true or could fully trust the person who had told them. He urged them to be sensible enough to behave especially well when the Germans came because they would not tolerate any stupidity and would punish people very severely. The children then went to their classrooms for the roll call. Jack was swamped with questions:

"Why haven't you gone sir?"

"When are they coming? Will it be this morning?"

"How long will they stay?"

"Are they going to kill people, sir?"

"Why can't we fight them?"

Jack tried to answer what he could and calm the fears, but keeping the children silent was clearly out of the question without playing the tyrant and one of those in the world was more than enough. Even after he dismissed them, most stayed around him still asking questions. ..why? why? why? Always the most difficult to answer. From the age of about three, children instinctively learn that 'why?' is the only question worth asking. The most painful was 'why has Mr Durridge gone?'

Jack had seen Kate briefly in the hall and now found her looking lost and sad-eyed in the staffroom. He went up to her and said: "Sorry, I just don't know what to say."

"You make it seem as if he's dead," said Kate.

"It does sound a bit like that, doesn't it? You never know, he might be back sooner than we think."

"Yes, he might." She didn't cry but it was an effort. "I didn't want to go over there with him joining the Air Force."

"I didn't know he was going to do that," said Jack, totally surprised.

"He told me just before he left, and only after I pressed him. He thinks being a pilot is the only way of actually doing something at the moment."

"We can be proud of him," said Jack, only too aware of his own desire to want to do something, and of his inability to find what it was.

"I am proud, of course, very proud and very unhappy."

"You must be. I admire him a lot. I was very sorry not to see him before he went."

"He did go to your place, didn't he?" said Kate surprised.

"Yes, Alice saw him. I had to go with a worried mum to the pier to try and find her son."

"Did you find him?"

"No."

"So, I'm not the only sad person after all," she said.

Jack thought this might be the moment to tell her of Alice's pregnancy. Kate was thrilled and wanted to go and see Alice straightaway. Jack walked with her as far as his front door, then seeing Cyril, the Constable's Officer near the churchyard wall, he left the ladies to it.

"I wonder how many more notices I'm going to have to pin up in the Parish Notice Box. D'you think anybody ever reads them, you, Jack?"

"Only if it is important and the word has got around that it's there. I must confess I've never seen anybody standing there reading one."

"Well, this one's important," said the Constable's Officer. "It's from the King."

"What! let me see," said Jack leaning forward. He read aloud:

" 'Message from the King to be Posted in Royal Square and at all Parish Churches.

For strategic reasons, it has been found necessary to withdraw the armed forces from the Channel Islands. I deeply regret this necessity, and I wish to assure my people in the islands that in taking this decision, my government have not been unmindful of their position. It is in their interest that this step should be taken in the present circumstances.

The long association of the Islands with the Crown and the loyal service the people of the islands have rendered to my ancestors and myself are guarantees that the link between us will remain unbroken, and I know that my people in the Islands will look forward with the same confidence as I do to the day when the resolute fortitude with which we face our present difficulties will reap the reward of victory...' "

"I suppose the next message will be from the Führer," said Cyril.

"Where's the Constable?" asked Jack.

"He's down at another meeting of the States. If the war was going to be won by the number of times the States met, then it would be over by now."

Jack smiled and asked if they had finished collecting all the stuff from the abandoned houses the day before.

"All that we know of, anyway."

"Ah te vlà, bougre," said Baptiste as he rode up and placed his foot on the bottom step of the War Memorial. "What are you reading there like that?"

"It's a letter for you from the King. He says he's heard what a bloody good postman you are."

"Laisse me vey tchna.Let me see that."

Baptiste read the proclamation, saying something like 'pah' every few seconds.

"That was written by a bloke at a desk in Whitehall, you can be sure of that. There's hardly a word of less than ten letters. Why can't he just say: 'Sorry lads, keep your pecker up, we'll smash the buggers soon.' Then we'd know what he was talking about."

Jack and the Constable's Officer grinned at the postman's irreverence.

"It could perhaps have been written a little more personally," said Jack.

"Look," said Baptiste, with a gesture which nearly made him come off his bike, "if my old woman had to read this, she'd need a bloody dictionary. You ought to hang one here, Cyril, on a little chain so that it doesn't get pinched."

"Ah bah," replied Cyril.

"Old Adolphe's not going to be pleased."

"Why not?

"He can only read Jersey-French and precious little of that. Can you imagine 'resolute fortitude' translated into Jerriais, you...."

By now a small crowd had gathered, as people came and went to the shop, the bus bringing a few more.

"Profit from the fact that a schoolmaster is here to translate the message from the King," shouted Baptiste.

Keen to escape, Jack asked him if he was going to the Royal, although it was obvious from his carefree attitude that he had just come from there.

"People are going to think I'm a regular," he said.

"Come on," laughed Jack. "I'll buy you a pint, I'd like a chat with you."

"You know me," he said later, after Jack had outlined his burgeoning ideas. "I don't go around poking my nose in other people's affairs."

"Don't make me laugh, Baptiste! Anyway, once the Germans are here some people are going to do things that the rest of us can't stand."

"Perhaps."

"You weren't too happy the other day when the food had been nicked from the larders of people who had changed their minds about going."

"Right, but we can sort buggers like that out," said Baptiste with a laugh.

"How?" asked Jack.

"How?" repeated Baptiste in amazement. "But you're not well then. First, there'd be a punch on the nose from Jacko here."

The publican was listening with interest.

"That should settle most of them."

"I was hoping we might avoid violence," said Jack.

"Eh ben merde, here we are in the middle of a bloody war and you want to avoid violence, you, that's a good one."

Jack could only laugh with the others then asked: "What other methods have you got?"

"One of my old favourites, for a start. Your brother-in-law reminded me the other day. You can smear cowshit on door handles and handlebar grips and on the grips of barrows, anything you are likely to grab. That upsets a lot of people I can tell you."

By now the whole pub was laughing.

"And if that doesn't work," continued Baptiste, "you can chuck great lumps of manure through their bedroom windows. The trouble with you schoolmasters is that you've got no imagination left. You ask the kids, they'll know what to do."

"I'll talk to you again when you're serious," said Jack.

"But I am serious, when do you want me to start?"

On his short walk home, Jack reflected that his hopes were little advanced. Perhaps Baptiste was right. You waited until somebody did something then you sorted them out with simple direct methods.

Kate and Alice were amused by Jack's account of his conversation with Baptiste and they went straight out to read the King's message.

"Well, I agree with Baptiste about the long words," said Alice when they came back.

Soon after eating, Kate had to get back to St Ouen's to help her mother who had been more or less obliged to take over the shop by the Parish Hall when the couple who owned it evacuated. As she cycled across the northern country parishes of Trinity, St John, and St Mary she had the idea of reviving the walk or cycle of the twelve parish churches as a challenge people might take up, for something to do in the times ahead. She would mention it to Jack. It was just the sort of thing he might want to organise.

It was still too cloudy for the beach, although sunnier than the previous day. Alice called up that she was going to her sister's. Henry was in the field, side shoots flying all around him.

"That's what comes from leaving them when it rains," he told Alice as she passed. "If Jack's got nothing to do ...?" he added tentatively.

"You'll be lucky to get him into a tomato field again," replied Alice, "even to help you out. He hated the wasted hours, as he calls them, tying and 'gourmanding' when he was a kid. He'll just say Sisyphus."

"What does that mean?" asked Henry.

"I don't remember, you'll have to ask him. There is another possibility though. His brother and Jennifer have finished working in their toms at St Brelade. Perhaps they could help you and sleep at our place?"

~

Jack decided to paint the upstairs windows, taking great pleasure in doing something useful and ordinary. When the Evening Post came hurtling up towards him, he caught it one handed to a loud cheer from the delivery van. The paper brought thoughts back to the 'existing conditions' and to the behaviour and attitude of some people. The owner of a field of tomatoes, for example, had actually taken the trouble to write to the newspaper about a woman worker who had told him that it was useless to go on looking after the plants, things being as they were. The man had written: 'She was told what I thought of her and her likes and she has returned to duty...'

It was one thing to say something like that but to actually write it in the Post! And the pompous ass had actually signed his name: Chas! Not, of course, Charles or Charlie. Strange thing war!

'I've never met Chas but the chances are pretty good that I would get on better with an ordinary German soldier than I would with him,' thought Jack. Still reading the paper, he nearly exploded. There was a letter from Mrs Riley, La Dame de Rozel no less, the feudal titular holder of 'Seigneurie' rights at the Manor, complaining about Sunday's sermon at St Martin's Church. What a pity he hadn't gone after all.

'Mind you,' he reflected, 'I'm not much keener on the Seigneurial system than I am on religion.' He read the letter: 'The preacher (not the Rector himself on this occasion) stood up before a congregation of Jersey farmers and their relations merely to give them his own petty views about Hitler's plans. He also instructed them about the growing of vegetables. Surely, at a time like this, he should have urged them to turn to God's providence and remind them of the simple words of the catechism? 'To do our duty in that state of life to which it has pleased God to call us but to do it with greater courage and resolve.'

Dame de Rozel

'She just wants to get her name in the Post in case we forget she's still there,' thought Jack.

More news. The States had talked again about abandoned houses. Also, two mailboats a week would continue to operate, so the links with England were not completely severed yet. People were still able to leave unless and until the Germans intervened. Jack, like everybody else needed constant reminding that they were bound to arrive soon. The evacuation the previous week had seemed almost like a culminating point in itself.

Alice returned from her sister's with Jojo and Louise to allow Jeanne and Henry to go to the pictures.

"Our turn tomorrow," she said.

"Fine, after we've been to the doctor's."

"Oh yes, I forgot."

"Liar."

"Listen," she said, happily changing the subject, "how about if Jim and Jennifer stayed here and gave Henry a hand, unless you want to work in the tomatoes?"

"No fear," said Jack. "Bloody Sisyphus, that is."

Alice laughed "I told Henry you'd say that. You'll have to explain it to him."

"I hope you noticed the smell of paint," said Jack.

"I did, well done, you can do downstairs tomorrow."

Jack sat down later to his journal.

*Journal extracts*

*... Yesterday I noted that England was desperately training young men to become pilots. Today I hear that Andrew has decided to join the air force and become one of them. What an exceptionally brave thing to do! It makes me all the sadder not to have said goodbye to him As far as I know, he has no flying experience. How long will it take before he is sent up in a fighter all on his own, into the infinity of sky, to meet waves of German bombers heading for London? I would be terrified out of my wits. We must tell the pupils what he is doing; as long as Kate doesn't mind.*

*... It was good to see all the children again. It keeps up morale in a funny sort of way. Surprisingly, very few of the class seem to have gone. Is it because we are in a rural country parish? Come to think of it, all the parishes apart from St Helier are pretty rural. It wouldn't surprise me, though, if the evacuation revealed town/country differences. Some people living in town have moved out for the moment to stay with relatives in the country.*

*... We had a bit of a laugh at the message from the King posted in the church notice box. A laugh at the language that is, not the content which, in effect says that the islands are now completely at the mercy of the invader. Baptiste was pretty scathing about it and I unwisely chose that moment to chat over my tentative thoughts on how we might behave under occupation. I had to laugh with the rest of the pub when he picked me up about not wanting violence in the middle of a war! His view is much more down to earth.*

*... I realise now that what I appear to be doing is making sermons. Perhaps I should have been a priest rather than a teacher. Better not tell that to Alice! I must confess that I have probably been looking for a role since that night I was asked in the pub to speculate about whether the Germans were likely to be coming or not. What has happened in the*

*subsequent ten days all seems like a bad dream. What should I do next? A letter to the Post? Or pin a notice up next to the King's letter? Would that be ' lèse-majesté'?*

*... Jokes aside, violent resistance is not an option. The implications of the King's letter are clear. The troops have been taken out to avoid carnage on a serious scale so it would be madness and futile to try to defend the island by ourselves. It would, I am sure, be equal madness, once the occupiers are here, to commit acts of violence against them. They would certainly respond in a brutal way.*

*... So, what would I want to say to people anyway? 'Don't fraternise or collaborate with the Germans or engage in black market activity'? Those seem pretty obvious. 'Don't hoard' and 'beware of rumours' are just morally sound truisms. I could list a lot more but whichever way you look at it, it smacks of the boy scout movement or Sunday sermon. No wonder nobody seems to get very excited when I discuss it with them. The curious thing about people like myself is that we are, of course, in favour of law and order, decency and good manners and all the rest of it, but we don't want a sanctimonious parade of the stuff or holier-than-thou statements about how people should behave. We also welcome individuality and mild forms of anarchy and, in doing so, might appear to condone irregular or spirited behaviour. In short, it seems practically impossible, to formulate any code of good behaviour for the occupation without sounding like the very people who irritate us so much.*

*... Henry's been out in his tomatoes. When he asked Alice if I would help him, she said I would reply 'Sisyphus' and she was right. In Greek mythology he was condemned by the Gods to roll a boulder to the top of a hill and just as he got it there it would roll down and he would have to start all over again. Thus it is with looking after tomatoes!*

*... Alice's idea that Jim and Jennifer come and stay for a few days, helping Henry at the same time, is an excellent one. It might also be helpful for all of us to be together when (I think I should drop the 'if' now) the Germans come.*

# THIRTEEN

*Tuesday 25 June, 1940*

Overnight, whilst everyone slept, malicious nature gave a macabre intimation of what might soon befall the populace. At dawn the badly-shaken owner of a stricken farm informed the authorities of an outbreak of foot and mouth disease and, within hours, the whole island was alerted. Men in white coats and wellingtons sped silently and efficiently to slaughter prime examples of the renowned Jersey herd. Road blocks were set up and basins of white stinking disinfectant awaited the boots of the vets and administrators who, alone, were allowed access to the farm.

Words of fear spread quickly among the farmers. Where would it strike next? No precautions were ever enough, no exemptions for champion cow or heifer collected from fields and driven into stables to wait with the anxious owners. Whenever it appeared, foot and mouth disease was a savage blow to the farming and breeding community. Years of painstaking planning and feeding, all lost in minutes. Once one member of a herd contracted the disease, the rest were systematically destroyed. On an island as small as Jersey, the potential disaster was calamitous and heartbreaking.

The light-brown and cream-coloured cows, with large twinkling eyes and lashes, are world famous. Prize winners at the major Island Shows had long been exported, accompanied by Jersey herdsmen, to New Zealand and the United States. This pure strain of cattle had spread the name of the tiny island further than the pullover, Lillie Langtry or even De Carteret, who had taken the name to New Jersey. The milk of the Jersey cow was everywhere acknowledged to be creamier and more delicious, the butter fat content the highest of any cattle in existence. But now, once more, on this small island, it was conceivable that every cow might have to be destroyed. And this, after such wisdom and determination to preserve the herd, as no cow of any description was ever allowed to enter the island, not even a Jersey born elsewhere.

Henry was panicking but with a positive panic which was crystallised in action, rather than in his fret and anxiety over evacuation. He fetched Jack early with a loud bang on the door, poured foul-smelling disinfectant, far above the necessary dose, into his tomato sprayers and, together, they soaked the stable, the doors, windows, feet of the cows, the yard, the wheel of the barrow and out into the road. Henry had seen his eight cows born and had written their names above every stall. He spoke to them, often more readily than he spoke to people. He washed them regularly, put their coats on when it was cold and milked them lovingly. Their slaughter was too terrible to contemplate.

The very words, 'foot and mouth', were enough in themselves to arouse feelings of horror in every adult and child in the vicinity of a farm. That such peaceful and productive animals could be shot and buried in lime pits was enough to turn the most hardened stomach. Farmers were helpless if, unseen, the fever struck. Often just as they thought all might be well, blisters were seen on the feet, then the mammary glands. The disease was not fatal in itself, but it reduced the cow to a skeleton and it spread quickly. The only real method of containment was by systematic killing.

Blame for the disease was quickly attached to starlings, the most common carriers. They came over from the same Normandy Peninsular, the Cotentin, where the Germans were now gathering. Fate was playing with the island, holding, for a little longer, unknown threats for the population, but first dispatching a horrific disease to its prized animals. It seemed a needless cruelty at such a time.

"We should phone papa," said Henry, "you'd better go down there Jack. I'll stay here to stop anybody walking into the yard. I wouldn't put it past Baptiste to ride in here as if nothing had happened. Tell papa to be sure to spray the little roof window in the stable, because the birds could easily come in there."

"Do you think he will have stuff to spray with?"

"Ah merde, you're right. I'll go in the lorry. Stay here, though, and keep everybody out."

Jack had great difficulty keeping up with this conversation as Henry, in spite of his heavy boots, kept moving in every direction as if about to do something. Jack stayed in the yard while Henry went for his keys, returning a moment later to say: "Suppose I pick up something on my tyres?"

Look, Henry, you can't barricade yourself against everything."

"Right," said Henry without much conviction.

Jack sat on a pile of upturned boxes near the little granite wall by the road and his reflections turned naturally to what the Germans might be doing. Did they actually know that the islands were just there for the taking? Perhaps they were not intending to come after all. Occupation could be a liability, people to feed and so on, unless they carted everybody off to France. He hadn't thought about that possibility!

He opened his eyes to a cough just near him.

"We don't normally see you lying about on walls, I must say," the headmaster told Jack, who was barely aware that he had climbed on to it.

"And I'm on sentry duty, too." laughed Jack. "My brother-in-law will court-martial me. Funny word don't you think? If the Commander-in-Chief, playing cricket, took a ball in the slips, would you shout 'well caught, Marshall'?.

"Oh dear, oh dear," said the Head. "I hope you don't use material like that in class."

"Much worse, I assure you."

"It may be a good thing that we have broken up early. But what are you guarding, may I ask?"

"The cows."

"Why, have any been stolen?"

"No, but there's an outbreak of foot and mouth disease about two miles away and Henry is very worried."

"I didn't know. I haven't been out today, until now of course. I almost expected to discover that the Germans were here, but it's foot and mouth instead."

"Let's hope the Nazis don't start slaughtering sick people," Jack heard himself say.

"It's a frightening thought, isn't it? But do you know, Jack, we've stopped worrying about what they are going to do. Nobody seems to speak about it any more."

"I agree. The other week I was wondering what would happen to men of military age, to the women and to the old... internment, deportation, brutality, starvation, massacre even. Then the evacuation took over and those fears seemed to recede somehow."

"That is very true. Few said that they were going to England to avoid being killed or anything like that. Going or staying seemed to depend on a whim or panic. For those of us who have decided to stay, it must be because we no longer believe our awful earlier thoughts are going to be realised."

"Yes, although doubts inevitably remain," said Jack, "but those who believe in omens won't have much comfort with this foot and mouth. It is a bit sinister, isn't it?"

Mr Stevens took out his pipe and banged it gently on the wall.

"Oh dear, oh dear," he sighed. "My wife will feel like that for sure. It will be all over the Post, I suppose."

"Bound to be."

"Well you know how she worries at the best of times, a fine fretter, I call her. She does rather tend to see omens everywhere and you can't win, you know, with people like that. They'll always find something to out-omen you with."

He lit his pipe and puffed.

"The other day she saw a single magpie," he continued, "and that set her off on a catalogue of imagined catastrophes."

"The one for sorrow, two for joy thing, you mean?" said Jack.

"Yes that's right, but she mixed it all up with predictions about the weather. You know how we say that it is going to rain if swallows are flying near the ground."

"Something to do with air pressure isn't it, forcing the flies down," said Jack.

"Exactly. Well, my good lady said they were flying down into the cemetery to give us a presentiment of death. Oh dear, oh dear."

Jack added, after a brief pause, that the presence of the cemetery so near to them, the War Memorial and the daily dose of the Evening Post, made it difficult for them to take their minds off the war.

"Very true," agreed the head, "but strange as it may seem, I've felt a sort of compulsion to read about war recently. It has always had a curious fascination. I've reread the terrible but beautiful and powerful poems of Wilfred Owen."

"We did a seminar on 'Dulce et Decorum Est' at college." said Jack.

"Very moving but the first line of 'Anthem for Doomed Youth' seems particularly apt to what has happened today. 'What passing bells for those who die as cattle?' Let's hope it's not an omen either. Now, I've just bought this."

"Hemingway," read Jack from the cover.

"'For Whom the Bell Tolls.' It's about the Spanish Civil War, marvellously written. Frightening, though, because it's so near in time and could easily happen to us. I'm going to find a little corner and read and puff at my pipe."

"I'm not reading much at the moment," said Jack, "but I'm trying to write a journal about all this."

The headmaster sucked at his pipe and beamed:

"I didn't know you were a writer, Jack."

"I wouldn't call myself a writer, I'm just writing. Finding what to say is not so bad because it is all there around you and you just have to observe it. The difficulty comes in organising it, shaping it and making it attractive to read."

"Indeed it does. Are you sticking to a factual account or are you trying to probe behind things a bit?"

"I'm trying to probe, as you put it, looking at different themes and so on."

"People are certainly behaving in extraordinary ways. I did myself, as you know, at that painful assembly. I've often thought about it since. I know you are not a religious man, Jack, but I've wondered if God didn't make me make a fool of myself, precisely to force me into a reappraisal of what I was doing and where I was going. He may be doing that for the whole island in a way."

Jack nodded that such a thing was vaguely conceivable. After another mighty puff which hid most of his face for several seconds, the Head continued: "It made me realise that I, and I'm sure, lots of other people of my age, that we'd..., well, stopped thinking. We were just living our lives, time-wasting towards retirement. The war will change that."

"It will jerk everybody from their rut, all right," agreed Jack. "I understand so well what you mean. In normal times on such a small island, it is difficult to stretch one's ambitions."

"There are so few peaks to get to, and, let's face it," continued Mr Stevens, "you are not always that high when you get on to them."

"It's very obvious in sport, isn't it? Our Island Champions don't usually get very far in the South of England, let alone National Championships."

"There's no political activity, either, to sharpen the mind a bit. To observe me now," said Mr Stevens a little sheepishly, "you might find it difficult to believe that I was a member of the Fabian Society when I was at college and even though I've been worn down by age and the system here, and am a churchgoing man, the idea of the twelve parish Rectors having seats in the legislative assembly still leaves me quite speechless."

"Is it wise to start me off on one of my pet subjects?"

"Indeed it isn't, but on this occasion, I am with you entirely. The clergy are there to run the church not to govern the place. Even England has packed its Bishops off to the House of Lords."

"Talking of rectors, did you see the letter in the Post last night?" asked Jack with a mischievous grin.

"About the sermon, you mean? Yes I did, quite extraordinary! First the lady in question doesn't usually come to church, she has her own chapel at the Manor, although I don't know who officiates there; and second, I wouldn't swear to this, but I thought I saw her leave early on in the sermon."

"Perhaps she walked out in protest."

"That is possible, but I am sorry to disappoint you, Jack, there wasn't much to protest about. I wonder if he will reply, He lives at Gorey; nice man."

"Much more fun to have a little controversy of this kind, than all the gloom we've got at present."

"Now, now, Jack. Ah, here's your brother-in-law to save you from provoking me, I can see the glint in your eye."

Henry came dashing from the lorry, his wellingtons catching every pebble and obstacle on the way. Papa had not known anything of the outbreak but took the view that if it got down as far as Fliquet, then it would be pretty well over the whole island.

"He's right," answered Jack, "but if the reverse applies, then the Germans might well decide to land down there. It's pretty well the nearest point to Carteret as the crow flies, after all."

Another wave of anxiety engulfed Henry.

"D'you think we should have them to stay here?"

"Who, the Germans or the crows?"

"Papa and Maman, you bloody tchu," replied a humourless Henry.

Mr Stevens calmed him a bit by suggesting that the Germans were almost certain to come by air. Several of their planes had been seen passing near the island apparently.

~

At the Birel front door Baptiste rode up, holding two letters aloft for Alice who was just coming out.

"The mail from England has started again, and it's all for you."

"For me, but who from?"

"The soldiers have voted you pin-up of the month and they are all writing to you."

"Stop being silly, Baptiste. Look, one's from Weymouth and the other one from Bradford, but it's the same writing."

Alice tore open the first one and looked at the signature.

"It's from the old lady," she said, excitedly.

"D'you mind if I stop to see what she says?" asked Baptiste.

"Of course not, it was you who sent me to see her, remember? It seems so long ago."

> Dear Mrs Birel
> I am sorry I didn't say goodbye properly but it is something you can't do well and I didn't want to upset you or myself by crying. Old women can be silly sometimes.
>
> If only you knew how much pleasure I had giving you those flowers. Perhaps my Renoir idea was silly too ,but it gave me contented feelings about beauty and capturing the moment and that is more important and real than all sorts of intellectual thinking about Art.
>
> I am writing this on the boat. The sea is wonderfully calm, a good omen, don't you think? The stewards are very nice and have wrapped me in a rug in a deckchair. We are due in Weymouth in

about an hour and a new life! I wonder if we'll see each other again.

Give my regards to your husband and to Baptiste, the postman. He is a nice man, always cheerful.

Thank you for coming to see me. It is something I won't forget. I hope I can write again.

Yours with affection,
Maud

PS: A seagull, an English one, has been very naughty. I hope I have rubbed it all off.

Alice had never seen Baptiste bashful. She almost detected a moistness in the eyes. She, herself, was unashamedly tearful.

"Poor old soul, I wonder what will happen to her?" said Baptiste.

Alice couldn't speak. She opened the other letter, which was longer. It described the arrival at Weymouth, where evacuees had only been expected on the Thursday, two days later. Maud, as Alice now knew her, had stayed in a small hotel before joining new arrivals for the train to Bradford where she was put up by a kind family.

'... when you've lived on your own in a big house with a garden and the beautiful sea not far away, Bradford is a bit of a shock. It is an industrial town and you smell soot wherever you go. But who am I to complain, my dear, when thousands of good people have been living here for years and years.

On the way up in the train I had another little whim. Do you think you could pick a flower, any flower, from my garden and press it in a book? When this dreadful war is over, I shall either come back and see it, as something which lasted in spite of armies, fear and time or, if I am too old or ill, perhaps you could send it to me then, wherever I am? I hope you don't find my request too strange. An old woman needs something to think about and I shall think of that flower.

Please write to me if you have time and those horrid Huns haven't arrived yet.

Yours tenderly,
Maud

"I'll go and fetch that flower, now," said Alice.

"D'you know," said Baptiste, "I'd like to come too. I'll pedal down there to join you when I've got rid of these other letters."

~

When Jim and Jennifer arrived from St Brelade's, almost simultaneously with Jack, back from Henry's, Alice was putting a bright red fuchsia into the Encyclopaedia. They, too, were moved by the letters and Jack remarked how strange it was that this flower, which, an hour before, had bloomed unheralded and virtually unseen, should now hold such significance in all their lives.

Jim was distressed to hear of the foot and mouth outbreak. He was at heart, a herdsman. On the few occasions when the more studious Jack had been pressed unwillingly to help him move their father's terrifyingly powerful bull, Jim used to shout and swear at his fear and ineptitude. Now Jim plied his brother with questions. Where was the outbreak? How far away? How many farms? Had they been sealed off? Had he seen any starlings? In which direction was the wind? What was Henry doing about it?

After dinner, they walked to the Constable's house.

"You're not at a meeting of the States today?" commented Jack

"Non est, mon vi, now that they've got this committee of theirs, they don't want blokes like me any more."

"But, that's ridiculous," said Jack heatedly. "You are one of 'them'. We voted you in to represent us. They aren't going to leave everything to the Rectors are they?"

"Ah no, at least they haven't done that. It's mainly the Jurats and a few Constables from around town."

Jack asked about possibly renting one of the abandoned farms, but for the moment no decisions had been taken about what to do with them. Meanwhile Jim and Jennifer could stay with them as long as they wanted. They would be a great help to Henry.

As they walked back, Jack gave his recent musings an airing with his brother.

"We've got the ten commandments, plus a few more the church has thrown in for good measure. We've got books and books of laws plus advice and opinions from teachers, doctors, parents, neighbours about what we can and can't do in life."

"Yes, yes, yes," said Jim impatiently.

"So, we all know how we should behave in normal times, but not when you are taken over by occupiers. Do you talk to them? Ask them for food? Go out with them? Disobey their orders? Make rude gestures at them? Paint slogans on their vehicles? Bash them on the head at night? Marry them? Nobody knows and, as far as I can see, nobody is going to tell us, apart from the Germans themselves."

"Calm down, Jack, or you'll have a bloody heart attack before they arrive. But surely, we've got a pretty good idea how to behave?"

"A good idea, yes, in the fairly obvious examples, but what about that middle grey area where most things tend to happen?"

"Like I said, I don't see we can do much before they arrive."

"What about food?" Jack carried on regardless. "What they call the black market? Those with money will be able to get hold of most things, but what happens to those who can't, especially in town? People will be prepared to betray a lot of principles to feed their children. I doubt if the law will be able to deal with it, nor will the punch on the nose that Baptiste and Jacko would advocate."

"You think too much for your own good, Jack, I've always told you that," chided Jim.

"Don't tell me you haven't been thinking, too, especially after you were carted down to the boat the other day."

"Apart from thinking about punching those responsible on the nose, you mean. Yes I have been thinking, but not as much as you," replied his brother dismissively.

Later, when the Evening Post arrived, the front page was full of news about Guernsey.

"I knew it," said Jack. "I'll read you that in a minute. Let's see first if the preacher has replied. Yes, here it is. Ho ho, it looks pretty good stuff."

"What are you ho hoing about?" asked Jennifer, "you sound like Father Christmas."

"Last night there was a letter from Rozel Manor complaining about the sermon at St Martin's Church on Sunday."

"I saw that," called Jim from the kitchen where he was washing some Jersey Royals, "I guessed it would tickle you."

"Well, here's the reply," said Jack. "Listen to this: 'Had Mrs Riley possessed the good manners to prevent her from leaving almost as soon as I began to speak ...' Nice start! Mr Stevens told me he thought she had left early. What a cheek! '...she might have discovered that the whole burden of my address was to do the very duty of which she writes. I understand she rarely attends the services, and, therefore perhaps, is not in a position to appreciate the value of topical illustrations in a sermon...' Neat little dig there, for a vicar!" said Jack.

"Well, I reckon she asked for it, if she left before the end," added Alice.

Jack continued: " ... I did speak of the growth of vegetables - today a very necessary part of our duty, with, as far as I know, two results. One was Mrs Riley's letter, the other the planting of 6 rows of beans by an old man who jumped out of his bed as I was outside his house tonight to tell me he had done as I suggested.'"

"I wonder who that was," asked Alice.

"Perhaps it was Adolphe, have you seen him lately?"

"He's not old!" laughed Alice. "Yes, as a matter of fact I saw him yesterday sitting on the wall during opening time. He told me he was practising being sober. Anyway, what else does the preacher say?"

"Unfortunately," sighed Jack, "he can't resist telling us that he's had a message from God. If God is dishing out messages, he might do better to explain why we are having a second war within twenty five years... Then he goes on to question her quote from the catechism."

"What was that again?"

"'To do our duty in that state of life to which it has pleased God to call us.' 'Mrs Riley,' the preacher says, 'grievously misquotes the catechism. The correct wording is 'shall call' not 'has called.' You may start life as a ploughman and God may later call you to be Prime Minister. In Mrs Riley's version, you would remain a ploughman forever.' He finishes off by saying that he was under great pressure to evacuate to England and that letters like that don't help very much."

"He sounds very upset," said Jennifer. "There's a fair amount of restrained anger there. Anyway, what's all this about Guernsey? You seemed very pleased with yourself when you saw the front page."

"The other day it said in the Post that the evacuation in Guernsey had gone off in orderly fashion. I pooh poohed the idea and Alice laid into me with accusations of cynicism. Well, just listen to this. The headline says it was no more orderly than ours. 'Latest reports disclose panicky conditions.'" Jack half read and half-paraphrased:

"What they published the other day was not wholly accurate. Copies of Guernsey newspapers have arrived at the Evening Post and they give a different story: 'scenes in town never to be forgotten, thousands thronged narrow streets, last minute arrangements, crowds besieged banks and registration centre. Throughout the night, schoolchildren have been leaving. People asked 'where shall we go?' and none could answer. The Procureur said: 'There is panic and unnecessary panic.'"

"So where did the story come from?" asked Jennifer.

"Most of the time the news from Guernsey we read about in the Post is taken from the Guernsey papers which are sent over here the next day. For the really up to date stuff, our Evening Post has a correspondent in Guernsey who phones it through. Anyway the regular bloke had left the island, in the evacuation I suppose, and they got a report from somebody else. It looks as if you can have his job, Jim."

"He's had the push, then, has he?"

"Yes." Jack continued reading. "The Post says it pointed out how misleading his report had been but he stuck to his story that what he had said in his phone call was accurate. 'It was clear to us that his conception of what constituted panic conditions differed greatly from ours. He no longer represents our interests in Guernsey.' I'm not glad exactly that it was just as bad over there," added Jack, "but it is a bit more comforting, even in a negative way, to know that we were not the only ones behaving like that."

"People are behaving funnily," said Jennifer." If you stay in the shop long enough you will hear contradictory reports about everything, and see people buying stupid things, 'in case it comes in handy,' they say."

"We've had some fights here, us."

"What, in the shop?"

"Yes," replied Alice. "Over bags of sugar and tea."

"Well, honestly, we're a bit more civilised than that in the West."

After they had eaten and made arrangements for the next day, Jack asked if they remembered the guessing game they had played in town while eating their chips some days ago now.

"When we tried to guess how near the nearest German was and what his name was and all that?" asked Jennifer.

"Yes, but, of course we have no way of knowing the answers, unless we ask all the Germans where they were that day. They wouldn't bother to answer in any case, even if they could remember. "

"Oh for goodness sake, Jack, say something sensible, if you've got to speak at all," teased Alice.

"Right, let's get some pencils and paper. We could put a few bets on, say thruppence a time and the winner of each question collects nine pence."

"Perhaps, teacher sir, you might explain first what we have to do," said Alice.

"OK, first write down which day you think the first ones are going to land here, then add morning, afternoon or night."

"What day are we today?" asked Jim.

"Tuesday."

"Is during the night Tuesday or Wednesday?" asked Jennifer.

"You're worse than the kids," laughed Jack.

"Well, tonight's for me," said Jennifer. "We'll see them when we wake up tomorrow morning, just like when it snows sometimes."

"I'd prefer snow any day," said Alice.

"We may have both if they stay till the winter."

"Let's hope the buggers aren't here that long," added Jim. "I'm for Friday morning."

Alice thought they wouldn't come until after the weekend and settled for Monday afternoon.

"That's just you left Jack."

"Sunday, whilst everybody is at church," he replied with a grin. "Now question 2, where will you see the first one?"

"At Fliquet on the beach," said Alice.

"You make him sound like a Colorado beetle."

"That's all we need, after foot and mouth."

Jack thought they'd be riding past the house on a motor cycle. Jennifer suggested the Royal Square, guarding the entrance to the States and Jim, in the pub, although he refused to specify which one.

Alice then said brusquely that they should stop playing the game before they began asking frightening questions or even thinking about them. The others readily agreed.

Jim said "It's half past nine. Shall we go and check that everything's all right with Henry's cows, Jack?"

Henry was calmer though still pacing about in the yard. Thankfully, there were no signs of disease and no bad news from elsewhere.

"It's a pity we can't disinfect soldiers in the same way," said Jack.

*Journal extract*

*Foot and Mouth*

*...All our nerves are on edge. Foot and mouth! As if waiting for the Germans wasn't enough. Is there a God just playing with us, sending us one awful scourge as the herald of another? Albany's speech, I think, in King Lear: 'As flies to wanton boys are we to the gods.' Henry is beside himself; the only positive thing is that it has taken his mind off the Germans.*

*...Had a conversation with Mr Stevens about omens and such like. I used the word surreal earlier, that was coined by a group of French writers and artists in the twenties. We are living in a totally unfamiliar, unnatural world full of menace where the abnormal has become the norm.*

*...We also talked a bit about war literature - the poems of Wilfred Owen in particular. I'm not sure, at the moment, that I want to read them again, too upsetting.*

*..Alice had two letters today from the Colonel's widow. She has arrived in Bradford which is a far cry from Jersey, but is remarkably stoic about it. She's asked Alice to keep a flower pressed from her garden. Baptiste, who is a big softee underneath, went to the Hall with Alice and they came back with a fuchsia. They are all over her garden so it seemed particularly appropriate.*

*...The reporting of events in Guernsey makes one fear for what lies ahead; a case of differentiating truth from fiction if ever there was one. It is said that Truth is the first casualty of war but how could the person passing on the news to the Evening Post in Jersey get it so wrong? And that's before the Germans even arrive! We won't be able to believe anything once Goebbel's propaganda machine gets going.*

*..The Post also carried a reply from the Gorey preacher to La Dame de Rozel's criticisms. At another time this kind of argument would be amusing. The debate, if that is the word, about the meaning of the catechism is something to reflect on, though.*

*Deep down I am wondering what I might be called to, with or without God's intervention. Andrew seems to have found his calling, so has Mr Stevens, so has the Bailiff.*

# FOURTEEN

*Wednesday 26 June, 1940*

Whatever the Germans were doing, gathering boats, assembling planes and perhaps transferring troops from other pressing needs, the farming community of Jersey was out in the fields at very first light. Foot and mouth fears had receded for the time being and the potatoes were being shipped again but it was probably the last chance to obtain much-needed cash. Henry had decided to switch his efforts from the tomatoes. The forks flew into the banked ground, flicked out the stalk; a quick shake and on to the next. Jennifer followed behind Jim, dividing the wares from the mids. Jeanne did the same behind Henry until she went in to prepare lunch. Mrs Duhamel, in fetching shorts, was helping to gather with the two boys Andrieu earning pocket money.

When the men had advanced far enough up the row, they came back and helped with the shaking and picking and carrying the baskets to the rapidly filling barrels. All were content with doing something therapeutic as well as profitable. No one actually mentioned the war and they worked and joked until about ten thirty when Jeanne re-emerged with a basket of sandwiches and scones and two cans of tea. Jim lay back on a pile of stalks and savoured the tea which always tasted better out of doors.

The Jersey Royal potatoes were almost as famous as the cow, and highly praised at Covent Garden and at markets all over England, with a taste worthy of being served at Maxims or the Café Royal, which indeed they were. Given reasonable weather in February they cropped early and in abundance in April and May in 'côtis', the name given to the small steep-sloping fields facing south, mainly at Rozel, St Catherine's and L'Etacq. The 'lates' which they were now digging, were main crop from the larger flat fields away from the coast. Those potatoes kept by the islanders for the following year's planting were usually stacked in sheds and lofts but Henry was not alone in planning security and hiding arrangements, determined that none should bring pleasure to Nazi palates.

While his relatives lifted the potatoes, Jack had managed to persuade Alice to return to the doctor. They sat together in the waiting room full of anxious-looking people. They were waiting twice over, in a sense, as the whole island had become a waiting room in itself.

The doctor had been able to reassure Alice that all was well. She would need to go back for regular check-ups and they made appointment dates. But he felt no more able than anyone else to speculate on how the situation would be in a few months time with regard to food and medical supplies. The tension in the waiting room, and especially the ten minutes or so while Alice had been in with the doctor had got to Jack. He was worried but did not want his fears to translate to Alice. Nevertheless, in the café near the market, once the bacon, egg and chips were in the care of their digestive systems, he said quietly:

"There is still time to go."

"Why are you saying that ?" asked Alice.

"What the doctor said to you about food and medical supplies and so on, I suppose."

"I don't think that changes anything. I can't believe the Germans won't supply the island with basic needs. In any case there's no knowing what things will be like in England. You haven't changed your mind about staying, have you?"

"No, I want to stay, but more than anything, I want to do what is best for you and the baby. "

"I know Jack," she said, kissing him, "but I don't want to leave my parents or the island." Then she added with determination: "I'm willing to risk it."

"I am too, but you must promise to tell me if you change your mind."

"Promise," she said with tears in her eyes.

They hugged each other tightly as they walked to the harbour to watch the potatoes now being loaded again. After the frenetic activity of the main evacuation days, all seemed quietly normal. From the wall at the end of the pier they gazed out towards the Minquiers, which could only be seen when imminent rain coincided with exceptionally low tides. Beyond the reef, about fifty miles from the island to the south, German troops might now be goose stepping where Jack and Alice, on trips to St Malo, had stood and gazed like this from the ramparts at Châteaubriand's tomb on the island of the Grand Bé.

The varying moods of the sea never fail to stir deep thoughts. When rough, it demands respect, and awe when calm; it makes one want to plunge in and caress it. The sea brought essential supplies and took away goods as witnessed by the potatoes being loaded from the long line of lorries, nose to tail on the pier. The sea took people away, as dramatically illustrated the previous week. It also brought people: many invaders over the centuries, farm workers, including Jack and Alice's grandparents and more recently, British holidaymakers. But now, once again, invaders were poised nearby.

The couple shared the beautiful view, pointing out landmarks to each other like honeymooners - Noirmont Point in the distance, the long sweep of St Aubin's Bay, likened by Queen Victoria to the Bay of Naples, the trees on the hill at Westmount and, dominating the town, the large Fort Regent, abandoned and silent. Seagulls, cranes, ropes, boats, the lapping of the sea on the steps - a peaceful harbour on a summer's day. They strolled down the line of lorries and Jack caught sight of the distinctive green and yellow vehicle of Alan Le Grand.

"Hello Jack, missus, what are you doing here, you?"

"Just come down for a look and to do a few things in town, like going to the doctor. Have I told you Alice was expecting?"

"No, but that's bloody good news, that. It needs celebrating. I'll be unloaded soon. Will you be in the Yacht?"

"Can be, but we'll stay here for a bit. It's nice to see other people working."

"Well, in that case," said Alice, "I'll sit on this bench and watch the seagulls while you get me a cup of tea from the kiosk."

"Nobody told me this fetching and carrying lark started this early. You can't even see anything showing!"

"And, no sugar, you know how they ladle it in given half a chance."

"Do you think it's safe here?" asked Jack seriously, suddenly losing his taste for banter.

"Why not?" asked Alice, looking round.

"The Germans could well fly over, think all these lorries are some sort of convoy and drop bombs on the harbour."

"Don't be silly."

"Sorry, it's just that everything looked so peaceful and normal then I suddenly realized what the reality of the situation was. Let's go and wait for Alan in the pub." Alice moved off reluctantly.

The Yacht Hotel bar was mainly full of farmers, who had already soaked enough rum and beer between them to fill one of their hundredweight potato barrels. Red faces called loudly for more of the same. Alan arrived and led Jack and Alice into the blue haze of the room. He elbowed his large frame to the bar and brought back the beers and lemonade unspilled.

"Well, cheers to you," said Alan. "It may not be the best time to have another mouth to feed, but there again, eh, it might be. If people are not going to rally round to find food for babies, we can all go and jump in the bloody harbour now."

To Alice's pleasure, Jack nodded.

"When you think of all the pain and misery people have already gone through in this war," she said, "how could we possibly be unhappy about the prospect of a baby?"

The noise in the crowded bar was almost too deafening for them to speak. After a moment or two, Alan said: "Well, there's another load gone, probably the last one, d'you reckon? This waiting for the Germans doesn't half get on your nerves, though."

Jack agreed. "People keep having second thoughts about whether they should have gone or not, but I don't think they are really afraid any more, more resigned."

"We've thought ourselves out of thinking, I reckon," added Alan. "I've had enough of imagining what might happen." Then suddenly he slapped his thigh as he remembered something.

"By cri, you talk about I made a mistake today, you. I don't know what came over me but I gave your neighbour, Belheche a lift into town. He'd missed the bus."

"That must have been an amusing journey," laughed Jack.

"A laugh a bloody minute, by cri. I don't mind people being miserable, I normally just ask them if they've got a 'ronche au tchu', a thorn in the bum, madame."

"I can understand Jersey-French perfectly well," smiled Alice

"Right, well he's got some pretty crazy ideas about the Germans. He's a real 'emmèrde'."

"You don't have to tell us," agreed Jack. "I never stay and argue with him now."

"I should have booted the half-baked twerp out of the lorry, like that I wouldn't have got as worked up as I did. The rubbish he said...'the pure will be spared ...the Germans are god-fearing people ...rid the world of scum... '"

"He's a pretty extreme case, but who knows what effect he might have on some people."

"You should have heard what he was saying about Adolphe - the gravedigger that is, not Hitler," Alan added with a smile. "He's never forgiven him for the time he fell in a grave, well you remember, you helped to pull him out. He regards him as a kind of filth that needs to be dealt with, as he puts it. Thank God for Adolphe, I say. He was a helluva laugh again in the pub last night. He told us that because of the early closing he was nearly sober and couldn't dig straight. He had another story about a cat which had pinched his tea off his plate. He's better than ITMA half the time. But to change the subject, when I went to the bar just now, I heard some blokes talking about digging air raid shelters near the airport."

"They haven't, have they?" asked Alice, amazed.

"Somebody they know hasn't dug his spuds because he was digging a shelter instead."

"We mustn't tell Henry, or he's bound to want to start digging them all round the field."

"He's not that bad is he?"

"He's got a bit better since Jeanne made him agree not to evacuate. He's got foot and mouth to worry about instead."

"That's no joke, I'm worried too, me," said Alan. "I've got a heifer in milk that should shake some of the regulars at the Show – if we have it of course."

"They might be judged by Germans who think a cow should be the same shape as Goering."

"That ugly, fat bugger, excuse my French this time, madame," said Alan.

"My brother spotted your heifer yesterday as we walked past your place."

"Well, that settles it. He knows what he's talking about when it comes to cows."

"So everybody tells me," said Jack. "Just shows how different brothers can be. I wouldn't know a bad one from a good one unless it had its udders at the front or something."

"Bougre tchu," laughed Alan.

"Jim's looking for a farm to rent around St Martin's. Do you know of any?"

"There are a few empty ones about, as you know; a good one near Faldouet. The Constable might take his finger out one of these days and sort them out; but I must go or the missus will put my dinner out in the stable again."

"She doesn't do that, does she?" said Alice, half-believing him.

"Only when it's oats and mangels. Do you want a lift back?"

They accepted with pleasure.

Back home Alice insisted on a visit to Fliquet. Without their car, halted by the new petrol restrictions, her parents would feel lonely and isolated. It promised to be the bus to Greencliff, a marathon game of nap and an overnight stay.

"I must write to the old lady, care of Bradford before we go," said Alice:

'..It was lovely to get your two letters. We were all moved by them and everybody wishes you good health and happiness in your new surroundings. Factories, coal and soot do seem a long way from our fresh, clean air. Sometimes we don't realise how lucky we are. A friend spent a walking holiday on the Moors not far from Bradford and thought it was lovely, so perhaps if you are able to get out a bit, you'll see some nice things.

Obviously the Germans aren't here yet or I wouldn't be writing. There was an awful panic to evacuate last week, just a bit after you left. Now we are just waiting again. It does get on your nerves.

I've got one piece of big news - big is the word for it, although not yet. I'm expecting. What a time! And after so long! We are thrilled though and Jack is fussing around like an old hen. If he reads this, I'm sure he'll ask how do old hens fuss around? He's not back at school yet and we went to the harbour this morning to see the potatoes being loaded again, but everybody thinks that's probably the last shipment. Perhaps some of them will find their way to Bradford.

I have collected a flower - I'll keep its identity a secret. It's in our Encyclopaedia A-H page 40 (for this year). Baptiste came with me to fetch it. I read him your letters when he brought them. Quite a surprise getting letters from England! I've never been. We always go to France if we go anywhere and I was at school in Brittany for a bit.

We are going to see my parents now. They are delighted with my news of course, although they have got a couple of grandchildren already from Jeanne and Henry.

We all send our love and kindest wishes.
Alice Birel

From the bus, they walked arm in arm down Fliquet Hill which held stirring moments of minor terror for both of them. On moonless wintry nights, the narrow road seemed the darkest place on earth as it descended through a kind of tunnel made by the trees meeting from the high hedges on both sides. In her youth Alice would run all the way home from the last bus, her heart pounding as audibly as her steps. Apart from the pitch black and the whistling and creaking of branches, the retired Brigadier from near the Tower was a menace in himself, all the more so if he was actually on the bus and offered himself as an escort.

Jack, in his courting days, would guide a grateful Alice home before facing the uphill climb back. On two of these occasions he had experienced gothic-like incidents which still tingled the blood.

Once, at the top of the breakwater path, there had been a galloping of feet and rustling of foliage before the sudden braying of an escaped mule as it hurtled out of the darkness into his bicycle. Another time, with only a last minute flurry of warning, a bat had landed on Jack's head. He stayed on the bicycle by good fortune alone. Revulsion and horror prevented him from the obvious, though ill-advised response of grabbing the bat and attempting to fling it from his head. A gamut of amateur experts on bat habits had subsequently told him that if interfered with, a bat will excrete a glue-like substance into the hair which becomes so entangled that desperate measures by a third party are needed to remove it. When Jack had arrived at the farm and told his prospective father-in-law of the incident, the latter had so doubled up with laughter that Jack thought for the moment he had felled the man who was going to pay for his wedding.

At the bend of the mule, Jack and Alice climbed through a little hedge which opened up to one of the best views of the coast of France, today very clear, the sun striking a bold strip of golden sand between Carteret and Portbail.

"Do you realise," said Jack, "that we might see the Germans come? It's sometimes difficult to realise that if they are going to come, they've actually got to get here."

"That's one of your best yet," laughed Alice. "Greek philosophy is it?"

"Thank you, and for my next trick, I'm going to make my wife disappear over this cliff! What I mean is, when we say they are coming, do we really visualise lots of boats leaving Carteret over there full of Germans and crossing that sea there, right in front of us to land somewhere here?"

"Will they arrive like the French visitors on the Gorey boat," continued Alice, "walking along the pier wondering what this or that is or will they jump out on the beach shooting and running for cover?"

"It must depend," said Jack, "on whether they've been told we are demilitarised."

"But will they believe it, even if they have been told?"

"They must, surely. They've got their own intelligence and we saw their reconnaissance planes flying over town the other day. Even so, they might still be a bit cautious."

"Well, I still find it hard to believe that a kind of armada is going to cross there," said Alice.

"It's too far-fetched."

"The act of their coming does seem incredible to envisage."

"I think it will be by plane."

"Perhaps the first ones, but you can't bring many that way. Do they know how to come in by boat? Wouldn't it be marvellous if they came at night, no lighthouse since the blackout, rocks everywhere around the town harbour, Demi des Pas, La Rocque. Imagine the people at Le Hocq or Green Island waking up one morning and seeing boats with swastikas high and dry on the rocks and soldiers shouting for help in German. Let's go in and tell papa, that will amuse him."

Maman was weeding near the portico door, where the scent of the eucalyptus was overwhelming. Jack tracked down Papa in the newly furnished sitting room, upstairs along a corridor away from the main farmhouse. Elbows firmly on the window sill, the old man was looking at the coast of France through binoculars.

"Have you seen one yet?" asked Jack.

The shock of hearing a voice nearly made the binoculars fall into the road. Papa, from his grandstand view, had been searching for trucks or boat activity at the little Carteret jetty, but it was just too far. He chuckled loudly at the thought of German boats running aground on their way around the coast to town.

"Dozens of boats have ended up on the rocks around there. They'll do well if they all get in. It could be the best fun we'll have for a while."

Jack eyed the binoculars like a child, anticipating excitedly what he might see through them.

"Have you spotted a little twerp with a moustache?" he asked.

Every hour or so for the rest of the afternoon and evening, Jack dashed up to the window and swept the French coast but to no avail. Elsewhere in the house preparations were made for the night's stay. Shrimps caught by Maman were eaten with butter then the card table was brought out and the old lady made a cast iron nap before they had barely finished getting their ha'pnies and pennies into little piles on the table.

~

In Henry's field the diggers had dug to their utmost. The lorry was loaded and driven off to the boat. Jim had milked the cows. No further outbreak of foot and mouth had occurred and all was well when Jennifer walked back to prepare a meal on Alice's grate. By then Henry had returned from the harbour having heard all about air raid shelters and was determined to set about digging one immediately. He called Jim from the stable and started pacing up and down the yard looking for a suitable site. Jeanne, who had been listening with some exasperation upstairs, finally shouted from the window:

"What's wrong with the cellar for goodness sake?"

Henry seemed disappointed that this worrying matter should find such an easy solution. Instead, he went into the stable and inspected the mouths and feet of the cattle again, then he measured the milk to see if there was as much as usual. Only then did he relax a little.

~

The headmaster's wife heard Henry talking about shelters as she returned from the shop and spent time seeking out her husband to persuade him into some sort of action on this front. He was happily hidden in a hedge reading 'For Whom the Bell Tolls.'

He looked up from time to time at the church on one side and the potato field on the other. The scene in the latter reminded him of Van Gogh's potato picking peasants, precisely because Henry and his helpers, especially the short-shorted Mrs Duhamel, did not resemble them in any way whatsoever. He knew it was old fashioned but it jarred with his idea of things that such an attractive woman should be roughing and soiling her hands and straining her back. But why not? There was no logic in this thought. Was he saying that only the plain and sturdy should work in the fields? The other woman was not unattractive either, far from it, but not, perhaps, as glamorous; pretty but not forward. He knew only too well as he thought of his pupils that certain girls were destined for a life in the fields and others for the town. How big was the step from trying on lipstick and flaunting yourself in front of boys to getting involved with the Germans?

That was a big problem to be faced. Life might become very boring and restrictive for the young, and soldiers in uniform, of whatever description, were always attractive. How many would succumb and what would happen to them, he wondered? Whatever Jack Birel might think, religion was the best bet for keeping them on the straight and narrow.

His thoughts turned to his conversation with Jack. Fancy telling him that he had been a Fabian! It had just slipped out. Still, what did it matter? The Labour people were untried in war but look at the record of the Tories! They had finally removed Chamberlain then didn't have the guts to give wholehearted support to his successor. But Churchill has proved too strong for them. Perhaps he would persuade the Americans into the war. How would Roosevelt deal with Hitler? The Russians might change sides again, not impossible. How could the Communists have made a pact with Hitler in the first place?

"Ah so that's what you are up to, sleeping in hedges and there was me thinking that teachers spent their whole time marking books," said Baptiste mischievously as he took a short cut across the field.

"Ah, it's you Baptiste, you've caught me daydreaming I'm afraid, about the war and Hitler."

"He needs his head examined, that bloke, preferably after it's been chopped off," replied Baptiste with some feeling.

"I tend to agree with you," smiled the Head, "although I don't hold much with the guillotine."

"It's a bit messy I suppose but it does a good job. If they chopped off the heads of all politicians at birth, that would stop a lot of wars if you ask me."

"It would help, I have no doubt."

"They all get too big for their boots, as Shakespeare said. By the way, Mr Stevens, Mrs Le Brun wants to know when school is going to start again," said Baptiste with a wicked little smile.

"That woman can be extraordinarily tiresome," said the head with some feeling.

"Those words are a bit long for me, Mr Stevens. I call her a pain in the neck, though I sometimes use another word. I was at school with her, so was Henry. What an 'emmèrde' she was, her beady little eyes were all over the place. The first sign of anything wrong she'd be off squealing to the teacher."

"Thank goodness her son is nothing like that anyway. He's a nice helpful boy and must be terribly sat on at home, poor lad."

"Like his father. He was at school with us, too, the poor bugger. Sorry, excuse the Shakespeare again. He's a bit short of speed upstairs is old Le Brun. I'm not a genius me, but you should have seen him doing multiplications. I've never forgotten it. He would add the numbers he was supposed to be multiplying and put a nought on the end. Every time! For ages nobody could work out what he was doing. He should be in the States."

The headmaster's rich chuckle echoed out once more and he told Baptiste that sadly, Mr Le Brun was not without his mathematical successors.

"By the way," said Baptiste, I wouldn't move from here if I was you."

"Why ever not, what's the matter?" Mr Stevens asked anxiously.

"Your wife is looking for you, she wants you to build an air raid shelter."

"Pull the other one, Baptiste, you nearly had me fooled for a minute there."

"In as much as 7 multiplied by 6 according to the Le Brun method is 130, an air...raid...shelter."

"But, but where did she get such an extraordinary idea?"

"From Henry, of course, he heard people talking about them in town and you know how he laps up stuff like that."

"But what about you, are you going to build one?"

"Me! But you're not well then. If there's a bomb with my name on it, then it will find me wherever I am. Adolphe's just told me he would shelter in a freshly d d dug grave as he called it. What are the odds on a direct hit on a gravedigger sheltering in a grave?"

The Head decided to pin his faith on Jack to help get him out of having to dig an air raid shelter. Why should the Germans want to drop bombs in the middle of St Martin's or anywhere else for that matter? If they were going to bomb then everyone should have been evacuated; but the island had now been demilitarised so that should not happen. He knew though that however cogent or persuasive the arguments against were, if his wife wanted an air raid shelter it would dominate her mind to the exclusion of all else until it was done.

Jack's absence from the house was a great disappointment, compounded by the fact that Mr Belheche emerged from next door. It was impossible to avoid exchanging a few words.

"Good evening, headmaster. No sign of the Germans yet, but it can't be long."

"You sound as if you actually want them to come," said Mr Stevens, bristling.

"I don't exactly want them to come but some people will have their come-uppance; there is only peace for the righteous. God finds a way to punish the evil doer."

The headmaster was rarely angry. This was one of the criticisms made of him by his staff; but now, he felt a surge of fire.

"I've got no intention of standing here listening to any more of your bigoted nonsense. It is treacherous talk and nothing else. People may well do something serious about it."

He walked briskly away leaving Belheche a little pale and pursing his lips. He soon found himself passing the farm where Henry and the postman were talking. Baptiste was holding a bucket of manure in his hand.

"It's fresh," he told the headmaster, pointing to one of the cows. "Marie Louise over there obliged with a smile."

"Is it for your garden?"

"No," laughed Baptiste, "it's a little surprise I've got planned for somebody."

"Oh!" said Mr Stevens, not understanding. "I've just been talking to that dreadful man, Belheche. He has got much worse."

"Ah, you too," said Baptiste.

"Why, has he said something to you?"

"No, he doesn't speak to me, but he had a go at Alan Legrand who was good enough to offer him a lift to town. It's for Belheche that I've got this present."

"What do you mean?"

"Bicycle handles, fork handles, door handles, I'll smear anything he's likely to lay his hands on."

The headmaster was quite taken aback.

"I'm not sure I approve of that," he said shaking his head, with a hint of a smile.

"Has Jack spoken to you about sorting people out?"

"He has mentioned it, yes, but I don't think he meant this sort of thing."

"He doesn't, you're right, but each to his own. I don't do things sut... what's the word?

"Subtly?"

"That's the one, bougre, I used to be a dab hand at this when I was a kid as Henry will tell you. In fact, and this could bring you round to the idea, I once smeared a streak of cat's shit on the pencil of Mrs Le Brun, or Gloria Bigot as she then was."

"You appear to be incorrigible, Baptiste."

"That's the word, too!"

While the postman performed the last al fresco deed before curfew, Maman was making yet another nap without even the ace or queen of trumps. In everybody's minds thoughts of the impending Germans were put off until restless moments between sleep.

After the old couple had gone to bed, Jack and Alice, sure that no one would be around to enforce any curfew at Fliquet, strolled down the rest of the hill to the tower near the beach and looked towards the dark shape of France with no sign of the flashing lighthouse near Carteret. Back at the farm, Jack found some writing paper and after a few pensive moments wrote a journal entry very quickly.

*Journal extract*

*..The wait for the Germans has created a state of pre-occupation in which even the most trivial acts are discussed in the context of their coming. There seems to be a temporariness about everything. I noted down a few remarks made around us as we had dinner.*

*'I'll have two lumps while they are going.'*

*'It'll be a bit tricky driving on the right past here.'*

*'We'll have to make another copy for them, I suppose.'*

*'Not having a German doctor prodding me about.'*

*'Keep going to the pictures while we can.'*

*'I don't understand German money.'*

*'We'll need a dictionary.'*

*'No jobs for anyone probably.'*

*..I'm worried about shortages of medical supplies should Alice require any at the birth. I'm getting as bad as Henry. Nevertheless I'm still certain that we have made the right decision to stay. I must make myself stop having doubts about it.*

*..It was good meeting up with Alan Legrand. He's the sort of chap to have alongside you during the occupation if that is the right expression. He's had a brush with Belheche as well. The more people have that experience the better, if something eventually has to be done about him.*

*..We've got something new to worry about: air raid shelters. If you build one, you are in effect believing that we are going to have air raids. Surely the announcement of demilitarisation, the departure of the soldiers and the King's message means that we won't be bombed? I do not intend to build one.*

*..We've all been moved by the fuchsia Alice has pressed for the old lady. It will be a symbol in the days ahead to remind us of happier summer moments to which we shall surely return.*

*..At Fliquet we had a good look at the French coast to see if there were any signs of invasion activity. Will they come across like the Spanish Armada? I think they are more likely to come by plane. However it happens, it should be a moment of high drama.*

# FIFTEEN

*Thursday 27 June, 1940*

The day promised to be beautiful, light and warm. Single wisps of cloud hovered for a moment over the island before moving on to what was now fortress Europe. Jim was up before six thirty and pumping the udders of Henry's cows. He had offered to do this to help Henry before leaving, spurred by his conscience to get back to the potatoes he had left undug at La Moye. All manner of fantasy came to him as the warm milk squirted into the bucket. He imagined the faces of the German hierarchy, Hitler, Goering and Goebbels on the stable floor when each lump of fresh dung dropped with a squelch. Then, after a breakfast treat of bacon, eggs and fried bread, he kissed his wife goodbye and set off towards the other side of the island on his bike.

Jennifer was staying a little longer to sideshoot the tomatoes, as promised, and she assured Jim she would be back on the 7 o'clock bus from town the next day.

Jack and Alice returned early from Fliquet but not before the coast of the Cotentin had been scanned again with binoculars for signs of a dawn raid. In the bus, air raid shelters were now the main topic of conversation: how deep to dig them, where to get the necessary material, how far to put them from the house. Jack, as usual made notes of the snippets he heard:

"I don't know what all the fuss is about."

"I reckon I could make a bob or two out of them."

"If one of them barks at me, I'll just bark back."

"They won't scare my Hilda, that's for sure."

"If one asks me for a cup of tea, I'll put rat poison in it."

But at about midday this north east corner of the island was stunned with an almost paralysing fear. Maman had been putting clothes out on the line and was one of the first islanders to see and hear the planes passing behind St Catherine's breakwater. In the fields the workers looked up and were cowed at the noise and sight of the large black crosses. For several days single reconnaissance planes had been observed flying over the town and harbour, but this was the first time that a formation of larger planes had been seen flying so low.

Jack, having slipped out to the shop, learned from a passing pupil who had taken a keen interest in military aircraft of both sides, that they were Heinkels. A second wave passed over as a small crowd gathered. More children plied Jack with questions. Some were crying.

What were they looking for? Was this the beginning? Were they going to land? Were they carrying bombs? Why did they keep coming back? Weren't they low. Would they crash? You could see the pilot.

The boys looked up into the sky, visibly excited as they watched the second wave of aircraft wheel south towards town.

"Are they Dorniers?" asked one.

"Dorniers aren't bombers, you silly fool," replied another.

"I know they aren't," said the first.

"Isn't he stupid, sir? I don't know why you bother to teach him."

"Is anybody going to shoot at them?"

"We haven't got any guns."

"They don't know that, though, do they?"

"Let's hope they do," interrupted Jack, "otherwise they may well start bombing us."

"My dad's gone mad about bombing. He keeps blowing a whistle and we have to run into the pigsty."

"Where do your pigs go? In your bedroom?"

"Shut your face, we haven't got any pigs, the sty's empty."

"It's got a pig in it when you run there, though."

"I'll paste your head in, Rimeur."

Jack leaned against the wall and listened.

"My old man's so sozzled half the time, he wouldn't even notice if a bomb landed on his head."

"You'd notice though, cos it would bounce off yours, it's so thick."

"How big are bombs, sir?" asked one of the serious boys.

"I'm afraid I don't know much about bombs, Denis," Jack replied.

"I mean, if one landed here, where we are, what would happen to the houses and things?"

"I would think that these houses would probably fall down and the church would be very damaged, not sure about the pub, though, it may be just too far."

"I bet the bottles would rattle a bit."

"I just reckon it would make a big hole in the road, me."

"Yes, eh, they would have to land on houses to knock them down."

"Why would they want to bomb here anyway, they'll only do the harbour or the airport."

"Don't be daft, they'll want to use those themselves."

"What do you think, sir?"

"I very much hope they won't want to bomb anything, I don't really see why they should."

"Are you digging a shelter, sir?"

"No."

"By cri, I wish we could put up a fight, don't you, Denis?"

"Let all their tyres down."

"Jimmy's got some pots of paint he's going to use."

Jack was aghast. Much as he approved the sentiments, he was still afraid that German retaliation for this sort of thing would be out of all proportion to the offence.

"D'you think we'll have to go back to school, sir?"

"Will we have to learn German?"

"The answer to both questions is I don't know" said Jack.

"I'm not learning German. They can't make you learn anything if you don't want to."

"You never learn anything anyway so you can be just as stupid in German as you are in French."

"What about you, you're as thick as a pig's backside."

Jack left them scuffling. The bell clanged as he pushed the shop door open. It took him a moment to realise how much it had changed. There was more room to move about and fewer items on display. Many of the shelves were actually empty. Mrs Pring had pinned a list above the counter of the things she had run out of: sugar, raisins, tea, margarine, lard. When she served him she said:

"Oh Mr Birel, I don't know how much longer I can go on refusing to sell things I'm trying to ration out. Some people get very angry. Then there's those coming in from I don't know where, never seen them before, usually well-dressed, in cars even, never mind the petrol. Normally people like that only buy cigarettes or something but now they want tea and sugar when they can see it's all gone anyway. Why don't you go to your own shop, I tell them."

"You mean," said Jack, "that some people are using precious petrol to go and buy things from different shops all over the island?"

"I think it's disgusting and something ought to be done about it," said the plumber's wife, one of the other customers standing behind Jack. "I reckon that while they're in the shop you tip us the wink, Mrs Pring, and we'll let their tyres down and go and fetch the Centenier."

Jack felt disheartened by all this, but before he could dwell on it there was a sudden brutal noise. He ran outside. Two planes passed over, terrifyingly low, just above the trees and the steeple of the church. Jack mentally noted the comments.

"What a racket!"

"It scares me enough just to see them. Where could we go if they start dropping bombs?"

"That's why people are building shelters. Have you got one?"

"No, but my uncle has; he's painted it red, white and blue."

"Aren't you supposed to camouflage it so that it can't be seen?"

"I'm sure we are better out in a field than indoors."

"Crouched behind the cemetery wall, that should be all right."

"A good place to die."

Gradually the little group found its way back into the shop, chattering but shaken. Not for the first time in recent days, Jack felt pangs of doubt about having stayed.

~

Even before getting up, the headmaster had known he was in for a trying day. Air Raid Shelters dominated his wife's mind. In the bathroom and at breakfast he tried arguing, staying sullen, wondering whether to use his most effective weapon, that of disappearing for the day, knowing full well that it would only make things worse when he got back. He held out for the morning, though having to waste it completely by putting up a pretence that he was collecting the necessary materials and tools with which to do the job.

Any thoughts that his efforts would suffice for the day, were quickly dispelled when the planes flew low, almost at ground level across the field behind the school, then up over the trees and the church. There followed a long miscellany of worry and complaint from his wife, before he realised the important ace he had up his sleeve. Since he hadn't the faintest notion of how to build an air raid shelter, all he needed to do was make a start, fail hopelessly, then persuade his wife either to abandon the idea or get someone in to do it. Before then the Germans would probably have arrived and the problem would no longer exist.

~

Adolphe, in the pub, had reduced Jacko, Mary and Baptiste to a state of weakness with laughter. Earlier that morning he had, as usual, been buying his flask of rum at the shop when Belheche had come in before catching the bus. He had said something about 'shit' which surprised everyone.

"W w we couldn't understand w what he w was on about. Then he looked at m me when someone mentioned air raid s shelters and s said 'the righteous have n n nothing to fear.'"

"So, what did you tell him?" asked Baptiste.

"I s said, s s since you reckon they are g gonna g get m me, and n not you, I'll c come and sh shelter on your d doorstep when they s s start b bombing."

"Good one Adolphe," laughed Mary.

"I tell you what," Baptiste added, with a wicked smile," at closing time tonight, let's all go and huddle up in his doorway and when he comes out, we'll tell him it's the best place for us to stand because we know the houses of the righteous are not going to be bombed."

Amid loud, agreeing laughter, more drinks were ordered but before they were consumed the drinkers, too, were drawn outside by the planes flying over. They were still discussing them and by how much they had missed the church steeple when Alan Legrand drew up and told them that the States had lifted the curfew.

"Why's that then?" asked Baptiste

"Don't ask me," Alan replied, "unless it's to allow people to go outside if the island gets bombed at night."

There were further jokes about being hit on the head and Adolphe promised to dig them good graves. The men walked briskly back to the bar to cheer their flagging spirits.

~

At Fliquet, Papa had seen the planes coming from France. He had difficulty keeping them in the sights of his binoculars, but once, briefly, he was shocked to catch a fleeting glimpse of a pilot, a young face of no more than twenty.

That evening, reading the 'Post', listening to the wireless, playing cards or dominoes, drinking in pubs or praying in churches, nobody felt safe. Blackouts were checked, neighbours quick to spot the slightest amount of light escaping like a leak from an offending window. Gas masks were fetched from cupboards, dusted and tested, revealing that elaborate hairstyles or beards undermined the very essence of the mask - that it should be airtight. Some families prepared to sleep in their shelters. Fear spread rapidly and many questioned the wisdom of their decision to stay on the island. Old arguments began again with the added bite of the bombing threat.

Although most people had now reached a numb resignation, prepared to take whatever came, others packed their bags ready to leave on the mailboat the following afternoon. Tension had built up to a new breaking point.

Geoff Le Balle, one of Jack's former pupils, now nearly twenty and working in an insurance office in Town, came round to tell him that his two elder brothers were going to join up and that he was leaving for England with them. He was a quiet, shy boy, difficult to imagine in uniform fighting anybody.

"We didn't go last week, you know, because my mother got upset and Paul didn't think much about the idea of going into the army."

"So why have you all changed your mind?" asked Jack.

"Just what we've read and seen and heard, I suppose. We've been talking about it every night and it now just seems the right thing to do somehow."

"Well, good luck," said Jack. "You've left it a bit late, though, haven't you?"

"I know, but in a way, I suppose, the Germans being so near to coming is probably what made us decide."

"Well, I hope they don't do anything to the boat tomorrow, Geoff."

"Now we've decided to go we're going and that's it."

"Have you got time for a drink to see you off, or do you want to get back home?" asked Jack.

"I'd love a drink with you, Mr Birel."

"I'll just see if my wife wants to come too, you know her, don't you?"

Alice agreed readily, not wanting to stay indoors on her own on an evening like this. They left a note for Jennifer who was eating at Henry's after a long day in the tomatoes.

Although the curfew had been lifted, it did little to bring people out. In the early days of the panic people had been grappling with the question of whether or not to leave. They needed opinions and answers to questions, reassurance. They seemed to thrive on rumour and doubt. Now, most of those remaining on the island were resigned to wait for whatever happened by retreating to their homes or shelters.

For those in the pub, the conversation was dominated by the planes and the continuation of the long ridiculous argument over the exact height they had passed over the church. Someone commented that he was surprised to see crosses on the planes and not swastikas. Adolphe claimed to have seen a swastika amidst general laughter that he had not even gone outside when they flew over.

"No wonder all the glasses were empty when we got back," said Baptiste.

"Geoff here is off tomorrow," announced Jack.

"Off where?" somebody asked.

"To England, you silly bugger. Come on Mary, give this lad whatever he wants before he goes off to war."

Geoff felt embarrassed to be the centre of attention.

"So your brothers are going too?" said Alice.

"Yes, I don't think any of us would leave if we didn't all go together."

They were interrupted by Jennifer, popping her curly head of hair around the door, tired and still smelling of tomato plant.

"It doesn't matter how hard you scrub, it takes ages to go," she said.

"Here's the only person doing any work around here," said Jacko, "I'll give you a drink on the house."

"By cri," said Baptiste, "all these planes must be affecting his head."

"I think he's just taken a fancy to her," said Mary.

"In that case, if he's going to leave you, let me know," chirped Baptiste.

"Changing the subject," said Alice, "it's a pity they can't broadcast 'Music While you Work' into fields. It's very good that new programme."

"I heard a bit of it this morning when I stopped somewhere for a cup of tea," said Baptiste.

"Oh yes, and where was that may I ask?" asked Mary.

"Never you mind, you. You're not the only one I've got my eye on; both eyes in fact. It's not fair that blokes like us who work outside miss out on these programmes. I reckon all the ladies should stand on their doorsteps and sing me a song when I arrive with their letters."

As she started her drink, Jennifer told them that Henry was becoming more and more obsessed with the fear of being bombed.

"He keeps saying that he should have joined the ARP because he doesn't know enough of what to do if the kids get injured. He went on and on about it, I had to tell him to shut up in the end."

"That ARP stuff is all right in town," said Baptiste, "but if anything happens here either we'll all be dead or someone will come out and help us."

Jennifer turned to Jack and Alice: "Anyway, Henry's got some books out of a cupboard, you remember the ones the English government issued last year?"

"The ones about blackout and gas masks you mean?"

"Yes. This one's called 'Protecting your Home against Air Raids.' He read us bits at tea-time, nice and cheerful, it was. It says things like 'the head of the house must be like the captain of a ship.' He's taken that to heart."

Baptiste, now slightly drunk at the bar, called for a packet of fags and looked eagerly inside for a picture of Clara Bow. He swore loudly as he held up the cigarette card. It was an ARP advert explaining how you put a broken leg in a splint. Baptiste was furious. He had heard more than enough of the ARP and bombing for one day. In his opinion everyone had gone bloody mad.

Donald Huquet, standing quite near him at the bar, said quietly but proudly, that he was in the ARP and that before long Baptiste might well be glad of his services. The postman was finally placated when Donald listed all the things he had been taught to do since he had joined: how to stop blood, put splints, carry injured people, deal with hysteria, the easiest way to move masonry, how to detect gas, recognise gas burns on the body, put out fires, throw incendiary bombs away from buildings using dustbin lids and pitchforks and even how to deliver babies.

As the others murmured their admiration for Donald's knowledge and calm, Baptiste reluctantly agreed that the ARP might render a useful service.

"I'm on call to go anywhere in the island where a bomb might fall," added Donald." I might even go to your place"

The atmosphere remained tense, though, with so many fears having been exposed in a raw state. Geoff said he had to leave and, for a few moments, some semblance of gaiety returned as they bought him another beer and wished him well.

At closing time the mood was subdued and they forgot their earlier plan of congregating on Belheche's doorstep. Adolphe was, in any case, way past congregating anywhere.

Henry finally persuaded Jeanne to bring the children down to sleep in the cellar. Many others did the same, although deep down, they could not really believe they would be bombed. The planes flying so low had terrified them and made them acutely aware of the devastating possibilities but the islands were demilitarised, undefended, the whole point of the King's letter.

Jack felt very twitchy as he started his journal for the day.

*Journal extract*
*Planes*
*...The wait goes on. It is beginning to get on everybody's nerves. All I want to keep writing is 'Will it be tonight?' But this could continue for some...*

*...Had another look at the Cotentin through papa's binoculars before leaving Fliquet. It was annoying because, although the weather was quite good, it was not one of those really clear days when everything is sharply focussed. There may be Germans with field glasses looking back at us. What do they know of Jersey ? Before they got to Carteret, from where they can see the island, did many of them know that Jersey existed?*

*...We all had a bit of a fright when the planes flew over. It was unsettling to see several in formation, to imagine them on a bombing raid. I happened to be talking to some boys from school and there is no doubt they were excited rather than scared by the planes. For mothers with young children, though, the noise and the menace was very upsetting. I was pleased that Geoff Le Balle came to say goodbye. Thankfully he didn't want me to speak to his mother. Three sons going off together, she must be beside herself with worry. Donald Huquet put Baptiste in his place describing all he had learned in the ARP. It made us apprehensive and reassured at the same time, in case his services are needed. Talk of air raid shelters is everywhere.*

*We can only hope that the news of the demilitarization of the islands has reached the Germans and that they will respect it.*

# SIXTEEN

*Friday 28 June, 1940*

The unease returned, as if uninterrupted, when people awoke, having again slept fitfully and fearfully. At bus stops and along pavements men and women informed each other with nervous little laughs, that they had survived the night. They spent much of the morning, however, stealing glances into the sky, as if ashamed at being caught looking towards the horizon, yet unable to suppress the need to do so. By dinnertime the scare of bombing had receded enough for the population to return to the previous worries of waiting for the Germans to land their troops.

Jennifer stayed at St Martin's for a midday meal of grilled salted cod, a treat generally reserved for cold winter evenings but Alice had exercised a pregnant whim to have some. She and Jeanne had been bolstered by Jennifer's presence, as had the regulars at the pub. She had large laughing eyes, curly hair and a friendly word for everyone. This exterior never entirely hid a romantic streak and emotional nature. She loved people deeply and cried as often in joy as in sorrow. Staying with Alice had turned her mind readily to the thought of having a child herself in spite of the uncertainty of the existing conditions, as the Evening Post kept calling them.

She was back to her good-humoured self after the shock and worry of those few hours when it seemed that her husband Jim had gone, perhaps for ever, whisked down to the boat in the back of an old lorry. She intended to shop in town later in the afternoon before taking the bus home from the Weighbridge to La Moye.

After Jennifer's departure Alice walked up to the farm where several wicker baskets of blackcurrants, picked the previous day, stood full and spilling, waiting to be coaxed into jam. When she arrived to help stir, sugar and put the dark liquid into jam jars, she was pained to see Henry pacing from kitchen to stable, his face unshaven, hands unable to rest. The German planes had given him something new and dramatic to worry about, now that his tomatoes were side-shooted, potatoes shipped, his cows milked and, thankfully, no sign of foot and mouth.

He threatened to be an unwelcome hindrance to the agreeable task of making jam, so the women were particularly grateful when Alan Le Grand stopped his lorry in the yard to borrow an extra rope to secure his load of potato barrels. He suggested that Henry might accompany him to the Weighbridge to see what new confusions were afoot for the island farmers. It was likely that fewer cargo boats would be available and merchants might be reluctant to buy produce and send it on the potentially hazardous journey to England, now that the enemy was entrenched in Cherbourg.

~

Jack sat at his desk and tried in his journal to do justice to the nature of the times. How did one reconcile the earnest hope that the Germans did not come at all with the opposite wish that the sooner they came the better, to put an end to worry and uncertainty? How did one reconcile also the fear of being bombed with the belief that such a thing could not possibly happen? With no lessons to prepare either, Jack soon became restless and distracted, looking for something to lure him away from the empty page.

A spot of low water fishing at La Rocque would not only supplement a dwindling larder but would provide useful practice for catching fish in the days ahead. He wasted no more time, called in at the farm and holding his nose away from the bubbling purple liquid told Alice where he was going. She was thrilled that he had even thought about finding food. "I won't settle for anything less than a lobster, or better still, two lobsters."

As he freewheeled down Gorey Hill, the majestic castle of Mont Orgueil came into view, high on an escarpment of solid granite rock guarding the channel between the island and France. Its long brave history of spirited defence, often under siege, would be of little use today in repelling the Germans. It would take more than arrows and cauldrons of boiling oil to stop this enemy. He turned the hairpin corner near the delightful little harbour which lay at the foot of the castle and continued cycling briskly past the old railway station, along the side of the golf course and about two miles on towards La Rocque. He parked his bike against the slipway near the Seymour Inn and headed through the gulleys between the rocks towards the Tower of the same name a mile or two off shore.

Alice had been joking about the lobsters but it made him realise that she was managing to supply meals without fuss. How long before they needed to rely fully on the resources of her parents' and sister's farms? The least Jack could do was forage for fish. If he didn't catch a lobster, which required the experience, skill and nerve displayed by fishermen like his uncle, who was known as the 'King of La Rocque,' he should, at least, come back with a feed of shrimps and winkles.

As he walked between the rocks his mind jumped to many things. This anarchy of the brain interested him; especially its ability to flit through half-thoughts, mental glimpses, sometimes clear, sometimes jumbled as if in a dream, triggered off unaccountably by a stone, a leaf, a noise, a gull or piece of seaweed. Jack had only read reviews of the recently published 'Ulysses' but he could understand something of what Joyce was trying to do.

The sun twinkled on the pools of water lying on the sand and he needed to shade his eyes to look straight across towards the French coast. Thankfully the sky was free of planes; only detached and shapeless clouds drifted about, parting and reforming in the blue. Nevertheless, he felt suddenly alone and apprehensive. He nearly turned back.

~

At La Moye, Jim was hot and kept wiping his forehead with his sleeve. From his vantage point in the field, he looked occasionally across towards the town.

Jennifer had told him that she would catch the seven o'clock bus from the Weighbridge but, having finished her shopping earlier and anxious to get home, she gathered pace along the pavement past the Post Office and was the last to step onto an earlier bus before it pulled away. With parcels and bags bouncing all over her, she sank back in her seat, quite out of breath but relieved at having saved herself an hour's wait.

Jim plied his fork into the potato stalks with a steady rhythm. Only a couple of rows remained along the privet hedge and he thought with pleasure that he would finish in time to meet Jennifer at the bus stop, something he was eager to do. As he lay alone the previous night, he had realised that this was the first time since their marriage that they had slept apart. He had stayed awake for a long period in a kind of delayed shock, his thoughts returning to the twist of fate which had taken him to the foot of the departing ship's gangway. How near to being separated from his wife for an indeterminate period! He usually treated life on a casual basis, mixing good sense with fatalism and easy goingness, rarely probing, like Jack, into philosophical niceties, but the recent events had forced him into worrying a little more deeply about existence. This confused buzzing in his head had made him miss his wife all the more.

~

In town at the Yacht Hotel, on the northern edge of the large open Weighbridge facing the harbour, Alan Le Grand and Henry were gratefully taking their first sips of Mary Ann. They had spent the best part of the afternoon queuing to get the potatoes loaded. Conditions on the pier had reverted to the near-chaotic by a rush of new evacuees frightened into leaving by the talk of air raid shelters and the low flying aircraft the previous day. Leavers and well-wishers, tearful girls and worried parents, milled to and fro in the vicinity of the mail boat, the 'Isle of Sark.' Alan wished 'good luck' to several acquaintances and 'good riddance' under his breath to a well-known local pest. Among the last to board were the three Le Balle brothers, Geoff following the two older lads after a last affectionate farewell to his mother on the quay. In this disorganisation, the potato merchants, already depleted in number, walked along the loosely-organised queues pointing at a single cargo boat. Nobody actually seemed to know whether any further produce was going to be taken aboard. Arguments flared over very little, accompanied by arm waving and shouting. Patience was at a low ebb. Alan and Henry were especially glad therefore at the eventual successful completion of business and now they were perched on bar stools wondering if they should have another.

At about a quarter to seven, Jack was on his way home with a variety of shellfish: winkles, razor fish, cockles, shrimps and a moderately sized crab but no lobsters.

He was pushing his bicycle up the steep hill from the harbour at Gorey and had stopped at the end of the small row of houses to take in the wide panoramic view of the bay of Grouville, given the title 'Royal' by Queen Victoria.

He heard the planes before he saw them. They were hidden behind the castle having come from further north up the Cotentin. Not the same type of plane as the day before, these looked larger and more menacing. The steady unpleasant rhythm of their engines took the ugly black bodies towards the far end of the bay where they turned inland over La Rocque. Jack had a sickening feeling in his stomach as he saw something fall from one of the planes and explode near the little jetty not far from where he had been just a short time ago.

~

A few minutes later, in the Yacht Hotel, Henry was just stepping off the bar stool to 'pay a visit' as he called it, when, without warning, there was a sudden deafening roar not very high up. Nobody moved. There was no time for reassuring words that these reconnaissance planes were starting to get tiresome. Distant crashes and cracking of wood were followed by an enormous ear splitting explosion and the shattering of glass on to the tables from all the windows near the door. Henry and Alan joined the others diving instinctively to the floor. The word 'bomb' was the only one to be heard above the screaming and breaking of glass. Further explosions interrupted the rat-tat-tat of machine gun fire not far away. People felt their hips and legs to see if they were still in one piece and made strangulated sounds as they coughed in smoke and dust.

Henry cried out at the sight of the four regulars who had been playing dominoes near the window. They were old men, passing the time of life with some of the few enjoyments they had left, a glass of stout and a game they were good at. Their drinks were spilt and the brown froth dribbled on to an ashen face near the table leg. The sight of him and the other three, blood seeping from gashes, limbs possibly broken, badly affected Henry.

'They were just sitting there playing dominoes' went round and round in his head. Next to him Alan said:

"At least they're not dead and nor are we."

Most of the customers remained dazed on the floor, having pulled a table or chair over their heads as a kind of makeshift protection. For a few moments nobody moved, numbed by the shock of it all and there was complete silence before a single sob startled the uninjured into beginning to tend to those who had suffered.

The worst fears had been realised. St Helier, small, undefended and helpless, had joined the growing list of towns to be bombed and strafed from the air, a grim innovation of the twentieth century. It was a clinical, efficient announcement of the imminent German arrival.

~

Jim heard the explosions from the potato field at La Moye. Black smoke rose from near the town and he could see large aircraft flying in his direction. The pickers with him also looked up, shocked by the noise of the engines and, a few minutes later, by the unfamiliar sound of what proved to be machine gun bullets whistling through the tomato plants in the adjoining field. One of the planes had given a final burst of fire as it left before crossing over the sand dunes which ran along the west coast of the island.

Jim glanced at his watch and his whole nervous system tightened with a knotting fear. It was just after a quarter to seven. Jennifer would be about to catch the bus at the Weighbridge. They must have been bombed. He could see even more smoke rising. She could be dead or injured. How could he find out? What could he do? Why had they chosen to come then? He got up, not bothering to dust himself down and told Dacourt who had come into the field a few moments before:

"Look, I'm going home, I don't know what to do, Jennifer might have been in that bombing in town."

By now, as panic gripped him, he couldn't think rationally any more and had persuaded himself that something awful had happened to his wife. He started to run, catching his foot in clumps of earth and potato stalks.

Then to Jim's relief and joy, he saw Jennifer herself run into the field. She had heard the noise and seen the planes as she was getting off the bus a few hundred yards down the road. She had stuffed her shopping in a hedge and run to Jim. As they hugged each other, two more planes flew over and they dived to the ground. Jennifer had her good dress on and, once the sky was cleared of menace, they laughed a nervous laugh at the incongruity of the scene.

They clutched each other and watched the Heinkels flying in formation towards Guernsey, where some minutes later large black palls of smoke rose to suggest that the fuel tanks by the harbour of St Peter Port had been hit. On the way one plane left the others and dived out of sight, guns firing, before climbing again to rejoin the formation.

~

In Jersey the real horror was at the Weighbridge. The large space near the harbour had presented an obvious target. Smoke and dust still clutched at throats and eyes. Glass fell periodically from the windows of the Premier Estate Agency on the corner. Alan and Henry emerged with others from the bar and saw people of all ages getting up with difficulty but several continued to lay injured and moaning. Pitiful screams came from Mulcaster Street where a crowd was beginning to gather on the pavement. The police were already there and two more cars sped, bells ringing, towards the pier itself. The scene was one of barely suppressed hysteria. An ambulance arrived and began to push the crowd to one side like a little boat advancing through seaweed. The word went round that two people were dead and many injured. The smell of smoke, the jostling, the cries, the falling glass all contributed to a new panic. More police arrived to cordon off the pavement and begin examining the bullet marks and blood stains. Large brown stretchers were lifted out of the ambulance and the crowd surged forward again with that morbid curiosity crowds have, to see horror at first hand, however appalling.

A young constable was doing his best to control the throng but he was just as shaken as everyone else. By now the ARP were on the scene and beginning to deal with the injured. Cries of hate mingled with the moans of pain; that so many innocent people were suffering for no reason at all. The savagery of what had happened surpassed the most fearful speculation. Even Henry, who had picked up a piece of stained glass blown from the Town Church window, had not, in his worst moments, imagined anything like this. He stared at the red and blue glass which he twisted in his shaking hands. Why hadn't he gone to England instead of listening to all the others? It was so obviously dreadful to have stayed. He always knew the Germans would bomb. He gazed about him, his whole system in a state of shock.

Alan's description of the crowd's behaviour would provide depressing material later for Jack's diary; many people gaping and gawking and pressing forward. Time had frozen into a grotesque tableau.

Only strenuous physical police effort finally edged the crowd out of Mulcaster Street into the open Weighbridge where they met a similar group being moved with equal reluctance from the pier itself. The two waves of people mingled, interchanging information, some real, some imagined. From the many figures quoted, Alan concluded that three more victims had died on the pier. Henry was prepared to believe it was many more.

A loud voice was heard to warn that there was nothing to stop the bastards coming back and, only then, did distressed parents start pulling their children towards places hopefully more safe.

Alan was steering Henry towards the old pier near the Commercial Buildings where Norman's Timber Store was on fire. In the smaller harbour a few yards in front of the store, masts and bits of wood were floating next to damaged little boats.

It was some time after the bombs had fallen that Alan thought of phoning their families but the few telephone boxes had long, terrified queues in front of them. Mary eventually took the call from Alan and was soon so white-faced and agitated that the customers at the bar stopped drinking, looked at her and waited. With tears in her eyes she told them that Alan and Henry were OK but that the Weighbridge had been bombed and there were many dead and injured.

"The bloody salauds," said Baptiste, "they must know we are demilwhatever it is."

"War is bloody war," said Jacko from behind the bar. "What's to stop them doing whatever they like?"

Someone suggested hopefully that it might be a warning of what would happen if Jersey didn't toe the line. Another saw it as just the beginning of being blasted out of existence.

"I'll go and tell Jeanne that Henry is OK," offered the postman.

Jeanne heard him ride into the farmyard and opened the door.

Baptiste said quickly. "Don't worry, Henry and Alan are all right."

"What do you mean they are all right, why shouldn't they be all right?"

Baptiste passed on as best he could the phone message about the bombing at the harbour.

Jeanne and Alice plied Baptiste with questions but he only knew the barest details. There was a long queue for the phone apparently and Alan needed to be quick.

"Are you sure people were killed?" Jeanne asked again in desperation.

"Alan said at least five. They saw two put in an ambulance."

Jack arrived from La Rocque just as Baptiste was getting back on his bike to take the message to Alan Le Grand's wife. He had been rehearsing how he might tell Alice calmly about the bombing at La Rocque but he felt his voice cracking as he pointed out how near he could have been. Alice clung to him trembling with the shock of what was happening.

Jeanne felt the full realisation of the effect it would have on her husband.

All morning he had gone on endlessly about bombing as he walked up and down near the shed scratching the back of his neck and the bridge of his nose. She knew all the signs. He would blame them all now for not wanting to evacuate and would redouble his gloom and foreboding.

"He'll want us to stay in the shelter all day and all night," she added tearfully. Her unhappiness began to drain Jack and Alice's emotional strength. All three sat in the darkening room, like mourners at a funeral, each with sad and confused thoughts; Jeanne to fret about her husband, Alice to fear for her unborn child and Jack to wonder once more if they had done the right thing by staying.

He shuddered as he thought of the hand of fate which had grasped at least five people. They had got up that morning and gone to work as on any normal day. Then one by one, they converged from different places, for different reasons, to a spot where they were singled out for a violent and historic death. He recalled his conversation with Andrew about the bombing in the Spanish Civil War and the picture he had seen in a magazine of Picasso's controversial painting, 'Guernica.' Only two days before, Alice had not taken seriously his questioning whether it would be safe to sit on the pier having a cup of tea.

He needed to leave the tension of the room and satisfy himself that the sky was not scarred with a new wave of bombers. Mr Stevens saw him emerge as he walked despondently back from the shop to the school.

"Have you heard the harbour has been bombed?" he asked Jack.

"Yes and I'm pretty sure I saw a bomb fall at La Rocque. I was coming back from low water fishing near Seymour Tower and was looking across the bay from below Gouray Church when I saw the planes in the distance and something dropped from one of them. I'd have been there had they come half an hour earlier. They were silent for a moment then Mr Stevens said with a sad shake of the head: "So what we thought wouldn't happen has happened. It's a terrible, terrible thing. What about the casualties, do you know?"

"Baptiste has just told us that five people were killed in town," said Jack.

The headmaster turned pale and placed his hands on the wall to steady himself.

"Oh no!" he said in a strong whisper, "such unnecessary, futile death. Pray God there were no children. What could they possibly hope to gain by it? We've declared ourselves to be demilitarised."

"Perhaps the Germans don't know that," suggested Jack.

"But they must know surely."

"I don't think Hitler is too bothered about protocol any more."

Their conversation was interrupted by the appearance, running towards them, of a hand-wringing Mrs Stevens.

"Oh dear, oh dear, I rather fear my wife has heard about it," said the headmaster.

"There you are!" she called as she got nearer. "Why aren't you at home to answer the phone? It's terrible, that poor boy, I just didn't know what to do, where were you? How am I supposed to manage things like that?"

"Calm down, Elizabeth, what is the matter?" he tried hopefully, but his wife clutched a little lace handkerchief to her mouth and began crying.

Jack thought it best to invite them into the farmhouse in spite of the heavy atmosphere. A tot of brandy was pressed on to the distressed Mrs Stevens and, in the tense silence each person wondered if the news she was about to impart could be worse than what they already knew.

"That boy who came to see you yesterday," she started, "the tall one with the fair hair."

"Geoff Le Balle, you mean?"

"I don't know his name, you know I never remember names."

"What's happened to him Mrs Stevens?" Jack asked uneasily.

"He's telephoned from Guernsey," she said.

"But why should he do that?" asked her husband, unable to stop himself from interrupting.

"It's terrible," said Mrs Stevens, sobbing again into her handkerchief, "the Germans bombed the harbour in Guernsey while the mailboat was berthed there."

She chewed at the lace as if trying to extract morsels of strength from it. Nobody wished to break this lengthening silence as they tried to imagine the horror of a boat full of passengers exposed to aerial bombardment. Mr Stevens could bear the silence no longer.

"Well, what happened? What happened?" he asked impatiently.

Jack added a more specific question. "Did the boat get hit?"

Mrs Stevens began a torrent of barely coherent sentences which, nevertheless, gave a graphic picture of the scene as she knew it.

"They dropped bombs everywhere, he said the boat wasn't hit, it's gone, that's the trouble, the boat had guns which fired at the planes, there are lots of dead he said, he ran with his brothers down the gangway to help the injured, he was sick, he said, he will never forget it, I don't wonder the poor boy, but the boat left the harbour and went out to sea, they thought it would be coming back but it didn't and he's stuck there with his brothers. He'd like somebody to tell their parents."

Attempts to elicit further information by questioning Mrs Stevens were met with more tears and despairing gestures. The essential facts appeared to be that the harbour in Guernsey had been bombed while the 'Isle of Sark' was berthed there and, because the boat had then left for England without warning, the brothers Le Balle had been stranded with a few others, after leaving the vessel to help the injured on the pier.

Jack went out to gather his thoughts, to mull on the dreadful irony of a simple act of humanity which resulted in the brothers being abandoned on another island as vulnerable as the one they had left, but without their homes, families or possessions. He was crouching in the yard flicking stones at an old rusty tractor wheel when Henry shuffled in from the road. They looked at each other for a few moments in silence then Jack said: "It must have been bad."

Henry only nodded and Jack became trapped in the painful frustration of finding something else to say. In normal circumstances words emerge as if by themselves, the mind seeming effortlessly to provide. Now faced with Henry's muted misery, Jack grappled with the need to say something, anything. The more he strove, the more it became impossible, his head filled with wordless air, black images and a silence which threatened to last forever. Fortunately the sound of his greeting had been enough to bring out Jeanne. She ran into her husband's arms and hugged him.

Back in the gloom filled room she sat him in the faded red armchair. Hands clasped under his chin, Henry stared at a point just below the mantelpiece and the others held their breath nervously, waiting for him to speak. Eventually Jeanne asked: "Where were you when the bombs fell?"

"In the Yacht," replied Henry in a way which suggested that brief answers to questions was the most they could expect from him. The children chose this moment to come in to greet their father. He clutched them soundlessly and tightly before Alice took them back outside.

"What happened in the pub?" asked Jack.

"The windows were blown in."

"Was anybody hurt?"

The memory of that moment was too much for Henry who finally allowed his pent up emotion to come out in loud sobs. "There were four old men," he eventually said, "playing dominoes and drinking stout. The explosion knocked them down. They just lay there with blood on their faces and beer dripping on to them from the table. We didn't know quite what to do to help, then the ARP arrived and they were wonderful."

He held his head in his hands and sank deep into the chair.

"After that I went out with Alan into Mulcaster Street. They had been firing machine guns there, you could see the marks on the wall. Look, I can't stop shaking," he added as he held out his trembling hands. "To see people dead like that who had just been walking down the road. It could have been any of us."

Now that he had started he went on to tell them of the police, the ARP and the ambulances, the scene on the pier, the fires and boats destroyed in the harbour, the smell, the smoke, the cries of pain. He had heard that someone had been killed up on Mount Bingham and that bombs had been dropped at La Rocque.

"I'll never forget it, never," Henry kept repeating. "Everything was thrown upside down in front of my eyes."

It seemed best to leave him to sit quietly with Jeanne. Alice said she would stay a little longer to look after the children. Mr Stevens took his wife home and Jack thought he would pass on these bits of information to the people in the pub. As he walked around the churchyard he was again struck by the irony that a beautiful Summer evening could settle seemingly undisturbed after a day of such awful horror.

Alan was the centre of attention at the bar where the day's events were being hotly discussed. Although the room was far less crowded than in the week leading up to the evacuation, Jack recognised two characteristics which remained unchanged. While the quiet introverts were totally quiet, looking down into their glasses, the talkers could hardly contain their opinions and questions. At a convenient pause, Jack asked if they had heard the news from Guernsey. They were already aware of the extensive bombing there and of the role played by the 'Isle of Sark' but surprised and dismayed to hear of the plight of the Le Balle brothers.

"And to think that Geoff was in here just last night, you," somebody said.

"At least he's alive," said another. "That's more than can be said for the poor blokes down the Weighbridge."

"A lot can happen in a day," mused someone else. "He leaves his parents and his home, gets bombed by the Jerries, sees people dead and injured all around him and gets left behind in a place he doesn't know. They probably won't get to England now and who knows when or if they will get back home? It's a good job his brothers are with him, the poor bugger."

At that moment Baptiste burst in. His face expressed that he had something important to say and he spat the words out angrily. "The bloody bastards have shot dead one of the crew in the lifeboat between the islands."

The others were stunned in horror. The unnecessary deaths by the harbour had been hard to take, but to attack a recognisable and defenceless lifeboat was barbaric. It was like attacking an ambulance. Everyone spoke at once to condemn this act of inhumanity. The more pessimistic saw it as a portent of worse to come and many, not helped by drink, began again to regret having stayed. Mary was terribly upset and left the bar to cry in the kitchen. At nine o'clock Jacko turned on the wireless and all the customers hardly dared breathe as the newsreader solemnly declared that although the Channel Islands were a demilitarised area, they had been subjected to air attack and many civilians had lost their lives.

"Well, they should know now that we are demilitarised, the bloody salauds. One of them at least must listen to the news."

"It won't make any difference to the bastards," said Baptiste loudly.

"I thought you were telling us the other day that they were just ordinary blokes like you and me," Jacko said more aggressively because of the tension.

"Well I was bloody wrong," Baptiste replied with considerable feeling. "No English pilots would bomb the crew of a lifeboat."

"I thought you said he'd been shot," somebody queried.

Baptiste turned on the man viciously. "What's the bloody difference, it was done deliberately and the poor sod's dead."

"I wish I'd evacuated, me," expressed a youngish farmer standing near the bar. "I would have gone last week but the missus didn't want to go. I bet she's changed her tune now."

"Why should you want to go now particularly?" Jack asked him.

"I don't want my head shot off that's why. I was in town too, me, you know. The only dead bloke I've ever seen was my grandfather and he was well over eighty and lying peaceful in clean sheets. The bloke I saw in town had blood all over him and was lying twisted on the pavement."

"It must have been bad."

Alan Le Grand returned from the toilet to catch the tail end of the conversation.

"But there's not much chance of them getting you, mon vi."

"Why not?"

"Well, think of the chances of you being just where the bomb falls," added Jacko.

"That's what you would have told the poor bloke I saw, I suppose. Well, go and tell him in the mortuary that his chances of being hit had been quite small."

The young man was getting worked up. Baptiste was still very angry and Jack tried to calm things down a bit.

"I'm sure they won't want to bomb anything around here," he said.

"That's all very well," continued the young farmer, "but what about those people who've got to go to town, and us, then, if we want to ship any more spuds? We are going to be targets every time. I don't want to give a Jerry bomber practice, me, I wish I'd gone, like I said."

"You may be right," replied Jack, "but you'll work yourself up into quite a state if you keep going on about what you should have done. It's too late now, so you'll have to come to terms with being here."

Unconvinced, the young man banged his empty glass on the counter and made for the door:

"I'm going to see if the missus is so bloody clever, now."

"He has got a point," said Jacko, I wonder how many people are going to go to town tomorrow."

"I'm glad I'm not working near the Weighbridge, that's for sure," somebody added.

Jack put his glass down and went out. It had clouded over, as if the forces of nature had realised that a beautiful sunset would not be in keeping with the events of the day. On entering the house he could see that Alice's eyes were very red as she hugged him fiercely to her. She had realised by now that he could so easily still have been at La Rocque when the bomb was dropped there. He stroked her hair and tried to murmur reassurance as best he could.

"I keep thinking about those poor families going to bed tonight," she said. "Just imagine what I would be like if I'd heard you'd been killed. How could they do such a thing?"

Later he tried to settle to his journal but could write little other than the bare facts. Too much emotion was welling up inside him. He could not find it in himself to describe the horror, brutality and destruction. As he lay back against the pillow he looked at his wife, now thankfully asleep, knowing that she would soon bring into this world a child among whose first images would be soldiers and guns rather than peace and calm. Yet the lapping of the sea, the yellow of primroses and daffodils and the love of parents and grandparents would remain and even intensify. So, in trying to go to sleep he forced himself to think of some happy moments of his life - his marriage, the first time he played cricket for the school and scored twenty two runs, his first bike, evenings at college drinking and playing darts and the many French meals he had eaten in Normandy and Paris. Thoughts of the French capital brought a momentary return to the Germans but he banished them from his mind as he took his memory like a film camera up and down the Eiffel Tower, along the Champs de Mars to the Seine, flicking through books and pictures at the 'bouquinistes', the windows of La Sainte Chapelle, the outside of the Louvre, then along the Tuileries to the Jeu De Paume where the glorious Monet awaited with his scenes of Argenteuil, La Grenouillière and the West Porch of Rouen Cathedral. If he were to be bombed, he would take all these memories with him.

# SEVENTEEN

*Saturday 29 June, 1940*

It had been another strange, silent night of newly-activated fear. Many people had slept, wrapped nervously under blankets out in gardens or open fields. Some lay awake for long hours under dark-stained tents. Most were up early, drawn indoors by feelings of embarrassed shame lest they be seen publicly to be afraid, though the owners of recently-built air raid shelters experienced no such anxiety as if a bona fide shelter offered greater respectability. But wherever and however they had spent the night, short in darkness but long in the mind, few had not tossed and twitched through waves of frightening images.

Henry had not even tried to close his eyes. After badgering Jeanne to help carry the children, already asleep, to the cellar, he sat with his back to the wall, chewing his lip and going over the scenes he had witnessed in town again and again.

Jack had just shaved, staring hard into the eyes in the mirror, to see what strength he could find, when there was a gentle knock at the front door. Worried that it must be bad news, Jack opened it gingerly to see Maman and Papa standing awkwardly on the step. There was no sign of the car and the flushed faces and laboured breathing confirmed that they had walked.

"We haven't slept a wink all night," Maman said, "and we've come to see how you were."

A resigned Papa followed her in. By this time Alice was down in her nightdress and hugging her mother. Jack said: "But we would have phoned from somewhere if anything had happened."

"That's all very well but what if the phone lines were cut or if you were buried under the house?"

"Don't be silly, Maman, we are perfectly safe here," said Alice, aware that this was not exactly what she had thought the previous evening.

"Well, I wanted to make sure. All those planes and bombs!"

Jack appreciated the old lady's concern and, after his first expression of surprise, said nothing more about the unnecessary worry she was giving herself. This period of restored calm was nearly upset by Jeanne's sudden arrival but she managed to speak to Jack quickly in the kitchen without the old couple hearing.

"Please come and persuade Henry not to be stupid, Jack. All he wants to do is go back to town and see the place where those people were killed yesterday. He wanted to go before daybreak even. I'm not sure what time it was, we forgot to take our watches into the cellar."

"You slept in the cellar!"

"Well, what do you think? He's spent enough hours getting it organised and, after what happened yesterday, nothing would have stopped him taking us down there to sleep. A lot of people had similar ideas; some have slept outside in the fields. I've seen them carrying their blankets in."

"What!" said Jack. "Here you mean?"

"Yes, here, the Kerdons from the cottage for a start. But forget about that for a minute. Since we got up, Henry's been going on about returning to the Weighbridge. I've tried to tell him that if the bombers come again, he might not be as lucky as last time, but this only seems to make him more determined to go. I don't understand him anymore. Why does he have to be like that?"

Jack had difficulty getting her to keep her voice down for the sake of her parents. "You stay here with them and I'll go and have a word with Henry."

He put on his shoes with the usual difficulty of a man in a hurry, first not opening the laces enough to slip the foot in comfortably, then pulling them open so hard that half the laces came out of the holes. He fought back agitation knowing he would need all his cool to placate Henry. He found him walking up and down in the farm kitchen, stopping only to tell the children to eat their breakfast and that mummy would be back in a minute. On seeing Jack he said: "Ah it's you, I guessed she'd gone to your place with all her nonsense."

"I don't know what you call nonsense, Henry, but Jeanne seems to think that you want to go back to the Weighbridge, is that right?"

"What has she got to make such a fuss about?"

"Do you want to go back there or not?" pressed Jack.

"Yes, I've got to. When I think of those poor people!"

"But what can you do for them, going back to gaze at the spot where they were killed? There will be enough morbid people who were nowhere near yesterday, gawking in the hope they might find a finger or something that hasn't been swept up."

"But I was there, me."

"All right, but what possible reason have you got for going back? Do you want to act as guide or something, telling the sightseers exactly where the bodies were lying?"

Henry sat heavily at the table and held his head in his hands, the veins standing high. First one child then the other started to cry.

"When's their mother coming back to look after them?" Henry asked peevishly.

Jack had promised himself to remain calm and reasonable, accepting that, in a way, Henry had a kind of sickness, but his blood boiled at this remark and he replied that she was being offered help and comfort and that it was about time he did the same. Henry's head sank deeper into his shoulders and his hands clung more tightly at his temples. The children, more and more bewildered, cried even more loudly. Jack felt momentarily helpless so the relief of Baptiste's arrival could not have been more welcome. To his credit Henry rallied and said:

"Ben, te v'là, you don't normally come this early."

"I'm not bringing letters," replied Baptiste. "There's nothing coming from England or France for a start. I've got a puncture and can't find a patch; have you got one?"

The children had stopped crying because the postman always amused them and was now lifting JoJo high above his head. Jack called on him for help in dissuading Henry from going to town.

"Eh ben, tchi bougre d'nouilîn est tchna, what bloody nonsense is that?" repeated Baptiste in English. "What the hell d'you expect to do down there?"

"Don't you start as well," said Henry. "I just want to go and see the place, there's no harm in that."

"I told him," said Jack, "that it wasn't healthy for a bloke in his state to go and wallow in something morbid like that."

"You're dead right there, mon vi, but you've lost your bloody pedals my poor Henry. There's a crowd of people not going to work in town today, you. Mrs Bull won't let Jane go, and the bus left nearly empty, on a Saturday morning as well, and yet you actually want to go to town, you, and to the Weighbridge as well."

Henry stayed silent knowing that his arguments were not logical but deep and difficult to put into words.

Baptiste continued: "I'm not scared of much, me, but if you tied two of Douggie Pallot's horses to me, they wouldn't be able to drag me down to the Weighbridge today."

Jack echoed these sentiments, aware of the irony that what Henry was proposing to do was courageous as well as stupid. He knew that other more logical attempts of persuasion would be long and ineffective so he used the easiest argument even though it felt mean.

"Look at your kids. You've been going on about wanting to take them away to safety and yet you want to take the risk of leaving them without a father for no reason at all. I'd understand if you had to go there to work, but not just to follow some silly idea in your head!"

Henry shrugged his shoulders wearily. "All right, you win again, you're going to drive me over the edge all of you before you're finished. Vein-t'en, Baptiste, there must be some patches for your tyre in the shed here somewhere."

After the postman's departure, leaving the air thick with swearing at the setbacks he encountered with the tyre, Jack asked Henry if he wanted to come down to the house.

"You take the kids down," Henry said. "I don't fancy getting into a hoohah with the whole family. If Jeanne and Maman get going together there'll be no end to the bloody thing."

"I take the point, but what are you going to do in the meantime?" asked Jack. "If I turn up there without you, they are bound to think that you are off to town."

"If I've said I'm not going, then I'm not going, that will have to be good enough for you and for them. I'll be tidying up in the shed."

"I accept that, but I think I'd still rather leave the kids here and send Jeanne back."

Again as he strolled down the slight incline to his home, Jack found himself lost in reflections on the dramas unfolding daily in the simple and regular lives of ordinary people. Outside the shop he stopped to chat to a couple of girls from his class and, as if a whistle had blown, five or six more children appeared, talking excitedly.

"They killed a man in the lifeboat sir... my father saw the bombs fall.... the mailboat in Guernsey... at La Rocque as well... slept out in the field... my feet were frozen..."

Jack stood, leaning against the shop door, a little tense, listening to the phrases which poured from the children.

"D'you reckon they are coming back today, sir?"

"I hope not, Jimmy, let's hope yesterday was meant to be a warning of what they could do."

"My old man's really scared," said somebody else. "He says look at what they did in Poland and Checko something."

"Czechoslovakia," said Jack.

"Sorry sir."

Jack laughed at his teacherliness coming out in such a way. It would be easy to say 'who cares what the name is' but it was precisely what the place was called and its very existence at all which was one of the underlying causes of the war.

"My sister hasn't gone to work today, my mum wouldn't let her go. She works near the Town Church. Some pieces of the window fell in the road near her office door."

"Did she see any of the dead?" another boy asked.

"No, they were too scared to go out."

"My father was on the pier, he was still white when he got home, he had to have a big brandy."

"I'm going down St Catherine's this afternoon with some binoculars."

"I'll come with you," said Jimmy excitedly. "We'll be able to practise with the slings again."

"What do you mean?" asked Jack.

"We set up a square box on the wall, sir, that's the German sentry, then we practise slinging stones at him."

"You're not going to start doing that when they are here, I hope," said Jack anxiously.

The boys laughed and ran up the road.

Jack went into the shop and saw, to his relief, that there were cigarettes on the shelf behind the counter. What would he do if supplies ran out? Could you easily grow your own tobacco? Would you be allowed to? The shop was full of women with large bags and, Jack thought unkindly, large behinds to match. The snippets of conversation confirmed his general views about wild rumours spreading. Although he knew no more about the events in Guernsey than the message brought by the distraught Mrs Stevens, he was quite certain that they did not resemble anything these women were saying: "bodies floating in the harbor... the mailboat, on fire... limping to England with serious damage to the engine... the Germans already landed and the Bailiff in prison..."

He was glad to get back into the sun, a Silk Cut hanging reflectively from his lower lip. How long would this tension continue? Regardless of his attempts not to scare his pupils, he could not help wondering if there would be more bombing. Time was weaving an uneasy pattern through what should have been a glorious, relaxing day.

Papa was standing on the step at the cottage, his face lined and tired. The sleepless night and remorseless worry all around him had wiped away much of his natural 'joie de vivre.'

"Ah te v'là Jack," he said, hardly raising his voice above a hoarse whisper. "Last time I was here it was for a funeral. Now more people are going to be buried after yesterday. I don't know if any of them were from around here."

"I don't know either," said Jack. "It should be in the Post tonight."

"I hope you don't think we're meddling or anything," Papa continued, "but Maman got very upset imagining things. She's a lot better since she's seen Alice and Jeanne. How is Henry?"

"Not too good, but I can understand it. He's been worrying for days about bombing and we all told him he was making too much fuss, then he sees people killed not twenty yards from where he was in the pub. It has just strengthened his natural pessimism that everything is going to turn out for the worst. Don't you wish the Jerries would make up their minds and arrive, then we'll all know the worst and be able to get on with it?"

Papa shrugged his large shoulders. "There goes the Constable," he said. "I suppose the States are meeting after what happened yesterday, not that there's much they can do."

"They might shut the pubs early again."

"That would upset a few people, by cri," Papa smiled. "I haven't been to the Royal for a few years. I used to call in there after taking the spuds to town. You talk about the beer and rum would go down, you. Is that space still there behind the bar billiard table?"

Jack nodded.

"Well, on Saturday nights that's where they used to lay the farmers on the floor. Then, at closing time, those still standing would lift the others each into their own carts and the horses would take them home. You can't do that now with lorries."

Jack knew the story that was coming, but it always amused him.

"One night Bigou's father was blotto as usual and they loaded him into his cart, led the horse into the road, pointed it towards La Mare and whacked it on the tchu. Nobody knew he had just bought a new horse from his brother at l'Etacq, right out at St Ouen, and old man Bigou ended up at the yard out there at about two in the morning. They never found out which way the horse went or anything."

Jack laughed. He didn't know whether to believe the story or not. Animals could do amazing things, dogs especially. They had now walked from the house and were leaning, elbows on the cemetery wall, gazing at the gravestones which marked the passage of the Anglicans of St Martin. Whatever upheavals they had lived through, they had not experienced aerial bombardment.

"It's a funny thing," Papa started again, pleased to be able to talk uninterrupted, a luxury not granted often to him in his retired domesticity, his eyes following the swallows, his fingers picking at the weeds growing from the wall.

"Last night when I was lying awake, I thought: 'the Germans are at Carteret and could be here at any minute and there's nobody guarding the telegraph cable at Fliquet. For the whole of the last war, even though the Boche got no nearer than the Marne, the militia mounted a guard on it day and night."

"I didn't know that," said Jack surprised. "There's been a bit of a fuss about it this time but I don't see much point in guarding it when the Germans are at the other end in any case."

The old couple were invited to stay for dinner and were joined by the early arrival of Jim and Jennifer, laden with food, this time to stay until they found somewhere to rent in St Martin's. Jennifer, naturally, spoke dramatically of how near she might have been to the bombing.

"When you think...I don't know why I decided...I had to run to catch the earlier bus..."

It seemed, just for a moment, that catching a bus would never be the same again. Jack recounted his own escape at La Rocque and Jim told them of his reunion with Jennifer in the field, including their dive to the ground when they heard the second wave of planes come over, guns firing.

"We watched them heading for Guernsey and saw one leave the formation. It must have been the one that strafed the lifeboat," he added.

This aspect of the German bombing again aroused the greatest fury and hatred for the enemy.

The conversation was interrupted by the throbbing arrival of a new wave of planes which swept low over the church and roared above the house. After a few moments' hesitation, Jack led the way outside just in time to see the dark grey shapes wheel towards the town followed, a few seconds later, by the howl of air-raid sirens.

Jack looked up and down the road at other people gazing up at the sky. A long silence was punctuated by a few whispered words, then followed by a greater and more enveloping silence with ears straining for sounds of a distant explosion. Everyone stood brutally alone, drawing into themselves with some dread.

"What are they going to do next?" asked Jim.

"We keep thinking that their troops are about to arrive at any minute," mused Jack, "but they may not come for some time. They don't really need to invade yet, they may not have enough men to spare, when you think of the huge area they've occupied. All they need to do is send over a few planes every now and again, and the occasional bombs to let us know they mean business and they could keep us quiet for a long time."

Before following the others back into the house, Jack sat alone for a moment on the cemetery wall, pulling dandelions as his father-in-law had done from between the granite stones. Left alone in seriousness, Jack unfailingly questioned everything - his reasons for being who he was, this teacher sitting on a wall in a tiny country hamlet of a small island awaiting the jackboots of the German Reich. What did it all mean? Could there really be a grand scheme of things of which this was a part? Was there any way in which the deaths of the previous day had been anything other than pointless?

"How is Alice today ?" asked Mr Stevens who had appeared next to him.

"Oh hello, a lot better thank you, better than me in many ways. She's got a lot of her father's stoicism in her."

"Good, good. Have you noticed, Jack, how difficult it is to fill the time, although normally we have so much to do. I really think we have suspended life, as it were, until the Germans get here, just in case what we do will be rendered futile by their arrival. That shouldn't be true of reading but I'm finding it very difficult at the moment. 'For Whom the Bell Tolls' is a bit too near the mark."

"I know what you mean," replied Jack. "I wanted to try and prepare myself and others for coming to terms with the occupation. You remember we spoke a little about it but they will be here any day now and I've done nothing. Sometimes I feel like a bit of cork that's been tossed into the sea."

"I feel helpless, too, but in a different way with my wife's anxieties and so on. I hope they have finished with this dreadful bombing."

"I found the atmosphere very strange just now when those planes flew over. It was as if some of the people who were out in the road actually wanted them to drop bombs."

"As a kind of death wish, you mean?" asked the Head.

"Perhaps. I don't know. Seeing themselves as victims. I can't quite explain it."

Mr Stevens drew reflectively on his pipe, the smoke drifting almost vertically into the air.

"I have a feeling you are trying to sort out your own thoughts, Jack and are allowing an over pessimistic view of human nature to run away with you. You, of course, make no allowances for religion."

"It depends the extent to which religious feelings are stronger than the subconscious ones which bring out basic instincts. When people are really cornered, I think religion will count for very little."

"You know I can't agree with that. Man does not want to die alone. Antigone's death was regarded as the most extreme form of execution - to be walled up and left to see and feel herself dying on her own."

"Shall we change the subject before we get too morbid?" suggested Jack. "How is your wife?"

The headmaster nearly choked on his pipe.

"Good job I've got a sense of humour, because if you think that enquiring after my wife at the moment is a more cheerful subject than Antigone...."

"Sorry," said Jack, laughing too.

"My dear fellow, it's the main reason I'm out of the house at the moment. Since that phone call from Guernsey yesterday she's been terribly upset and imagining all sorts of things you wouldn't credit if I told you. I wish the Evening Post would hurry up and come because she believes the young man who phoned her is dead or wounded. When I feel my patience going, rather than speak crossly to her, I prefer to pop out for a bit of tobacco."

"People will start accusing you of hoarding if you're not careful." laughed Jack. "But I must go in and help with dinner. My in-laws and brother and his wife are there. It's like Christmas."

"It might be an idea to treat it like Christmas, it's difficult to know what Christmas itself will be like this year."

Jack brought in some white, light blue and dark red sweet peas, his favourite flower. Their wonderful fragrance might just help to dispel the brutal sights and noises that they were all experiencing. Nevertheless the meal was subdued and the bread and butter pudding was interrupted by angry shouting outside the front window.

Jack looked out at arms and legs moving in ungainly shapes as two men jostled each other in an aggression which stopped just short of actual fighting. The thin erect figure of Belheche, the solicitor's clerk, screeched like a demented bird as he attempted to push Baptiste, but the postman moved surprisingly quickly and Belheche tripped over the bicycle lying on the ground. The laughter of the bystanders did little to calm his temper and he picked up the bicycle and threw it viciously against the wall.

Baptiste, angered by the damage to his machine, shoved Belheche into the gate pillar of the cemetery and continued shouting abuse at him: 'traitor, bloody fascist, hitlerite!' Belheche's mouth curled in hatred and his black popping eyes glared into Baptiste's angry face a few inches from his own. The increasing number of onlookers took their chance to display their hostility to the clerk who thought better of issuing his customary warnings of how the Germans would soon sort the scum out.

An underlying cause of this painful scene was highlighted by the return of the German planes, seemingly lower than ever. Jim, following his experience in the field at La Moye, shouted to everyone to dive behind the wall. Baptiste took the opportunity to thrust Belheche roughly to the ground where his face struck a vase of faded flowers on the grave near the gate.

"Here come your friends," spat Baptiste.

Jack viewed them in two minds, glad that Belheche was having a come-uppance yet sad that the incident demonstrated only too clearly the undercurrents of strife within the community, waiting for unknown threats to provide a catalyst.

Belheche, bleeding from the lip and only just controlling his trembling fury, got up and dashed for the house, slamming the door viciously behind him. Inside he would no doubt fuel his rancour, welcoming all the more in his heart the invader under whose shadow he might feel more secure.

The others got up and strained to listen again for the noise of explosions.

For Jack the most immediate concern was to calm the red-faced postman who was shaking his fist at the closed door. He called to Jim to bring Papa with him to the pub. The old man needed little encouragement.

Jack took Baptiste by the arm saying:

"Vein-t'en bethe une fais, mon bougre, laisse chu tchu-la. I val pon la peine de tourner les sangs. It's just not worth it"

The offer of a drink was just enough to move the postman away from hurling more abuse at the door. The pub was empty apart from Jacko's enormous presence behind the bar and Adolphe who had managed to be first there after the fracas. The black Labrador lay puffing gently in the space behind the billiard table.

"When the bloody Germans arrive, I'll charge them for a couple of glasses," said Jacko.

"How come?"

"They fell off the shelf when the planes flew over, the whole bloody place shook."

"It could be worse," said Jack. "According to Henry and Alan, there was a helluva mess in the Yacht yesterday after the bombs."

"I know where I'd like the next one to fall, if you didn't live next to him," said Baptiste with feeling.

"Well," said Jack, "now that you've got a drink in your hand, what was going on out there?"

Baptiste placed his glass deliberately on the bar and stepped back a little. He needed room around him for his indignation to grow.

"Adolphe was digging a grave and I stopped to ask him who was being buried. I thought, me, like a twerp, that it might be somebody who was killed yesterday - but they wouldn't bury them that quick. I just leaned my bike against Belheche's wall. He must have been looking out of the window because the silly sod was out straightaway shouting: 'Take that bicycle away from here.' You can imagine what I told him, the bloody tchu. The next minute he grabs my bike and chucks it down into the road. I haven't looked at it yet, you saw him chuck it against the wall as well. He's going to pay for it and properly too."

The others could only agree and gradually, after a few more gulps of beer, they began to speak of less troublesome topics - tomatoes, potatoes and the chances of finding an abandoned farm to rent. Then Jacko asked Papa what he thought of the war and the old man, stimulated by the unaccustomed freedom in these surroundings and helped a little by the beer began to speak quite readily.

"I can't talk properly about it. I've sat for a few hours thinking and gazing out to sea from the windows of the sitting room. You've got no idea how sad I feel inside that another war has come so quick. War to me means seeing my son get up early, he never liked that, and coming to milk the cows with me, then to see him take the cows up into the field whilst I went indoors to find a letter on the mat in a posh envelope telling him to pack his bags and go to the war, for two years it turned out. Everybody has told me I was lucky he came back and I suppose I was, but it broke my heart to see a boy who was always smiling, calm and gentle as you like, come back home, wounded, bitter and hard. I don't think I saw him smile from the day he came back until the day he died ten years later. That's what I think about war."

Nobody spoke. Papa took a sip of his beer, his quiet dignity radiating a profound sadness. He continued, as if glad to get something off his chest: "You know Jack, that we go over to France every year. I enjoy myself certainly. The Lamonts, you met them, six years ago was it, when they came? They feed us well and we get through a bottle or two, but I always find a few moments to go off and stand on my own looking at the little war memorial by the Mairie, and I read the names and I think of those boys who had been working in those fields all around and who were told to walk off up the long straight road out of the village to the Marne, the Somme and Verdun. Every time I've been to France I've stood there on my own and cried."

A single tear hung now to his eyelid.

It was some time since Papa had spoken uninterrupted for so long. Most of his contemporaries were dead and, in his retirement with Maman at their granite farmhouse, the days moved by leisurely in the quiet understanding of each other's presence. They had said most of the things they wanted to say to each other. It was the realisation that this tranquil existence might soon be broken, that especially preoccupied the old man's mind.

"Where are the Germans going to live, Jack? The Lamonts have got this huge house they inherited from an uncle, near the coast at Barneville. It wouldn't surprise me if the Germans have moved in there, which makes me wonder about Fliquet. It's near the beach and the tower."

"But they are not going to move into people's houses surely?" said Baptiste, surprised at a notion which had not occurred to him, though realising at the same time that his meagre smallholding would be pretty safe in that regard.

"That's a good question." said Jack. "They won't want to rough it in tents whilst the population goes on living in their comfortable houses."

"There are the hotels," suggested Jacko.

"That's true but there may not be enough of them and they might not be situated in the best places from their point of view."

"Do you think," asked Baptiste again, "that they will force people to move out or will they just come in ones and twos to live with the families?"

Jack was annoyed with himself that he had not even considered all these possibilities, that some people, for example might have to feed German soldiers who were living with them the whole time.

Baptiste spoke again: "If any of them come to live with me and the missus, they can whistle if they want anything done for them. They can cook their own bloody meals, I'd rather chuck the Aga into the sea."

"Like that we'd c c catch the f fish already c c cooked," observed Adolphe.

Later that evening as each meal ended, the Evening Post was hurriedly collected from boxes, pipes, flower beds, wherever it had been placed or thrown. The headlines gave the stark message. Most readers stared in disbelief at the dark black print before reading through the details again and again. The simple facts were that six Heinkel bombers had flown over the islands at 6-45 pm the previous day, and had dropped a large quantity of bombs and machine-gunned several places. Two men and a woman had been killed at La Rocque where Jack had seen the bomb fall.

"I can't help shuddering when I think how near you were. It could easily have been Uncle Denis too, the hours he has spent down there, coming up the slip with a lobster in his box," said Alice speaking for all those like Henry, Jennifer and Jack who had come near a confrontation with death. One man was killed on top of Mount Bingham, somewhere near the fort, before the Heinkels swooped down on the harbour, killing two more men in Mulcaster Street.

"There were another three men killed on the pier." added Jack. "That makes nine dead on the island and ten with the lifeboatman."

In Guernsey the situation had been worse, far more bombs and twenty two people killed, including many waiting to board the mailboat which had fired at the planes with its few anti-aircraft guns.

"There's been a lot of damage to buildings here as well," added Jack. "The store at Norman's has been virtually gutted and there are pictures of shattered windows everywhere."

In every household the newspaper reactivated conversations and fears about the bombing. Ten deaths, ten families and friends coming to the end of their first full day of grief, almost too stunned to take in what had happened. The arbitrary descent of death from the air gave too many cards to the hand of fate. The only relief for the frightened population was the knowledge that although German planes had again flown menacingly over the island today, no further bombing had taken place.

The news of the States' sitting was relegated down the columns, although the three further defence measures they had taken would radically affect everyone's lives: restrictions to deal with the rapidly diminishing supplies, the reintroduction of a curfew and the complete ban on private motor vehicle movements.

Jack sat up long into the night, filling page after page of his journal with tiny writing.

*Journal Extract*
*The bombing*
*...Suddenly everything has changed. We had just drifted into the mentality of waiting for their arrival, apprehensive yet not too alarmed. But the flying over of German planes and the subsequent panic rush to build air raid shelters has disturbed this fragile peace of mind. Without warning yesterday the bombs fell and thirty two of my fellow Channel Islanders are now awaiting burial after a callous aerial attack on a demilitarised area. This followed hard upon the capitulation of France and the almost certain severance of travel links to England.*

*...Many people have lost loved ones or people they know. Many more were close enough to the bombs to have felt, at first hand, the fear and horror..*

*...What would Andrew, a practising Christian, make of all this? He has left the woman he might have married to follow a course of duty by becoming a pilot. If he flies bombers, his duty will take him into the cockpit of an aircraft bringing the same terror to ordinary German people as the Heinkels have brought to the peaceful island he has left behind. Could God be on anyone or everyone's side, sitting in every bomber, or in none? How can anybody be sure of what they believe when I, allegedly intelligent and educated, am so totally bewildered?*

*...Then there's Belheche! The more I think of him the more I am amazed that he exists. A novelist would be laughed at if he introduced such a neatly packaged Nazi sympathiser into our midst. But he does exist, he is there and that's all there is to it. What will happen to him? What will happen to others because of him? I don't know. How easy to catch oneself thinking it's a pity that it wasn't him rather than the other victims in Mulcaster Street on Friday.*

Before going to bed, Jack opened the window, looked out and savoured the air of a free Jersey, albeit cut off from the mainland and probably the other Channel Islands too.

# EIGHTEEN

*Sunday 30 June, 1940*

Would this last day of June be the last day of freedom? Another Sunday for the faithful to assemble in their churches and ask their God for guidance. Another Sunday for vicars, priests and lay preachers to resolve the strains that war and the deaths of the innocent placed on Christian belief and the concept of a just God.

Jack took breakfast to Alice in bed. She lay on the pillow, her gentle face of pregnancy a sleeping Raphael. Her first thoughts on wakening were that Jack go and see how Henry was. He hesitated for only a short selfish moment, as he was looking forward to opening a new pot of loganberry jam, and set off up the road.

Henry was reading the Post for the umpteenth time with Jeanne saying: "You must know it by heart."

"When I think how near I was."

"Look, Henry," said Jack, "whatever happened on Friday and whatever is going to happen today or tomorrow, none of us can do anything about it, so there doesn't seem to be much point in worrying oneself sick over it."

But he detected in Henry's subdued lethargy a resignation which suggested that he might have worried himself out, that in the course of another sleepless night he had pushed his anxiety to the limit. They sat at the table toying with their cups of tea.

"Well," asked Jack, "d'you reckon it's for this afternoon?"

"What?" said Henry without looking up.

"The Germans landing."

"How the hell do I know?" said Henry aggressively, "what sort of question is that?"

"It seems as good a question as any."

"And you, then, what do you think?"

"It could be at any moment but there again they might be happy to leave us dangling here for a while. They must have found out by now that we are demilitarised. Apart from a few shots from the 'Isle of Sark' in the harbour in Guernsey, nobody has fired at them, unless Baptiste has been catapulting cow dung in the air."

Henry smiled in spite of himself.

"That sacré Baptiste, I'm sure Belheche knows it was him who smeared his door handle the other day. That's why he was so upset."

Part of Jack could not help feeling amused at Baptiste's actions but he knew that sorting people out in this way would not be without consequences.

The conversation lingered on but Jack felt able to leave the farm relieved, to some extent, that his brother-in-law's nerves would survive until the next crisis. The waiting was difficult for everybody, the not quite boredom, the normal relaxing mechanisms stuck in abeyance, the 'putting things off until they were here and you knew where you were.'

As he walked back, distracted by the occasional bird or wild flower, Jack wondered again what might happen to schools when they arrived. Would they insist on German being taught instead of, or perhaps as well as French? Would they introduce German money? And measurements? Driving on the right? Take over the Evening Post with their Gothic script? What was happening in France? Would they import enough food for everyone to eat; all those damn sausages? Would the population have to salute them or address them in German?

Jack had his notebook with him so, brushing aside a few twigs, he sat back on the hedge and scribbled, almost illegibly, all these questions and others as they came.

Would they be allowed to listen to the radio? Would the Germans buy things or just take what they wanted? Would young Jersey men be rounded up and put in camps as hostages against hostile acts? Would the States continue to function? How many Germans would there be? Hundreds? Thousands? Where would their headquarters be? Did many of them speak English? Would they ever be out of uniform? Did they smoke different cigarettes? Would they go into pubs? Would the pubs be allowed to stay open? How long were they going to stay? Would the coast be a kind of military zone, no more going on the beach? Would inhabitants from Germany or other occupied countries come to the islands on holiday? Would islanders be allowed to go to France? Would there be a curfew? Would German soldiers try to go out with Jersey girls? What should be the reaction to this?

His thoughts continued to buzz. What about work? Farming would remain extremely important but it was possible that the Germans would take over the farms and use the islanders as cheap or even free, labour. The tourist industry had obviously come to a complete halt. Had the posters at Waterloo Station advertising a holiday in sunny Jersey been taken down? The building industry would be at a standstill with so many houses abandoned. Shops could not last very long as every available commodity became scarce then non-existent. The Germans would have to be relied upon for everything. How would anyone whose source of income ceased as a direct result of occupation, find money to feed their families? Would the States even continue to pay teachers?

Down the road the church door was opening to release its soothed congregation. Jack felt forced to move as the sight of him sitting on a hedge scribbling might arouse some puzzlement in the people returning home to whatever would now pass as Sunday dinner.

How could he repeat to them all: 'I'm just sitting here jotting down a few questions about what might happen when the Germans arrive.' So home to render vigil to another afternoon and evening of imminency! How many other people in history had known that occupation was on its way like this? Had not invaders tended to just arrive suddenly like the horsemen of the apocalypse?

The Germans did not arrive before dinner.

Another plane flew over in the afternoon, very, very low. Was it always the same pilot? Would he try to land? Was he being sent deliberately on these flights or was he just flying over for some personal kick?

Later when Jim joined Jack to sideshoot a few tomatoes in the garden, a plane flew over, not so low and a little distance away.

"That's a British plane," said Jim excitedly.

"Pull the other one," replied Jack without looking up.

"I hope you don't think that because I haven't been to college like you, I can't tell the difference between red, white and blue rings and a bloody black cross."

"Well, bugger me," said Jack, looking at the plane in astonishment. "I'd never have believed it."

Immediately he wondered if it might be Andrew, then dismissed the thought as too much of a schoolboy comic story to imagine him flying over the old island.

"The last thing I expected," he continued, "was a possible air battle."

"I wonder if they've seen each other."

"I don't know. It's quite extraordinary, isn't it? Every day there is some twist or turn. It may be that the islands are not as undefended as we thought. There might be a fleet in the Channel somewhere ready to intercept a German invasion and fighters patrolling to establish mastery in the air."

"Pigs might fly, more like," said Jim. "One little British plane does not make a summer and a defensive fleet would have to move jolly quick to intercept anything crossing the sixteen miles from Carteret."

Jack tried one last effort. "The Germans are more likely to come from Cherbourg, in which case our boats may be waiting for them around Alderney somewhere."

Jim didn't comment.

"The plane must have been on a reconnaissance to see if the Germans had got here yet. But it can't be too safe for a British plane to venture this far on its own."

They stopped talking for a moment and concentrated on sideshoots, weeds, creepers and brambles, Jack's restless mind finding a parallel in the way the Nazis were reputed to treat people; plucking out the suckers, the chokers and the frail. In a very short time, Alice, Jim, Jennifer, Jack himself and all those he knew and loved would become subjected people; to new, possibly arbitrary laws and justice.

Jim had been thinking too. "Should we have gone to join up?"

"What makes you ask that?"

"Well, since I nearly got carted off the other day, I've wondered a few times whether I should have gone."

"I've thought about it too." Jack paused to apply a dock leaf to the little white spots left by a stinging nettle. Until about a week ago it looked as if the choice was fighting here or going to the mainland to escape. Now it looks as if we shall escape any fighting by staying here. For all we know there may not be any fighting to defend England either, the way things are going. So where would we be if we left? Also, imagine the island, with only the old, the young and women left on it. It might not be so bad on somewhere safe like the Hebrides, if all the men left, although it would be dreadful if they all got killed, as happened in the Great War, but for a little island which the Germans are going to occupy, it just seems wrong to abandon it without men between eighteen and fifty. Anyway, since I've known that Alice is pregnant, it just hasn't occurred to me to go away leaving her to face the occupation on her own.

At that moment the face of Baptiste appeared over the wall:"Ah te v'là à gourmander les tomates."

"Ah, it's you," said Jack. "Have you recovered from your prize fight yesterday?"

"Don't talk to me about it, he's bent six spokes in my front wheel, he's going to pay for them the sod."

"Calm down, Baptiste, he might hear you," smiled Jim.

"That's exactly what I want him to do. He wasn't at church this morning, they tell me. Didn't want to show off his black eye!"

"You'd better be a bit careful," warned Jack. "He could do something nasty when the Germans are here."

"Ah that's a good one. If you think the Jerries are going to have time for a bloody twerp like that."

"From what I've read, Baptiste, he is exactly the sort of twerp they do have time for. Someone who'll do all their sneaking and reporting for them."

It was clear from his reaction that it would have taken little for Baptiste to have gone banging on the door to resume where he had left off. It was difficult for all of them to stomach the possibility of a potential collaborator already in their midst. The nature of events would create enough potential collaborators, created by hunger and fear, without those fuelled by rancour or prejudice. To change the subject Jack asked Baptiste what was new.

"I tell you what" replied the postman, "my sister has heard from her sister-in-law who's heard it from God knows who, you know how it goes, that the best thing to do is to bury your valuables in the garden. Henry must have heard about it because when I passed there just now, he was off behind the house with a sack and a spade."

"You mean people are actually burying stuff? But some of it is bound to get lost surely."

"That's what I told my sister, either the bloody cat will want to piss there or the kids will dig it up or you'll forget where you've put it."

"But why?" asked Jim, as he lit another cigarette.

"Because they say that the Germans will melt down everything they can lay their hands on and send it all back to Germany for God knows what."

"I suppose there might be something in that," said Jack. "But it does seem a bit extreme. So when they leave, everyone will be walking around with maps like in 'Treasure Island?"

"When I told Adolphe about it, he had his usual daft reply. He said 'M m me I'm g g going to b bury a f f fart.' Tu parles d'un tchu."

The Germans had not arrived by teatime.

After tea, the two couples went out for a walk around the perimeter of the field, picking wild flowers and throwing green potatoes at the trees. Back indoors they played '500' until Alice, her eyes closing, said that she must go to bed. Jim and Jennifer also retired to their room and Jack sat at his desk before another page. He counted the pages he had written. Sixty! He could hardly believe it, nearly a whole notebook.

When the war was all over, people might be interested in reading about these dramatic days which preceded the German arrival as a kind of preface to the day by day chronicles of life under the occupation – his next journal perhaps?

He recorded the events of the day, the planes passing over, the thoughts on air and sea defences, the burying of valuables.

Then he added:

*'These words are being written on 30 June 1940, nearly three weeks after I started keeping this journal. I am writing this while I am still a free man. All of us have had to make a fateful choice; either to abandon all we have known, worked for and loved by evacuating to England, or to remain here and wait, an interminable wait, for the Germans to come and change our lives, perhaps for ever.*

*Will any of us know whether we have made the right decision? If you are reading this at some time in the future without the benefit of hindsight, what would you have done?*

Jack put the notebook in a box. He thought of burying it but decided instead to hide it somewhere in the loft when the Germans came. Tomorrow he would look for a place.

He found Alice, still awake, and glad to just hug him when he got into bed.

# NINETEEN

*Monday 1 July, 1940*

It was Baptiste, as usual, who had the news. When Jack emerged after a leisurely breakfast 'à quatre,' the postman, looking surprisingly like a serious official in his neatly pressed uniform and clean white shirt, was speaking excitedly to a crowd of people outside the shop. He was waving a large brown envelope to cries of 'ahs' and 'noes' of amazement. Jack called to the others that this might be worth hearing.

"Get on a box," somebody shouted and Mrs Pring, almost on cue, brought out a beer crate.

"What's happened, Baptiste? Get on with it, I've got some spuds to dig," yelled a farmer from the cab of his lorry.

The Germans had flown over again very early that morning, before six o'clock, and had dropped copies of an ultimatum instead of bombs. They were in canvas bags, weighed down with sand and with long red streamers attached. One was found in town, caught in some railings near St Mark's Church. The others fell at the airport.

"I was told," said Baptiste, "that they were taken to the Bailiff."

"What do they say?" yelled the farmer again.

"Patience, patience, don't get excited," said Baptiste, milking the situation for all it was worth. "The ultimatum was in bloody German and nobody knew what it said."

"So what's happened?"

"They phoned Maison St Louis. Apparently one of the Jesuits at the seminary comes from Alsace, where they speak German, is that right, Jack?"

Jack could not shirk his 'teacher' responsibility, although he was becoming as impatient as anyone to know what the ultimatum had said.

"Alsace and Lorraine were taken by the Germans after the Franco-Prussian War and were given back to France by the Versailles Treaty after the Great War, so most of the inhabitants speak both French and German. But, get on with it Baptiste, or you'll have a bloody riot on your hands."

Baptiste waived again the brown envelope on which a postman colleague had scribbled down what he could from the translations which had been posted in prominent places in town.

The first few points had been copied in full, the rest was in abbreviated note form.

"Come on, Baptiste," several voices shouted.

"Right then," he said, "are you listening?

To the Chief of the Military and Civil Authorities, Jersey (St Helier)"

"They've addressed it to Adolphe, " the farmer said, to general laughter.

"ONE: I intend to neutralize military establishments in Jersey by occupation."

"What does that mean, neutralize?" asked a woman with a shopping bag.

"Don't you know English, you?" replied Baptiste.

"I know enough to know that you don't know what it means either."

"It's what you do to bloody cats," said the voice in the lorry.

When the nervous laughter died down, Baptiste continued:

"TWO: As evidence that the Island will surrender the military and other establishments without resistance, and without destroying them, a large White Cross is to be shown as follows from 7 am July 2nd, 1940:

a) in the centre of the Airport in the East of the Island."

"But, they're not well," said Mrs Quérée with the shopping bag.

"What d'you mean?" asked Baptiste. "Is anybody going to let me finish reading or what?"

"But the airport's in the West," she said.

"By cri, yes, sis-t'i tchu," the postman added, "unless they think the airport is the golf course at Grouville."

"They must know where the airport is," said Jim. "They've flown over it enough times. Somebody at their HQ must have got his map upside down."

"b)" shouted Baptiste, " if I can carry on, a white cross on the highest point of the fortifications of the port,

c) on the Square to the north of the Inner basin of the Harbour.

Moreover all fortifications, buildings and houses are to show the White Flag.

THREE: If these signs of peaceful surrender are not observed by 7 am July 2nd heavy bombardment will take place:

A. against all military objects.

B. against all establishments and objects useful for defence."

This point was greeted in total silence.

"Now for the rest," said Baptiste,"I'll just read what's written here in notes and you'll have to work out for yourselves what it means.

White flags to stay until they arrive...authorities to airport...radio and telephone to outside the island hostile act...bombs. Hostile acts to any German...bombs. If peaceful surrender then lives and property guaranteed.

It is signed by the Commander of the German Air Force in Normandy and you can read his bloody name for yourself," added Baptiste finally.

The crowd, because it had now become quite a crowd, sank back on to their heels. The late arrivals began pestering Baptiste to read the first part again and he, eventually, in frustration, got a nail from Mrs Pring and nailed his envelope to the shop door.

"So if we surrender we should be OK," said Jim.

"That shouldn't take the States long to decide then we'll have to wait until they actually arrive before we know their day to day orders."

It gave some comfort at least for the populace to know that a peaceful surrender should bring reasonable treatment. There was no talk of arbitrary bombing, of imprisonment or of hostages.

The familiar aroma of the pipe informed Jack that the headmaster was approaching his left shoulder. He had received a message from town that all communications with England had stopped at eight fifteen that morning to comply with the German ultimatum. The States were meeting to decide what else to do.

Jack wasted no time. He wanted to be there, notebook in hand. He barely knew what to think or feel. The diarist and historian in him was excited and wanting to be at the centre of things as they happened; the Jerseyman, shattered that his island was about to be lost; the husband, desperately fearful about what might happen to his wife and unborn child;

the vulnerable human being, worried about what might soon envelop him.

Jim agreed to come with him and, after a quick word to reassure their wives that there should be no further danger from bombing, the brothers pedalled off to town. Jack took particular pleasure in reciting to himself the names along the way in case and before they were germanised...La Préférence, Poplar, Three Mile, Maufant, The Lodge, Eden Chapel, La Ronde Porte, Five Oaks then down St Saviour's Hill past the church, the entrance of the now empty Government House, down Stopford Road, into David Place, Bath Street, right into Beresford Street, around the Market, up Halkett Place, round the back of the Peirson and into the Royal Square.

Not many people had gathered yet. Perhaps other outposts of the island did not have a Baptiste sniffing every grapevine. The States sitting was already over and news was emerging of two important decisions. First, there had been little alternative to acquiescing to the surrender demands and second, the sale of alcohol was temporarily withdrawn.

The sun now flickered through the trees, placing here and there, little shapes of bright light. A baby was crying inconsolably as if he had just heard the news, a cat slept unmoved on the faded window ledge of the corner shop and the Town Church struck twelve thirty. As if called by unseen criers, shopkeepers, customers, children, passers-by, workers, employers, Jersey men and women, Breton farm workers and a few English residents gathered in the centre of island life as the Bailiff appeared on the steps of the Royal Court.

A rope had been hurriedly placed in position just after Jack and his brother arrived, to cordon off the middle of the paved area. Word spread that this was where the white cross would be painted.

The Bailiff announced there would be another cross near the Weighbridge and a third on the runway at the airport. Already white flags were being flown on all the States buildings and the Bailiff urged the population, when they returned to their homes, to find some way of hanging something white at their windows.

This request provoked murmurs and some grumbling in response. It was one thing for the island to surrender officially but not the same thing to mark a personal surrender in the way suggested. Many would grasp the opportunity to show some sign of rebellion, of self-respect, however small.

The island's leader looked tired. He had known for some days and nights that to protect the territory under his charge and the lives of his fellow islanders he would have to call on them to accept the inevitable, however unpalatable. He appealed for calm and warned sternly of the dangers of disobeying German orders. His face told the whole story of the tension and worry of not knowing what the occupiers might do or what some islanders might do to provoke them. Jack hurriedly made notes in his little book.

The Bailiff declared that he and the Crown Officers, the Attorney General and Solicitor General, would hold themselves in readiness to go, as required, to wherever the Germans arrived. Meanwhile he had arranged for the Union flag to be taken down at Fort Regent. Whatever happened he would do everything in his power to best represent the island with the Occupying Forces.

Lastly he said to the now silent gathering, that places of amusement would remain open and that there would be no curfew that night. However, to ensure that nothing detrimental to the safety of the islanders took place, all intoxicants were to be withdrawn from sale and all arms had to be handed in at the Parish Halls. He stepped back up another step and said:

"Keep calm and obey orders. God's blessing upon you all."

He did not wait for a reaction but turned and walked hurriedly into the building, his chin firmly set. Many people in the square were in tears and lots were praying silently and aloud. They gathered in little groups, sharing their fears and feelings of resignation. On such a fine day many of them would normally be happily mingling with tourists on beaches with picnics, buckets and spades. Instead, they were waiting for the most menacing of visitors to join them.

The crowd, several deep all around the square, in the shadows of the trees, stayed to watch as four States' workman came out of the side of the building carrying buckets and brushes. Were they fully aware of the historic significance of the few brushstrokes they were painting in the square? Two simple white lines in the shape of a cross sending a hieroglyphic message to an enemy in the sky that Jersey, Channel Islands, British territory since 1204 was surrendering its sovereignty to the German Reich.

"D'you know Jim, the way the Bailiff spoke I reckon they could easily arrive today. You needn't come if you don't want to, but I'd like to go to the airport to see if anything happens."

"OK," replied Jack's brother, "but won't Alice and Jennifer be worried if we don't get back?"

"I'll ring Mr Stevens to pop round to tell them. I'm sure he won't mind and he'll be happy to hear what's been going on here."

"You don't think there's any danger of us being rounded up or anything up there?" asked Jim.

"Let's hope not, but I'm prepared to take that small risk. Having got this far with my journal, Jim, I can't pass up the chance of being an eyewitness to the actual arrival."

~

At the airport several policemen were keeping members of the public either in the waiting lounge or on the flat roof of one of the buildings where family groups usually gathered to see people off. Today, if too many came to the airport, something would no doubt be done to move them away, but at the moment, there was only a handful on the roof when the two brothers dashed up the steps.

Back in town, the buying intensified, quietly at first, then dramatically as neighbours called on neighbours and told them what was no longer to be found in such and such a shop. Frustrated customers told tales to other frustrated customers. Packets of tea, coffee, sugar, tins, boxes, sticks of this, strips of that, a gallon of this, a pint of the other, a square, a bagful, a lump, a little, a gross, a dozen, as much as you've got all disappeared into bags and containers. Cyclists took to the country looking for more shops. Mrs Pring sent messages to her local regulars to come quickly and get what they could. She tried to hide as much as possible in her small cellar, knowing that a serious crisis must be near.

Jack and Jim had time to take in the horizon and the view of the sea beyond the cliff at the end of the runway and, in the distance, Sark, Herm, Jethou and Guernsey. There were no planes parked anywhere on the airport but the smells brought memories back to Jim. He pointed to the petrol tanker standing idle near one of the hangars.

"You remember I used to drive one of those."

"That one?" asked Jack.

"I don't think so, it looks a bit new."

"You didn't have a licence, if I remember."

"No, and it all came out, I know I've told you this dozens of times, when the weather was so bad up here that the plane bringing the papers had to land on the beach near First Tower. Until then I hadn't needed a licence to drive the tanker within the airport but when my boss told me to drive down to the beach, I had to tell him I couldn't go on the road. He wasn't too pleased. He had to drive it down himself!"

"Look," said Jack suddenly, "over there!"

The brothers watched the grey shape gradually come nearer and over the airport where they were able to identify it as a Dornier 17. It circled round once more then came down on to the runway and taxied up below them. Almost immediately, a tall, young pilot with a rounded face, jumped from the plane, took his pistol from its holster and walked slowly towards the airport building.

As he looked down, Jack felt the thrill of participating in something momentous but it was impossible not to see its incongruous aspect.

"If we survive," said Jack, "what a tale for our grandchildren! The day we went to the airport and saw the island captured by just one bloke, barely out of short trousers."

"Put like that, it does sound pretty amazing," Jim agreed, "but he's got everything going for him - the island bombed last Friday, white crosses all over the place, threats of more bombardment if anything is done to a member of the German Armed Forces, him obviously."

"That's true but look at him there all on his own. It must still take a lot of courage for a kid like that to calmly walk up to the airport building as if he was arriving on holiday. I wonder what he's thinking. When Alice and I went down to Fliquet the other day, we stopped at the 'pièche', you know, her father's field overlooking the breakwater, and wondered whether the Germans would land at the harbour at Gorey, or come running up Grouville Beach, or parachute into St Aubin's Bay or even something like twenty planes carrying soldiers landing here at the airport but never, for one moment, did we imagine a kid with a pistol landing on his own. I can barely believe it. It's so humiliating."

"I doubt if Churchill will be too pleased at the way a piece of British Territory has been taken," said Jim with a sad shake of the head.

"Who's that going out to meet him?" asked Jack excitedly.

"That's Charles Roche, he's in charge of the airport."

"I wonder if the pilot speaks English. I'd give anything to hear what they are saying."

The other people on the roof, who had kept up a similar steady chatter of amazement at the turn of events, now raised their fingers to their lips as they also strained to hear something of what was being said. As the usual polite openers to visitors about their flight and the weather were inappropriate, the conversation did not last very long. The pilot turned and walked back to his plane. The Jersey representative stayed outside for a moment and watched him climb into the aircraft. The propeller started quickly, the wheels moved forward, the plane taxied to the runway, turned and gathered speed over the white cross, then away into the sky towards Normandy.

One of the children on the roof waved before his father asked him crossly what he was doing.

Jack and Jim came down into the airport lounge where they heard Mr Roche saying that the pilot's name was Oberleutnant Kern, who had landed after seeing the white crosses of surrender. "I told him what the Bailiff had instructed me, that the island was ready to comply with their demands and he's flown back to report to his Commanding Officer. They want the Bailiff and other people in charge, the Crown Officers, I suppose, to come to the airport without delay."

Somebody said loudly "I don't like the bloody Germans but that kid must be brave after what happened to their envoy in Paris."

It was clear that a force of German troops would soon be arriving and Jack was determined to stay until then. He was aware, though, that they had not eaten and that their wives would worry the more with each passing hour they did not return.

"Look," said Jim, "I don't really mind whether I stay here or not. I'm not writing a book! I'll go back and tell them you are in the front line."

"Don't put it like that, Jim, for God's sake."

They cycled to the nearest shop where Jack was hoping to buy a ham roll or something to eat, but to their astonishment, there was quite a crowd outside shouting to those inside not to take more than their share. The shopkeeper was in tears, repeating over and over again that there was nothing she could do. Jack banged his handlebars in frustration and returned, unfed, to his vigil at the airport. There were now surprisingly few people around. He climbed the eighteen steps back on to the roof where a few scattered groups were debating whether to stay or not. Jack thought it best to warn them about the run on the shops, a message met with a mixture of disgust and concern. For some, this settled their decision and they set off briskly to add to the larder-filling, tin-gathering and shelf-cramming.

Jack sat leaning against the wall, brushing a stone or two from under his buttocks. He took out his little notebook. A couple of slashes of his penknife brought the pencil back into use and he began a fresh page, writing what came into his head.

He entitled it: 'To my unborn child.'

> 'I don't know when you are going to be born or if you will be a boy or a girl, or who people will say you look like. When you cry for the first time, the Germans will be here. You don't, of course know who Germans are and why they shouldn't be here, or why it is something worth writing about. By the time you can read, you will know all about it. I wonder how old you will be when they leave.
>
> I am sitting on the roof of the airport. A lot of them will probably be landing soon. I was with your uncle here a little while ago and saw one young pilot land and talk to the man in charge of the airport. He must have been scared, to land on his own and get out of the plane with only a pistol in his hand. What an anticlimax after all our speculation about the dramatic ways they might come.
>
> He has gone away again to tell his superiors that the island is

prepared to surrender and that the Bailiff and senior dignitaries are coming to the airport to meet the German officers who will shortly be arriving with troops.

This means that we are going to lose the thing we treasure most, our freedom, but that is something we will have to learn to live without for a while.

I hope that all of us will behave properly when they are here. By that I don't mean that we do everything they tell us but that we don't do anything that we will remain ashamed of all our lives. We will probably be hungry and cold at times and one of the greatest tragedies of war is the way subjected people behave in order to be better clothed or better fed or better heated. I don't want you to grow up under a German occupation but, even worse, I hope you won't have to grow up in a society torn apart by the way it behaved when they were here.'

The arrival of the troops was sudden. Jack couldn't remember later whether he was absorbed in his diary or lost in reverie but planes were suddenly landing across the airfield. They turned and moved swiftly to the concrete parking area, then stopped. The doors opened immediately and soldiers began jumping out. One of the first, in a different uniform and clearly an officer, led thirty or forty men of the first wave to the apron in front of the building. Planes were continuing to land and soon more officers and well over a hundred men in mouse grey-green uniforms and soft military hats, had followed them.

In no time at all, a group of German officers were gathered in a little circle where they were joined by the Bailiff and Attorney General. The Germans looked quite normal, no shouting or barking of orders. Most of them were smiling. Jack noticed one holding a dog in his arms and gently stroking its ear. It looked like a poodle. 'Goodness knows where it came from,' he thought. 'Did he bring it with him?'

Transport planes landed, from which troops jumped down onto the grass before getting into military formation. Jack had never seen so many planes before. Like most islanders he and Alice had occasionally taken a Sunday picnic to the airport to see the plane to Croydon come and go. To witness so many landing together was both frightening and exciting. A Junkers JU52 transport aircraft landed and disgorged motor cycles and sidecars.

Jack didn't see any cars. Perhaps they were going to commandeer the Bailiff's. Surely they wouldn't make him walk back! Perhaps taxis were being ordered from town.

Shortly afterwards a policeman came up the stairs to tell Jack and the others that they had to leave the airport which would now be out of bounds. He was very tempted to go back via town because that was obviously where the Germans would be heading but it would take quite a bit longer and Alice would become seriously worried if he didn't get back soon. So, reluctantly, he set off across the country parishes, past the attractive granite parish churches of St Peter, St Mary, St John and Trinity. Everything looked the same, glorious countryside, meadows patched with daisies and buttercups, cows grazing, farmers farming, children playing, birds singing. For most people, so far, it had been a day like any other.

Back at St Martin's, as he neared the school Jack was stopped by a girl in his class, nearly bursting with excitement, who told him that her father had phoned to say he had seen a German sentry standing outside the States Building in the Royal Square.

At the door Alice hugged Jack before admonishing him for being so foolish. How could he think it was perfectly safe to go to the airport! The Germans might have done anything when they arrived. But relief at his return soon prevailed and a cup of tea and welcome cheese sandwich were pressed upon him.

He just managed a few sips and a bite before the questions started again. How many Germans were there? What did they look like? Was there any shooting? Did they give any orders on their arrival? What did the Bailiff tell them?

Jack realised just how little he knew. His short inadequate answers were met with further questioning.

"Come on Jack, it can't have been as simple as that," said Alice, "they must have done something more than just walk from their planes and disappear on motorbikes towards town."

"I think they left a few soldiers to guard the airport," said Jack "but do you want me to start making things up, or what? I'm glad nothing more happened, even though it might be more comfortable if they had met with some kind of resistance."

"Then we would have all been bombed again," said Jennifer.

"Exactly," replied Jack, "but subconsciously people might feel better if somebody else had shot at the Germans and somebody else had been bombed because of it. Then they would feel able to take communal credit for having defied them."

The Germans had paid scant attention to the publishing time of the Evening Post, so the headlines that day said nothing of the their arrival, but, in thick black letters, the Paper set out the ultimatum which had first come to the people of St Martin via the brown envelope waved by Baptiste outside the shop. The only small comfort was to be found in Point 8:

'In the case of peaceful surrender the lives, property and liberty of peaceful inhabitants are solemnly guaranteed.'

It was signed by the Commander of the German Air Force in Normandy, Richtofen, General.

~

During the course of the evening, Jack spoke to Henry, when he nipped up to the farm to see if things were under control; to the headmaster, who he met near the gate and to Baptiste, who popped in for a beer because, in his words, 'the bloody pub was shut.' The feelings of all three made a varied and interesting picture. For Henry it was a kind of relief that nothing more could now be done and that there would be no more bombs. The headmaster felt energized and ready to start a new life. For Baptiste it was immense frustration that he would not be able to carry on with life as normal.

Re-reading the Post before settling down to his diary, Jack spotted something he would have preferred not to have seen; an announcement by the Public Instruction Committee that the Elementary Schools would re-open the next day, July 2nd. He cursed that his recent 'holiday bonus' was about to end just when he wanted to be at the centre of events and not have to rely on reports almost certainly distorted from mouth to mouth.

A little advert also caught his eye and gave him a moment of amusement:

'French and German conversation and coaching for all examinations. Swift method of teaching by certified Swiss Master.'

'He must be daft,' thought Jack,' to allow such an advert to stay in the paper at a time like this. He's even got a German name to go with it.'

"Anyway," said Jim. "what about that game you made us play, writing down when they would come and where we would see the first German and so on. I don't think the airport really counts."

"I put our bits of paper in the kitchen drawer here, let's have a look. Well Jennifer is the furthest out, she went for last Tuesday. Jim went for Friday morning, the day of the bombing. I suggested yesterday, when everyone was at church. And the champion, who, settled for Monday afternoon, absolutely bang on, is Alice."

"I won't win the 'where will we see one' competition," said Alice, "with my suggestion that they might land at Fliquet. And you won't see one in a pub, Jim, since they are all closed. So it remains to be seen whether one is going to ride past the house, Jack's idea."

"There goes one," said Jack.

"Where?"

"He's gone round the corner, you've just missed him."

They all laughed as Alice punched him playfully, but the atmosphere quickly changed to a tense silence which seemed to unleash the enormity of what had happened.

After a few moments Jack said: "Well, I've got lots to put in my journal and there's school tomorrow, I'd better get on with it."

*Journal extract*

*...Well, they are here and I saw them arrive. I've started to go all shaky as I write this although at the time, I felt more curious than afraid.*

*..Where shall I begin? I'd better do it chronologically or I will be all over the place, so much is buzzing in my head.*

He wrote of Baptiste reading the ultimatum outside the shop, the need for it to have been translated, the ungermanic error of saying the airport was in the east of the island, the Bailiff addressing the large crowd in the Royal Square...

*... several workman came out and painted a large white cross in the middle of the square. It looked for all the world as if they were painting the popping creases on a cricket pitch. At that moment I don't know why but I noticed that practically everyone, men and women, seemed well-dressed and were wearing hats. How I wished that I were a capable artist rather than a humble wordsmith! The people, buildings, trees and shadows just cried out to be drawn and painted.*

He wrote of the anticlimax of the single plane landing at the airport and the arrival of the first troops and officers.

*...so what we have speculated about and feared has happened, quickly and simply. Are these the same people who invaded Czechoslovakia, Poland and Holland with such butchery; the same people who burst into Belgium and France, strafing refugees walking along the roads; the same people who needlessly bombed the Channel Islands a few days ago?*

*...As I pedalled along I wondered several times whether I should shout to people 'Did you know that the Germans have landed at the airport?' But thought I'd better not. I might just be scaring them out of their wits before disappearing around the next bend. When I had to stop in a narrow bit of road to let a farmer go past with a horse and cart, I did mention it. He replied:*

*"I thought as much, I've never seen so many planes."*

*...How do I feel about all this? I must confess that my emotions are all over the place. During my ride back from the airport, I thought myself into confusion. I felt a kind of guilt, guilt that my island homeland had given itself away, guilt that my co-islanders were hoarding, guilt that ordinary, nice, moral people were just accepting the state of things as an inevitable consequence of war; guilt that I hadn't left the island to join the army; guilt that I hadn't demonstrated in some way at the airport. By doing what?*

*...Unfortunately I spotted the announcement that the schools would be starting again tomorrow. I hadn't expected that. Were they just waiting for the Germans to arrive? How strange!*

*Will any of them come into the school tomorrow? Now is the time for everyone to be counted. At the very least, we, as teachers, must resist all attempts to germanise our children, especially anyone trying to turn them into collaborators or informers.*

# TWENTY

*Tuesday 2 July, 1940*

For the second time since 'existing conditions' had existed the school was reassembled and again a babble waxed almost uncontrollably in the playground. The Head thought it wise, as on the previous occasion, to allow the children to work the excitement from their systems. Some had seen German soldiers, others had seen the bombing, friends had evacuated, all had something to tell. The headmaster eventually got them into the hall and silence achieved. This was his moment. Jack waited, hoping. He could see Kate a few chairs away, grim faced, looking directly at the lectern, not allowing her eyes to stray elsewhere. Returning to school without Andrew must have been painful for her especially as there would be no more mail from England.

The headmaster coughed. He was dressed in his suit. He stood holding the lectern with both hands. When every child was quiet he began:

"So we are back at school (groans) but probably not for long (muted cheers) but while we are here I want you to do some thinking. War is a terrible, terrible thing and it makes children grow up too soon. You see things and you hear about things which make you realise what a miserable business life can be if the wrong people are running it. First, I want you to pray with me for a few moments in silence for those poor people who were killed by the bombs last Friday and those who were injured and for their families and friends. Stand up please."

The children stood, as if one person, and bowed their heads in a silence which went on until it was broken by a little sob. At that point the headmaster asked them to sit down.

"Next, is to remember those who are not here today. The first is Mr Durridge."

Jack watched Kate's face tighten. Had Mr Stevens told her he would speak about Andrew? Did he even know of their attachment?

"Mr Durridge came to see me the other day and said that he wanted very much to stay with us and that he was very happy here, but he thought it was his duty to go back to England, his home, and join the RAF. To do this required great courage and he will soon be fighting on behalf of us all. I want you to pray for him. I want you to pray too, for the safety and well-being of all the children who were pupils here until a couple of weeks ago and who have gone with their parents, for whatever reason, to England. I would like you, too, to pray for all of us; for me, for your teachers, so that we do the right thing because it will not always be easy for us to know what the right thing will be anymore.

Lastly, there's you, all of you. Life is going to be very difficult from now on and I'm going to talk to you like adults because you will have to behave like adults. First let us pray."

They stood again.

After a minute or so the headmaster paused, looking slowly from one side of the hall to the other. He took a step back from the lectern and returned, setting his face forward with determination.

"You have got to behave like decent, civilised people at all times. All of you are capable of being silly or childish; sometimes one or two of you do something particularly naughty and need a slipper on the bottom to remind you how to behave. But things will be different now. The Germans are soldiers. They have taken the island by force. They will not stand any nonsense from anybody so if you do something naughty to them, it might not be just a telling-off or a couple of whacks anymore, it might be a lot worse. So I urge you not to misbehave towards the Germans.

But, and this is why you have to be adults, you must not treat them as your friends either. They will probably make a lot of rules and laws which your family or neighbours might break. Normally when people break the law, the good citizen has a duty to tell the police but, in this case, it is different. We already have our own very good laws and if they come along and make horrible laws that nobody wants and nobody has voted for, then people you know may feel they are allowed to break them."

Here Mr Stevens raised his voice.

"Whatever happens you must be on the side of Jersey people, the people you know and you must never take bribes or sweets or anything from the Germans to make you say or do something which would be very wrong. Don't ever forget that."

The headmaster turned and was out of the hall before anyone could even think he was going. He left behind him a long, stunned silence.

Jack thought: 'I wonder what the German Commandant would think of that?'

The peroration had helped Jack clarify many of his own thoughts. If the Germans were going to influence the minds of children then these minds must be closed to them in advance and the Head had started well. Jack felt he should continue where Mr Stevens left off but how much of it could the children take? Nevertheless, without frightening them unduly, they must be made aware of the dangers that now existed. Soon he'd have a child of his own to bring up in these conditions.

He walked into the classroom ahead of the children for a lesson of French. Suppose the French had invaded instead of the Germans, as they had done many times since 1204 when the islands chose to remain loyal to the British Crown? Many of the pupils were at least half-French and spoke French or the Jersey-French patois at home; witness their names, Le Guen, Pallot, Billot, Le Grand, Le Roux, De La Perrelle. There were still many Bretons working on the farms. Suppose Pétain and Laval, who, according to the news, were now hand in glove with Hitler, had taken over France in the thirties and had started invading neighbouring countries, what would the Jersey people have felt if these men had landed at the airport in similar circumstances to the Germans the day before?

The children were sitting down looking at Jack. Most were clearly fearful. They needed further reassurance. Jack put trust in his instincts. He had not prepared a speech but he couldn't stay silent.

"Before we start the lesson, I want to make a few comments about what Mr Stevens said. You are all old enough to accept responsibility. Things could get very difficult for you. You may get cold and hungry this winter. What would you think if some people could get more food by paying the Germans a lot of money that you haven't got? What would you think if somebody else had new shoes and warm clothing because they had told the Germans where somebody they were looking for was hiding? How would you feel if your father was taken away to prison because of something silly and childish that you had done, like letting down the tyres of German cars? What would you think if Mr Stevens was not allowed to stay as headmaster because he was trying to make good Jerseymen and

Jerseywomen out of you? You must not be frightened by everything but you must be scared enough to behave properly.

As Mr Stevens said, you cannot trust the Germans. We are at war with them. Even if a German soldier is nice and kind when you meet him; he may show you pictures of his wife and children of your age, he is still the enemy. He is only here because the Germans seem to have more guns and tanks and planes than everyone else. So far. Remember the British are still fighting."

Jack felt that he had said enough and threw himself into the lesson determined to make the children laugh with as many silly questions he could think of. 'Combien de bananas est-ce que le singe mange? Combien de moustaches Hitler a-t-il?

At break he sat next to Kate.

"How is it going?" he asked her.

"Miserable."

"It can't have been too good for you this morning, but I'm glad Mr Stevens said something about Andrew."

"I am too, but I would have preferred not to cry in front of the children. It is too much to hope he can survive the war, flying planes. I know I won't see him again, whatever happens, but I can't bear the thought of him being killed. He's too nice to die, Jack."

Her eyes welled up again with tears. Jack put his arm around her, not quite knowing what to do and was grateful when she sat up, wiped her eyes and changed the subject.

The afternoon seemed very long. Addition and multiplication were not enough to take the mind off the Germans. Was Alice all right? What orders were they going to give? Would he have to report somewhere on a regular basis or even be interned? Nothing seemed familiar any more. The usual noises of the classroom seemed far away, the smells felt strange. It was as if he was concussed.

After a cup of tea later with Alice it took Jack nearly half an hour to persuade her it would be quite safe for him to go to town. "I must find out what is going on. I want to see for myself where they all are," he said.

So, with Jim again in attendance, he cycled off on a similar route to the previous day, but this time, going down Mount Bingham to check out the rumour that the Germans had made their headquarters at the Ritz Hotel, near Howard Davis Park. Right enough, there were several sentries outside the building and motorbikes in the forecourt. Field grey uniforms were going in and out. Policemen were also on duty moving people on, so Jack was only able to get a quick look at the sentry near the entrance looking very young and very bored.

In the town centre they saw people dashing about in all directions. There were further sentries outside the Post Office and the Telephone Exchange. In the Royal Square he overheard more snippets of conversations which he scribbled down, so different from the remarks of previous days. One girl, giggling to another said:

"He told me his name was Hans, so I said, you can keep your Hans to yourself." And they shrieked with laughter.

"You should have seen the way he looked at me," remarked another.

"The one at the Post Office is awful, he keeps pushing people with his gun."

"...nearly run over by a motorbike."

"they are driving on the right, they don't care about other people."

"...it's awful if you want to telephone."

"...saw one in the toilet."

"I must get some fags," Jack told his brother.

In the tobacconists in King Street, the lady behind the counter was talking excitedly to the customers.

"You talk about I had a shock. I was just serving Mrs Dobbs when she touched me on the arm and I looked up and there he was standing in the doorway. I just didn't know what to do I can tell you. In the end, I couldn't bear him just standing there grinning. I said 'yes' and he said 'Madam, I require matches,' in a very polite voice."

"How awful," said one of the ladies sympathetically. "So, what did you do?"

"Well, I thought, matches aren't very expensive so I gave them to him. By then he had walked right up to the counter here. I could have touched him."

She came round the counter and took Jack by the arm and moved him a little nearer the mahogany.

"He was standing just there, very tall he was, over six foot. Anyway he says to me: 'How much please?' I was so surprised because I thought he was just going to take them. My husband's been saying for weeks: 'Lucy they will just come in and take what they want. For gawd's sake don't do anything to stop them.' So I says a ha'penny. 'Is that a half penny?' he says and I had to laugh, the way he said it, so did Mrs Dodds, you can ask her. Anyway I says yes, a half penny and he reaches into the pocket of his tunic and pulls out a brand new shining ha'penny. Here it is here, I've kept it in my pocket."

She passed the glistening coin around and everyone looked at it with curiosity. Jack was surprised and amused. Would we all be collecting souvenirs of them? Where had he got the coin from? Had they been issued to them in France? Did the Nazis have a special mint where they produced the currencies of the countries they were going to occupy? Could they flood England with bank notes through secret agents to render the money worthless?

At last Jack was served. He sat with Jim on a bench in the Royal Square and told him the shopkeeper's story. This small incident was a good sign at least that the Germans were going to pay their way. A cat rubbed against Jack, not caring whether it was a Jersey or a German leg. A motor cycle passed behind them and they turned to see a soldier in grey with another in the sidecar disappear around the corner towards Woolworths. An old man on a nearby bench said 'bastards' and spat on the paving stone. A few moments later Jack's blood nearly drained as something hard jabbed him in the back and a voice said 'stand up.' He did as he was told and turned to see Baptiste standing there, a pipe in his hand. Quite shocked, Jack poured a torrent of abuse on the postman who desperately tried to say it was only a joke.

Eventually Jack asked him what he was doing in town.

"We all had to come to a meeting about not sabotaging the mail and I decided to have a look round to see what was going on."

"Well, what have you seen, you idiot?"

"I've seen a bloke who's lost his sense of humour, for a start. Apart from that a German soldier said good afternoon as he passed me on the pavement. I nodded and said 'mon tchu' to him. That's 'my arse' he said to a 'townie' who was listening to the conversation. With a bit of luck he'll go round saying 'mon tchu' to everyone he meets. He might even teach it to a few others," Baptiste said with his customary roar of laughter.

"You don't change, Baptiste, I'll give you that."

"One thing I won't forgive them for. Look, the Peirson's shut. What a miserable sight, you, a pub door closed, merde!"

Mention of the Peirson could but remind Jack again of the sacrifice of the young English officer thwarting the French invasion of 1781 in this very square.

The three men wandered down to the harbour and saw groups of German soldiers taking in the sights and making themselves at home. They did not seem to be armed. Some were taking photos, perhaps to send back to their loved ones at home. Jack felt an almost irresistible urge to talk to them but knew it would not be right. What could he say in any case? Did you have a good flight? Where are you staying? How long are you going to be here? Why did you bomb us last Friday?

It soon became apparent that there was not much to see and Jim suggested they go home. They all came back together. As they pushed their bikes up St Saviour's hill a convoy of cars passed at speed and turned into Government House. They paused for a moment.

"We'll see on the Post if they've issued any new orders," said Jack. "What do you think they are going to do?"

"I bet they keep the pubs shut, the 'salauds'," replied Baptiste, "and they'll want guns handed in I suppose. I spect they'll stop us listening to the wireless."

"Perhaps not," wondered Jack.

"A bloke at the Post office told me they would."

"I imagine they won't want us to hear the English news."

"Why not?"

"They probably believe it's all propaganda and what if we actually start winning a battle somewhere, they wouldn't want us to know in case we tell their soldiers."

"Fat chance we've got of winning anything, they're unstoppable, the sods," added Baptiste.

"It's not like you to be defeatist, Baptiste. I reckon Churchill might be the man to do it," said Jim.

"You may be right, he's our only hope, good luck to him," agreed Baptiste. "I could listen to him all day."

"There you are, you see," said Jack. "The Germans won't want you to keep up your morale by listening to Churchill."

"Don't tell me we'll have to listen to their bloody maniac instead. I can't understand how any of them know what he's talking about, screaming and shouting like that. He's worse than my old woman when I've had a skinful on a Saturday night."

Later when Jack and Jim were back at the house and were having tea, the Evening Post arrived. The whole of the front page was given over to the new German orders in large black type. Jack began reading aloud to the others:

> ONE All inhabitants must be indoors by 11 pm and not leave their homes before 5 am

"Well, that's not as bad as it could be," said Jim.

Jack agreed, pointing out that it was better than Jersey's own curfew, imposed during the panic.

> TWO We will respect the population in Jersey, but, should anyone attempt to cause the least trouble, serious measures will be taken.

"Frightening but hardly unexpected."

THREE All orders given by the Military authority are to be strictly obeyed.

FOUR All spirits must be locked up immediately and no spirits may be supplied, obtained or consumed henceforth. This prohibition does not apply to stocks in private houses.

"If yesterday's anything to go by," said Jim, "all the stocks are in private houses already. Still Baptiste won't be too pleased, it doesn't look as if the pubs are going to reopen."

"I don't know," said Jack. "It doesn't say anything about beer and wine."

FIVE No person shall enter the Aerodrome at St. Peter.

SIX All Rifles, Airguns, Revolvers, Daggers, Sporting Guns and all other Weapons, whatsoever, except Souvenirs, must, together with all Ammunition, be delivered at the Town Arsenal by 12 noon tomorrow July 3rd.

"Have we got anything?" asked Alice. "What about carving knives?"

"Don't be daft."

"You could easily kill a German with one, couldn't you? Anyway I'm surprised they say 'except souvenirs.' Couldn't you just say that anything was a souvenir?"

"I agree, awfully sorry Herr Capitain or whatever, but this machine gun is a souvenir my father brought back from the Great War. There aren't any soldiers left on the island, surely," added Jack.

"Why do you say that?"

"Point seven."

SEVEN All British Sailors, Airmen and Soldiers on Leave, including Officers in this Island must report at the Commandant's Office, Town Hall at 10 am tomorrow July 3rd.

"Do they really expect to see anybody?" Jack asked incredulously.

EIGHT No Boat or Vessel of any description, including any Fishing Boat shall leave the harbour or any other place where the same is moored, without an Order from the Military Authority, to be obtained at the Commandant's Office, Town Hall. All Boats arriving in Jersey must remain in the Harbour until permitted by the Military to leave. The crews will remain on board. The Master will report to the Harbourmaster, St. Helier, and will obey his instructions.

"Who on earth is going to come here, now?" asked Jack, "and, if they do, how will they know they've got to stay in the harbour if they're not here already to read the Post?"

NINE The sale of Motor Spirit is Prohibited, except on Essential Services such as Doctor's Vehicles, the Delivery of Foodstuffs and Sanitary Services where such vehicles are in the possession of a permit from the Military Authority to obtain supplies.
The use of Cars for private purposes is forbidden.

"So, that's that, said Jim.
"What are Papa and Maman going to do?" wondered Alice. "Will the buses be allowed to carry on?"
"It doesn't mention buses."

TEN The Blackout Regulations already in force must be obeyed as before.

ELEVEN Banks and Shops will be open as before.

TWELVE In order to conform with Central European Time all watches and clocks must be advanced one Hour at 11p.m. TO-NIGHT.

"Ah," said Jack, "the first plan to germanise us. What will they do if we refuse to change our clocks?"
"Remember Order 3 Jack," said Jennifer, who, until then had been very quiet. "All orders must be strictly obeyed."
Alice looked at the clock on the mantelpiece.
"What does that mean then? Instead of being eight o'clock tomorrow at this time, it will be nine o'clock, so we will get dark earlier."
The others thought for a moment and Jack said: "No, it won't, it will be light until an hour later. In fact it could virtually still be daylight when the curfew starts at eleven."

THIRTEEN It is forbidden to Listen to any Wireless Transmitting Stations except German and German Controlled Stations

"We guessed as much," said Jack.

He went on to speculate on how the ban might be enforced. Since very few islanders understood German, it was unlikely that they would listen to it on the radio. Most would be hard-pushed to find the right station. He thought it likely that the Germans would soon start searching houses on spot checks, seeing who lived where, looking for weapons and at the same time hoping to catch people listening to the English stations. If they just burst in, it would be very difficult to switch stations suddenly. The best thing would be to listen under the covers at night.

"At least we can show a bit of defiance by not changing our clocks and by listening to the BBC."

"Last point," said Alice, "they didn't stop at thirteen, perhaps they are superstitious like us."

FOURTEEN The Raising of the Price of Commodities is Forbidden.

"Well, that's good news, I bet the Chancellor of the Exchequer would like to be able to do that as easily in England."

"It must be to try and stop a black market starting up," suggested Jack.

"So far, thank goodness, there is nothing about anyone being carted off to places of detention or having restriction of movement."

All the German points were mulled over again and again as they finished their tea. Jim noticed that nearly all the nouns were in capital letters. Jack remembered vaguely that this was the German way of doing things and noted this down at the head of what could be a long list of 'germanising.'

- Capital letters all over the Evening Post
- Move the clocks forward to Central European Time
- Only listen to German radio stations.

After they had cleared and washed up, Jack sat back in the armchair reading the rest of the Post.

"They haven't closed the pictures yet. How about going later in the week? It's important not to just sit around getting depressed. We should take Jeanne and Henry with us; Papa and Maman would love looking after the kids."

"Let's see what's on at Wests: 'The Chinese Bungalow' with Paul Lucas and Jane Buxton.

"Don't like Chinese stuff much," said Jim.

"Forum: It's 'Chasing Danger' with Preston Foster and Lynn Bari, sounds a bit like a thriller. The Opera House looks promising: Ray Milland, he's good, and Akim Tamiroff in 'Untamed.'"

"I vote for that," said Jennifer.

"So do I," agreed Alice.

"That settles it, now what else is on the Post? The leader urges us to read carefully the orders of the Germans. Well, I think we've done that pretty thoroughly, don't you? The town was crowded, it says, with people looking at the troops. It's a bit like going to the zoo to see the animals. That's me saying that, not the Post," laughed Jack. "This is sad, in the Deaths Column, two of them say 'as a result of the air raid.'

'Oh dear, look at this. It's going to upset Henry. There's another case of foot and mouth at Maufant."

Then he said:

"Jim, look outside"

"Why?"

"Are there any Germans about?"

"No."

"Right, let's switch on the BBC, leave the clocks alone and have a drink of spirituous Calvados to toast the little person inside his or her mother."

He gathered four glasses and poured generous helpings of the fiery apple spirit in the bottle without a label they had got from a cousin of Alice's father on their last trip to the now-occupied Barneville. Jack raised his glass.

"First to us, all still here together, then to you, young Birel, I hope you are listening. We pin all our hopes on you, male or female, to build a better world in which there are no maniacs with thousands of men and machines telling other people to push their clocks about, stay moored in harbours and not listen to Winston Churchill."

Alice hugged her husband tearfully.

"D'you think they'll be gone before the little one is born?"

He could only hug and murmur in reply.

That evening, Jack wrote a few more lines.

*Journal extract*

*...Well that's the first full day of occupation over. It is surreal and unreal as I look back to the night I first started the journal, that night in the pub when we began to realise that the war was increasingly likely to reach even the small hamlet of St Martin in this north east corner of Jersey.*

*...We've been through so many mental and emotional upheavals since then which I have tried to do justice to and comment on. Looking through other pages of the diary I am conscious of asking a lot of questions. Some of those have been answered: we know that the Germans are here and when and how they arrived. We know what their first set of orders is.*

*...We will be judged by our actions. War places people in extreme situations, often of life and death, of heroism or cowardice. The best I can do for the moment is share the determination of the headmaster that teachers and those who have influence over the young, must show leadership and courage at this time. I hope I am up to it.*

*...At the same time I must continue with my role as witness and recorder of events.*

*...As the Occupation starts in earnest, I have completed the first notebook of my diary which I will hide in the loft. I am calling it 'An Island Preoccupied.' What will happen to the notebook? Will the Germans find it? Will my child or grandchild find it in the future still living in a German colony or will I be the one to get it out and read it again with the Germans gone?*

*Meanwhile tomorrow, on with notebook two: 'An Island Occupied.'*

# Jersey-French Glossary

These notes are a rendering of Jersey-French colloquialisms and oaths into 'good French', as it is known on the island, to allow readers to make a linguistic comparison. The English meaning of the Jerseyisms is often clear as used in context in the book. Translated into English, or even French, the oaths can appear stronger than they actually are.

In 1940 most farming and fishing communities and many people living in the country parishes would have spoken or certainly understood the Jersey-French patois. During the Occupation Jersey-French was often used by the locals to confuse and annoy the German occupiers.

*Jack Huet* – Jersey equivalent of Jack Robinson, origin of expression unclear

*ternelle mille bougre!* – generalised oath: bloody world!

*si bas tchu quand i pète i fait l'ver l'ponsi* – fr. son cul est si bas qu'il fait lever la poussière quand il pète: he is such a shortarse, when he breaks wind he blows up the dust

*foutaise* – fr. gâchis (from fr. foutre): mess up

*bougre* – expression of annoyance or surprise: I'll be damned (*lit* bugger)

*ch'est la dgerre* – fr. c'est la guerre: it's war

*by cri* – my goodness (*lit* by Christ)

*niolîn* – fr. niaiserie: nonsense

*tchu* – fr. cul: twit (*lit* bum)

*tchéthue à tchians* – fr. charrue à chiens: a right old mess (*lit* a dog plough)

*reste pas là à gober la leune, co-d'pise-li dans le ventre* – fr. reste pas là à gober la lune, donne-lui un coup de pied dans le ventre: don't stand there gawping at the moon, kick him in the guts

*les St. Ouennaises* – girls from St Ouen's parish

*tu n'as pas acuou veu* – fr. tu n'as pas encore vu la grosse bête qui te mangera: you haven't yet seen all there is to see (*lit.* you haven't yet seen the beast that is going to eat you).

*merci ben des fais* – fr. merci bien des fois: thank you many times

*mon vier bougre* – fr. mon vieux: my old mate

*mon vi* – fr. mon vieux: my old friend

*une bande de feunmyi* – fr. une bande de fumier: a useless bunch (*lit.* gang of manure)

*salaud* – fr. salaud: bastard

*salope* – fr. salope: nasty (*lit* slut)

*foutu la bouche* – (from fr. foutre): finished

*un pic, un cap, une péninsule* – a peak, a headland, a peninsula

*un côti* – fr. coteau: small sloping field

*laisse me vey tchna* – fr. laisse-moi voir cela: let me see that

*te vlà* – fr. te voilà: there you are

*nonnais* – fr. il n'en est pas ainsi: it's not like that

*une ronche au tchu* – fr. une ronce au cul: a thorn in the backside

*emmèrde* – fr. emmerdeur: pain in the arse

*sis-t'i tchu* – fr. que je suis bête: what a twit I am

*vein-t'en bethe une fais* – fr. viens boire un coup: come and have a drink

*i vaut pon la peine de t'tourner les sangs* – fr. il ne vaut pas la peine de te vexer (*lit.* turn the blood): it's not worth getting upset

*gourmander* – fr. enlever les gourmands: to sideshoot

*la pièche* – fr. la pièce: piece of land

# Background notes on constitutional and administrative matters relevant to the novel

The Island of Jersey is a Crown Dependency of the British Crown, which is responsible for its defence.

The **Lieutenant Governor** is the representative of the British Monarch and acts as the de facto Head of State. He liaises between the Government of Jersey and the UK. In normal times the duties are primarily diplomatic and ceremonial.

**The States of Jersey,** the legislature of the island, makes its own laws which have to be ratified by the Queen in Council. The States derives its name from the French 'états' or 'estates' made up of:

- **the Crown** represented by the Bailiff (qv) and Jurats (qv),
- **the Church** represented by the rectors of the 12 parishes and
- **the people** represented by the elected Connétables (Constables qv) of the Parishes (qv) and 14 deputies.

**The Bailiff** is the first civil officer of the bailiwick of Jersey combining the roles of President of the States' Assembly and Chief Judge of the Royal Court. He or she is appointed by the Crown and is almost invariably selected from among those who are occupying high office such as Attorney General or Solicitor General.

The particular and dramatic events of the German Occupation in 1940 called upon the Bailiff to display leadership, integrity and courage as he dealt with the Germans and sought to preserve the life of the island and the safety of its inhabitants.

**Jurats,** given the appellation Judge, were senior and influential lawyers and politicians elected for life by islandwide, as opposed to parochial, suffrage. They tended to become Presidents of the main committees of government as well as presiding over cases in the Royal Court. In 1948, after the Occupation, there were a number of constitutional reforms which began to separate the legislature from the judiciary and Jurats were replaced in the States' Assembly by Senators elected for 9 years (now reduced to 6).

For administrative purposes the island is divided into 12 **parishes** each electing its **Connétable** as head of the Parish, roughly equivalent to a Mayor. In addition he has a seat in the States' Assembly and is responsible for the policing of his parish. To help him in this task he is supported by three categories of elected Honorary Police - in order of seniority, the **Centenier**, the **Vingtenier** and the **Constable's Officers**.

Each of the parishes has a church, Parish Hall and elementary school, usually' but not in all cases, forming the nucleus of a parish village. This is true of St Martin where Jack lives. It is situated in the north east corner of the island and is the nearest parish to the Cotentin, as the Normandy Peninsular is known.

The **Seigneurs** go back to the Middle Ages and and the feudal system whereby the supporters of the King or Duke of Normandy were granted lands, often with an imposing manor House, and a fiefdom with tenants who worked the Seigneur's land. By 1940 they had no legislative or legal powers but still retained an important influence in the lives of the communities around their Manors.